Steadfastness in the Covenant

Responding to Tests and Tribulations

Steadfastness in the Covenant

Responding to Tests and Tribulations

Abdu'l-Missagh Ghadirian

GEORGE RONALD
OXFORD

George Ronald, Publisher
Oxford
www.grbooks.com

© Abdu'l-Missagh Ghadirian 2014
Reprinted 2015

All Rights Reserved

*A catalogue record for this book is available
from the British Library*

ISBN 978-0-85398-579-2

Cover design: Steiner Graphics

Contents

Preface and Acknowledgements   ix

Introduction   xiii

1 The Covenant of Bahá'u'lláh: Its Significance and a Brief History   1
    Significance of the Revelation of Bahá'u'lláh   4
    Seven Stages in the Unfoldment of the Bahá'í Faith   6
    Understanding the Power of the Covenant   7
    Twin Covenants of Bahá'u'lláh and 'Abdu'l-Bahá   9
    Twin Institutions of the Guardianship and the Universal House of Justice   13
    The Infallibility of the Guardian and the Universal House of Justice   14
    Interpretations of the Guardian and Elucidations of the Universal House of Justice   15
    Metaphors in Understanding the Covenant   18

2 Responses to the Covenant   20
    Two Witnesses to Divine Revelation   22
    Sufferings of Bahá'u'lláh and 'Abdu'l-Bahá   24
    Mysterious Forces which Expand the Faith   30
    Tribulation as 'Horizon to Revelation'   31
    Crisis and Victory   32
    A Blessing in Disguise   33
    Servitude and Certitude   34
    Warning and Preparation for Challenges Ahead   38

3 Opposition and the Capacity to Respond — 40
    The Nature of Opposition — 40
    The Forces of Opposition — 42
    Dire Contests, Both Internal and External — 44
    How Severe Will the Forces of Opposition Be? — 46
    What Should Our Attitude Be Toward Opposition? — 46
    How to Respond to Opposition — 47
    Love and Unity as a Protective Force — 53
    Internal Opposition — 54
    Internal Opposition: Recent Challenges — 61
    External Opposition: Enemies of the Faith — 62
    Protection of the Faith — 64

4 Persecution, Resilience and Heroism — 66
    The Power of Faith — 66
    The Triad of Oppression, Resilience and Faith — 68
    Transformation of Hate into Love — 69
    The Covenant and the Persecution of Bahá'ís in Iran — 70
    Psychological Terror Used in the Persecution of Bahá'ís — 71
    Steadfastness in the Face of Tribulation — 73
    Martyrdom and the Bahá'í Faith — 74
    Inciting Hatred — 77
    Education under Fire: Heroism of young Bahá'ís — 82
    Response to Persecution — 89

5 Steadfastness in the Covenant — 93
    Profiles of Steadfastness in the Covenant — 95

6 Scholarship and the Covenant — 110
    Revelation, Knowledge and Scholarship — 111
    Understanding Bahá'í Scholarship — 113
    Firmness in the Covenant and the Defence of the Faith — 115
    Priesthood and the Bahá'í Faith — 117
    The Spiritually Learned — 122
    Attributes and Attitudes of the Learned — 123

7 **Tests of the Covenant among Scholars and Teachers of the Faith** 133
    Intellectual Pride and Arrogance 135
    Taming the Ego, Learning Humility 142
    Pursuit and Purpose of Scholarship 146
    Freedom and Responsibility 148
    Scholarship and Authoritative Interpretation of the Writings 149
    The Role of Religion in Acquiring Knowledge 151
    Knowledge and Firmness in the Covenant 154
    Materialistic Methodology and Spiritual Reality 155

8 **The Covenant: The Individual, the Community and the Institutions** 159
    Spiritual and Moral Requisites 162
    The Relationship between Bahá'í Scholars and the Community 166
    The Challenge of Detachment in a Consumer Culture 173
    The Insidious Influence of Materialism 176
    Bahá'í Youth and the Covenant 181

9 **'Abdu'l-Bahá: Centre of the Covenant and Perfect Exemplar** 184
    Significance of the Station of 'Abdu'l-Bahá 184
    Personal Relationship between 'Abdu'l-Bahá and Bahá'u'lláh 187
    'Abdu'l-Bahá's Life of Servitude 188

10 **'Be Thou Assured'** 193

Bibliography 197
References 205
Index 225

Dedicated to the martyrs, heroes, heroines and lovers of Bahá'u'lláh whose resilient spirit, obedience to the Covenant and unshakeable determination enabled them to remain steadfast and to withstand the storms of opposition

Preface and Acknowledgements

This book's primary focus is firmness in the Covenant. Excerpts from the Bahá'í Writings are presented with stories of the lives of some of the heroes and heroines from past and present – blessed souls who remained staunch and faithful in the face of persecution and suffering to uphold the truth of the message of Bahá'u'lláh. It is not my intention to repeat what has already been written about the Covenant, as there is already a wealth of material available. Instead, I have chosen to concentrate on the nature of steadfastness and the capacity to acquire it for the defence and protection of the Cause and as our response to tests and tribulations in the path of God.

The book begins with a review of the nature and scope of the twin Covenants of the Bahá'í Faith described by Shoghi Effendi, followed by reflections on the significance of the Revelation of Bahá'u'lláh and the suffering of the Central Figures of the Cause. It examines the nature and characteristics of oppression on the one hand and the resilience and heroism of countless believers throughout of the history of the Faith on the other. The crucial role of firmness and faithfulness to the Covenant as a measure of love for the twin Manifestations of God is discussed, while the plight of those who arose in opposition is examined. Why did most respond while others failed, and what are the requirements of faithfulness to the Covenant?

The Bahá'í Writings tell us that persecution and trials will occur and intensify as the Cause emerges from obscurity to full recognition. But there are alternating periods of crisis and victory. A prime example of firmness in the Covenant amidst the fire of ordeals during our time is the Bahá'í community of Iran, to which part of the book is dedicated. The book also discusses what the Covenant means to the present generation of young Bahá'ís, and what are the challenges in one's individual and community life in relation to the Covenant of Bahá'u'lláh. Two chapters of the book consist of analysis and discussion about issues related to scholarship and the Covenant: what is the meaning of scholarship in the Bahá'í Dispensation and what do the Bahá'í Writings say not only about acquiring knowledge but also about individual virtues and character development of the learned which would distinguish Bahá'í academics and scholars from their colleagues in a world submerged in a competitive drive for entitlement and superiority? What is the role of these souls in the defence of the Cause and extending our knowledge toward a deeper understanding of firmness in the Covenant and the application of the Bahá'í teachings in response to questions arising from current issues of society? The Revelation of Bahá'u'lláh will guide and shape the concept and evolution of Bahá'í scholarship far beyond what we understand it to be today! We are still humble students of this Dispensation, learning about the immensity and the implications of knowledge made available through this mighty Revelation.

Through the Writings discussed in the book we also recognize that beyond the dark forces of external and internal opposition to the Faith, there is another kind of hidden and pernicious test which we need to reckon with in our daily life. This is the insidious but devastating influence of egotism, selfish pride and passion for leadership. Living the Bahá'í life and obedience to the laws and institutions of the Cause at the individual and community levels in relation to the Covenant are addressed.

The concluding part of the book turns to the life of 'Abdu'l-Bahá as the Perfect Exemplar and the Centre of the Covenant of the Faith. The last section draws on a compilation of excerpts from the Bahá'í Writings compiled by the Continental Board of Counsellors in the Americas and published by the National Spiritual Assembly of Canada and White Mountain Publications as *Be Thou Assured* (1996). I would like to thank the National Spiritual Assembly for their copyright permission. I also wish to thank the Association for Bahá'í Studies for permission to include an adaptation of part of my article on persecution and suffering, published in the *Journal of Baha'i Studies* (1994).

I would also like to express my deepest appreciation to Dr May Hofman for her invaluable suggestions, skilful editing and insightful comments in organizing and improving the chapters. My heartfelt thanks to Mr Brent Poirier for his review of the manuscript and his

PREFACE

thoughtful comments and recommendations. I am also deeply indebted with abiding gratitude to my dear wife Marilyn for her loving support, encouragement and selfless assistance to complete this work.

Abdu'l-Missagh Ghadirian
October 2013

Introduction

> The Hand of Omnipotence hath established His Revelation upon an unassailable, an enduring foundation. Storms of human strife are powerless to undermine its basis, nor will men's fanciful theories succeed in damaging its structure.
>
> *Bahá'u'lláh*[1]

In the Formative Age of the Dispensation of Bahá'u'lláh we have come to a point where the expansion of the Cause coincides with accelerated crisis and convulsions in the world. These calamities, with their associated suffering and confusion, herald the advent of the transformation in the consciousness of people and their receptivity to the teachings of the Faith. With the awakening of humanity to the emergence of the World Order of Bahá'u'lláh and its implications for the progress of civilization, there will be positive responses of large numbers of receptive souls around the world as well as negative reactions and intensified hostility and attacks from leaders of religions and enemies of the Cause. As 'Abdu'l-Bahá has prophesied: 'How great, how very great is the Cause; how very fierce the onslaught of all the peoples and kindreds of the earth!'[2] However, as He also tells us, 'The power of the Covenant will protect the Cause of Bahá'u'lláh.'[3] And He wrote:

> Know that no soul is quickened except through the spirit of the Covenant, no eye is illumined except by the light of the Covenant, no ear is thrilled except by the melody of the Covenant, and no heart shows forth the divine sentiments except by the bounty of the Covenant.[4]

No wonder, then, that Bahá'ís have been encouraged to study the Covenant and to acquire steadfastness in it, as this is 'their Fortress, their greatest protection'.[5]

In a world beset by dangers – whether physical, psychological or spiritual – it is no wonder that protection is needed. In the Bahá'í Writings such dangers are often referred to as 'tests', and they afflict every human being. In the Tablet of Tests (Lawḥ-i-Fitnih):

> Bahá'u'lláh . . . affirms that every atom, every created being, every accomplished man of learning, the servants of God and His sincere lovers, the angels that enjoy near access to God, the Concourse on high, every righteous man of discernment, every mature embodiment of wisdom, every prophet sent forth by God – all will be tested.[6]

The Master warned the Western Bahá'ís of the '"severe mental tests" that would inevitably sweep over His loved ones of the West – tests that would purge, purify and prepare them for their noble mission in life.'[7] All of this underlines the critical importance of understanding the dynamics and wisdom of the protection of the Cause and the role of firmness in the Covenant. Deepening the Bahá'í youth in the Covenant is also of paramount significance. The Beloved Guardian stressed that the youth 'must ponder deeply over the significance and implications of the Covenants of Bahá'u'lláh and 'Abdu'l-Bahá, for these form the hub of the Bahá'í wheel, so to speak, the point of unity and strength for all the believers all over the world.'[8]

In recent decades the persecutions suffered by Bahá'ís in Iran since the dawn of their Faith in 1844 have become institutionalized in government policy, while in the West Bahá'ís are increasingly suffering from intellectual ridicule or materialism. This book focuses on both kinds of tests in the context of the need for steadfastness in the Covenant.

Steadfastness in the Covenant is the hallmark of this Revelation. 'This is the Day that shall not be followed by night,' Bahá'u'lláh tells us.[9] And 'Abdu'l-Bahá affirms that this Covenant is 'so firm and mighty that from the beginning of time until the present day no religious Dispensation hath produced its like.'[10]

As the Cause of God emerges from obscurity it is bound to attract opposition. These forces of opposition are blessings in disguise and become the motivating power of progress of the Faith. The tests that individuals suffer become meaningful when one recognizes the divine Manifestation. Through this recognition the soul is educated, inspired and transformed. Therefore, in each dispensation of a new prophet

INTRODUCTION

there is lightning and thunder, a leap of knowledge of the mysteries of life and a test of ego to distinguish those who are sincere. Bahá'u'lláh states: 'Busy not thyself with this world, for with fire We test the gold, and with gold We test Our servants,'[11] while in the Qur'án we read, 'Do men think that when they say "we believe" they shall be left alone and not be put to proof?'[12] Bahá'u'lláh writes:

> Verily this is that Most Great Beauty, foretold in the Books of the Messengers, through Whom truth shall be distinguished from error and the wisdom of every command shall be tested. Verily He is the Tree of Life that bringeth forth the fruits of God, the Exalted, the Powerful, the Great.[13]

At each level of service to the Cause, one is tested and each test becomes a new opportunity for empowerment and personal growth. Like in a school, without tests and hard work progress and perfection cannot be achieved and measured. There is a tradition in Islam which sets forth challenges and perils encountered by the traveller on the journey of life. It describes 'how all men will perish and die except the believers; all the believers will perish and die except those who are tested, all who are tested will perish and die except those who are sincere, and those who are sincere will be in great danger'.[14]

Not all tests which believers are subjected to are for their faithfulness in the Covenant. Indeed we are confronted by tests in many different circumstances. Let's take the example of serving on an institution such as a Spiritual Assembly. The standard set forth by 'Abdu'l-Bahá in participating in one of the Assembly's most basic functions – consultation – becomes 'the greatest testing ground for its members'.[15] Engaging in consultation while keeping in mind its spiritual requirements is a very challenging task. 'Abdu'l-Bahá states that the prime requisites are 'purity of motive, radiance of spirit, detachment from all else save God, attraction to His Divine Fragrances, humility and lowliness amongst His loved ones, patience and long-suffering in difficulties and servitude to His exalted Threshold.'[16] Each one of these qualities stands as a test of sincerity for the consultation process. But each one of them also provides a precious opportunity to exercise our will to overcome weakness, egotistical inclination and other shortcomings, and to become a more mature and noble human being, imbued with certitude. The experience can also create emotional pain and discomfort. But this discomfort paves the way for self-evaluation and perfection. The more we are detached from the insistent self, the more we feel liberated; while the more we act upon the dictates of our ego, the more we may feel frustrated, discontented and more vulnerable to self-deception. Prayer elevates our soul to a new height of consciousness of the purpose of serving and of consultation, a purpose which should be aligned with that of the Revelation of Bahá'u'lláh and the betterment of humankind. As the Universal House of Justice writes:

> No one should expect, upon becoming a Bahá'í, that faith will not be tested, and to our finite understanding of such matters these tests may occasionally seem unbearable. But we are aware of the assurance which Bahá'u'lláh Himself has given the believers that they will never be called upon to meet a test greater than their capacity to endure.[17]

Tests often serve as stepping stones for personal growth and progress. We need to reflect and meditate about the meaning of each test that we experience. Prayer and asking for divine assistance may facilitate this process and strengthen our faith. We also need to be mindful that as human beings we are not perfect, but we do what we can to be worthy of this station.

'We must not only be patient with others, infinitely patient!, but also with our own poor selves, remembering that even the Prophets of God sometimes got tired and cried out in despair!',[18] we read in a letter written on behalf of Shoghi Effendi, and,

> Perhaps the greatest test Bahá'ís are ever subjected to is from each other; but for the sake of the Master they should be ever ready to overlook each other's mistakes, apologize for harsh words they have uttered, forgive and forget. He strongly recommends to you this course of action . . . and you should show them a strong example of Bahá'í discipline and the unity which can and must prevail amongst the Community of the Most Great Name.[19]

With this in mind, let us now turn to the Covenant of Bahá'u'lláh and its significance both for the future of the world and for our individual lives and be assured that the power of the Covenant will unite and

INTRODUCTION

strengthen us in our efforts to overcome tests and trials in the path of God.

I

The Covenant of Bahá'u'lláh: Its Significance and a Brief History

The pivot of the oneness of humankind is the power of the Covenant, and this power quickens every distinguishing element of Bahá'í life.

The Universal House of Justice[1]

The Covenant of Bahá'u'lláh and steadfastness in it are closely intertwined: steadfastness is the essential outcome and the active component of faithfulness to the Covenant. Study of and immersion in the Covenant are part of a dynamic process which releases its potential when a believer's love and obedience to the laws and ordinances of the Manifestation of God are tested. Thus, translating knowledge of the Covenant into the act of faithfulness testifies to the depth and strength of the bond between the believer and the Beloved. In this context the Covenant is like a mighty tree and firmness is the fruit of the tree.

In the history of the Bahá'í Faith there have been some believers who in ordinary times were devoted to the Cause and admired by the community; but who, when the winds of tests and tribulations blew could not withstand them and denied their allegiance to the Covenant. On the other hand, there have been many others who remained resolute and firm as a mountain. In the same way as the Covenant and steadfastness are interrelated, so there is a connection between the Covenant and tests and trials; these distinguish the faithful from the waverer.

In the opening paragraph of the Most Holy Book (Kitáb-i-Aqdas) Bahá'u'lláh defines the role of the individual in relation to the Manifestation of God:

> The first duty prescribed by God for His servants is the recognition of Him Who is the Dayspring of His Revelation and the Fountain of His

laws, Who representeth the Godhead in both the Kingdom of His Cause and the world of creation. Whoso achieveth this duty hath attained unto all good; and whoso is deprived thereof hath gone astray, though he be the author of every righteous deed. It behoveth every one who reacheth this most sublime station, this summit of transcendent glory, to observe every ordinance of Him Who is the Desire of the world. These twin duties are inseparable. Neither is acceptable without the other.[2]

Based on this statement, recognition of His Revelation is conditional upon observance of His commandments, otherwise it is incomplete. Accepting one without the other is like separating the body from the heart; it loses its viability and meaning. Recognition is basically a spiritual and intellectual acceptance of the truth of Bahá'u'lláh's station, while obedience is a commitment to act. It gives meaning to the new knowledge of recognition. If it were not to function in this manner it would be like a researcher who has worked hard to make a discovery, but after achieving it, does not know what to do with it. Likewise, if a traveller who undertakes a journey longing to reach a destination, finds after arrival no actual purpose in being there, he would be a lost soul, feeling unfulfilled.

Firmness in the Covenant sustains and safeguards observance of the twin duties of recognition of and obedience to Bahá'u'lláh. 'Abdu'l-Bahá emphasized that 'Today, the most important affair is firmness in the Covenant'.[3] Therefore it is of utmost significance that we study and deepen ourselves in the power of the Covenant and come to a broader understanding of steadfastness in the Cause. 'Abdu'l-Bahá, as the Centre of the Covenant of the Dispensation of Bahá'u'lláh, expounds upon the significance of firmness in the Covenant in these words:

> . . . know that steadfastness and firmness in this new and wonderful Covenant is indeed the spirit that quickeneth the hearts which are overflowing with the love of the Glorious Lord: verily, it is the power which penetrates into the hearts of the people of the world![4]

> Were it not for the protecting power of the Covenant to guard the impregnable fort of the Cause of God, there would arise among the Bahá'ís in one day, a thousand different sects as was the case in former ages . . .[5]

THE COVENANT OF BAHÁ'U'LLÁH

The Covenant is a hallmark of the Bahá'í Dispensation, and the appointment of 'Abdu'l-Bahá not only as the Successor but also the Centre of the Covenant of Bahá'u'lláh distinguishes the Bahá'í Faith from all divine religions of the past. The Covenant rests upon two mighty pillars: steadfastness and obedience. These two obligations of every follower of Bahá'u'lláh are endowed with much wisdom, as He elucidates in these emphatic words:

> A twofold obligation resteth upon him who hath recognized the Day Spring of the Unity of God, and acknowledged the truth of Him Who is the Manifestation of His oneness. The first is steadfastness in His love, such steadfastness that neither the clamour of the enemy nor the claims of the idle pretender can deter him from cleaving unto Him Who is the Eternal Truth, a steadfastness that taketh no account of them whatever. The second is strict observance of the laws He hath prescribed – laws which He hath always ordained, and will continue to ordain, unto men, and through which the truth may be distinguished from falsehood.[6]

A 'dynamic process, divinely propelled, possessed of undreamt-of potentialities, world-embracing in scope, world-transforming in its ultimate consequences' was set in motion with the declaration of the Báb in 1844, writes Shoghi Effendi.[7] The forces released at that time were then channelled through the institution of the Covenant, a divinely ordained instrument established by Bahá'u'lláh prior to His ascension. The principles of the institution of the Covenant were expounded by Bahá'u'lláh in the Kitáb-i-'Ahdí (which in Persian means 'Book of my Covenant', also known as the Kitáb-i-'Ahd). It is sometimes referred to as 'the Book of the Covenant', Bahá'u'lláh's 'Most Great Tablet' and the 'Crimson Book'.[8] It is basically the Will and Testament of Bahá'u'lláh. In this mighty document Bahá'u'lláh makes the following unequivocal statement: 'It is incumbent upon the Aghsán, the Afnán and My kindred to turn, one and all, their faces towards the Most Mighty Branch ['Abdu'l-Bahá].'[9] This is the foundation of Bahá'u'lláh's Covenant with the Bahá'ís of the world.

The Universal House of Justice in its Constitution further elaborates:

> Bahá'u'lláh, the Revealer of God's Word in this Day, the Source of Authority, the Fountainhead of Justice, the Creator of a new World

3

Order, the Establisher of the Most Great Peace, the Inspirer and Founder of a world civilization, the Judge, the Lawgiver, the Unifier and Redeemer of all mankind, has proclaimed the advent of God's Kingdom on earth, has formulated its laws and ordinances, enunciated its principles, and ordained its institutions. To direct and canalize the forces released by His Revelation He instituted His Covenant, whose power has preserved the integrity of His Faith, maintained its unity and stimulated its worldwide expansion throughout the successive ministries of 'Abdu'l-Bahá and Shoghi Effendi. It continues to fulfil its life-giving purpose through the agency of the Universal House of Justice whose fundamental object, as one of the twin successors of Bahá'u'lláh and 'Abdu'l-Bahá, is to ensure the continuity of that divinely-appointed authority which flows from the Source of the Faith, to safeguard the unity of its followers, and to maintain the integrity and flexibility of its teachings.[10]

Significance of the Revelation of Bahá'u'lláh

'In this most mighty Revelation all the Dispensations of the past have attained their highest, their final consummation,' writes Bahá'u'lláh, and again: 'That which hath been made manifest in this preeminent, this most exalted Revelation, stands unparalleled in the annals of the past, nor will future ages witness its like.'[11]

In order to fully appreciate the station of Bahá'u'lláh and His Dispensation, we may turn to the Báb, a Prophet Himself, Who was the Herald of a new Age. As 'the inaugurator of the Bábí Dispensation' the Báb was, Shoghi Effendi tells us, 'fully entitled to rank as one of the self-sufficient Manifestations of God . . . in His person . . .the object of all the Prophets gone before Him has been fulfilled . . .'[12] The Báb's perception of and attitude toward Bahá'u'lláh was infused with a profound humility and lowliness before 'Him Whom God shall make manifest'. In His book the Bayán, the Mother Book of the Báb's Dispensation, the Báb states that 'all that hath been exalted in the Bayán is but as a ring upon My hand, and I Myself am, verily, but a ring upon the hand of Him Whom God shall make manifest'.[13] Further, the Báb viewed the entire book of the Bayán as only 'a leaf among the leaves of His [Bahá'u'lláh's] Paradise.'[14]

To raise the awareness of the Bábís of the significance of the Dispensation of Bahá'u'lláh, the Báb impressed upon them that in that

THE COVENANT OF BAHÁ'U'LLÁH

Day a 'thousand perusals of the Bayán cannot equal the perusal of a single verse to be revealed by Him Whom God shall make manifest'.[15] In another place in the Bayán, the Báb explains that 'the year-old germ that holdeth within itself the potentialities of the Revelation that is to come is endowed with a potency superior to the combined forces of the whole of the Bayán'.[16] Moreover, He prophesied: 'The newly born babe of that Day excels the wisest and most venerable men of this time, and the lowliest and most unlearned of that period shall surpass in understanding the most erudite and accomplished divines of this age.'[17]

In one of His Tablets revealed in Adrianople, Bahá'u'lláh gave us a glimpse of the immensity of His station:

> Know verily that the veil hiding Our countenance hath not been completely lifted. We have revealed Our Self to a degree corresponding to the capacity of the people of Our age. Should the Ancient Beauty be unveiled in the fullness of His glory mortal eyes would be blinded by the dazzling intensity of His revelation.[18]

Shoghi Effendi explained the extent of knowledge bestowed upon humankind by each Divine Revelation: 'Indeed the measure of Divine Revelation, in every age, has been adapted to, and commensurate with, the degree of social progress achieved in that age by a constantly evolving humanity.'[19] Bahá'u'lláh, revealing the importance of the station of a true believer, wrote, 'This is a Revelation, under which, if a man shed for its sake one drop of blood, myriads of oceans will be his recompense.'[20] Furthermore, He tells us that:

> Such is the station ordained for the true believer that if to an extent smaller than a needle's eye the glory of that station were to be unveiled to mankind, every beholder would be consumed away in his longing to attain it. For this reason it hath been decreed that in this earthly life the full measure of the glory of his own station should remain concealed from the eyes of such a believer.[21]

Elaborating on the depth of the vision of Bahá'u'lláh in creating the Administrative Order in this new Dispensation, and its fundamental distinction, Shoghi Effendi remarks:

... this Administrative Order is fundamentally different from anything that any Prophet has previously established, inasmuch as Bahá'u'lláh has Himself revealed its principles, established its institutions, appointed the person to interpret His Word and conferred the necessary authority on the body designed to supplement and apply His legislative ordinances. Therein lies the secret of its strength, its fundamental distinction, and the guarantee against disintegration and schism. Nowhere in the sacred scriptures of any of the world's religious systems, nor even in the writings of the Inaugurator of the Bábí Dispensation, do we find any provisions establishing a covenant or providing for an administrative order that can compare in scope and authority with those that lie at the very basis of the Bahá'í Dispensation.[22]

Seven Stages in the Unfoldment of the Bahá'í Faith

In 1953, at the beginning of the Guardian's Ten Year Plan and in his message to the Bahá'í World, Shoghi Effendi elucidated various stages through which the unfoldment of the evolution and progress of the Cause would take place (emphasis added):

> This present Crusade, on the threshold of which we now stand, will, moreover, by virtue of the dynamic forces it will release and its wide repercussions over the entire surface of the globe, contribute effectually to the acceleration of yet another process of tremendous significance which will carry the steadily evolving Faith of Bahá'u'lláh through its present stages of **obscurity**, of **repression**, of **emancipation** and of **recognition** – stages one or another of which Bahá'í national communities in various parts of the world now find themselves in – to the stage of **establishment**, the stage at which the Faith of Bahá'u'lláh will be recognized by the civil authorities as the state religion, similar to that which Christianity entered in the years following the death of the Emperor Constantine, a stage which must later be followed by the emergence of the **Bahá'í state** itself, functioning, in all religious and civil matters, in strict accordance with the laws and ordinances of the Kitáb-i-Aqdas, the Most Holy, the Mother-Book of the Bahá'í Revelation, a stage which, in the fullness of time, will culminate in the establishment of the **World Bahá'í Commonwealth**, functioning in the plenitude of its powers, and which will signalize the long-awaited

advent of the Christ-promised Kingdom of God on earth – the Kingdom of Bahá'u'lláh – mirroring however faintly upon this humble handful of dust the glories of the Abhá Kingdom.

This final and crowning stage in the evolution of the plan wrought by God Himself for humanity will, in turn, prove to be the signal for the birth of a world civilization, incomparable in its range, its character and potency, in the history of mankind – a civilization which posterity will, with one voice, acclaim as the fairest fruit of the Golden Age of the Dispensation of Bahá'u'lláh, and whose rich harvest will be garnered during future dispensations destined to succeed one another in the course of the five thousand century Bahá'í Cycle.[23]

My understanding of the above statement is that various Bahá'í national communities will evolve not necessarily in the same chronological order from the stage of obscurity to an eventual stage of 'emergence of the Bahá'í state'. In some countries of the world the Faith is still in the stage of obscurity, while some others have already achieved a certain degree of recognition of the Faith by the civil authorities. In Iran, the Cradle of the Faith, the Cause, which was in obscurity, began to emerge as a result of open opposition and systematic repression by the theocratic government of the Islamic Revolution.

On the other hand, in many of the western countries, including, Australia, Canada, the United Kingdom and the United States, the Faith has not suffered the repression we observe in some other countries, and is recognized as an independent religion.

The ultimate goal of the Bahá'í international community is the 'emergence' of the Bahá'í state that 'in the fullness of time, will culminate in the establishment of the World Bahá'í Commonwealth'. The 'final and crowning stage' of this evolutionary process of the unfoldment of the Bahá'í Faith will be the 'birth of a world civilization'. Until then, the Cause of Bahá'u'lláh will march forward through the dialectical process of crisis and victory toward the divine civilization promised in the Writings.

Understanding the Power of the Covenant

The Covenant of Bahá'u'lláh has been likened to an ocean, vast and mysterious, and to fathom its depths and content requires decades of study, reflection and understanding. Here, some brief quotations are provided in order to prepare a path for greater understanding of steadfastness and constancy in the Covenant which, as we have seen, is of the highest significance after recognition of the Manifestation of God.

> A Covenant in the religious sense is a binding agreement between God and man, whereby God requires of man certain behaviour in return for which He guarantees certain blessings, or whereby He gives man certain bounties in return for which He takes from those who accept them an undertaking to behave in a certain way.[24]

There are two types of Covenant, the Greater Covenant and the Lesser Covenant. The Greater or Eternal Covenant is the Covenant

> which every Manifestation of God makes with His followers, promising that in the fullness of time a new Manifestation will be sent, and taking from them the undertaking to accept Him when this occurs.[25]

The Lesser Covenant is

> made by the Manifestation of God with His followers concerning His immediate successor . . . In the *Kitáb-i-Aqdas* and later in His Will and Testament known as the *Kitáb-i-'Ahd*, Bahá'u'lláh made such a covenant with His followers. Through these writings Bahá'u'lláh established a mighty and irrefutable covenant unprecedented in the annals of past religions. Never before has a Manifestation of God left behind an authoritative statement in which He has explicitly directed His people to turn to someone as His successor, or follow a defined system of administration for governing the religious affairs of the community.[26]

Furthermore, it is pointed out that the Covenant is

> an institution which protects the Cause from individuals who, through the assertion of their own wills, would try to force God's Cause into the paths of their own preference and thus divide the faithful and subvert the world-wide establishment of divine justice.[27]

Another aspect of the Covenant of Bahá'u'lláh is the appointment of the Centre of the Covenant. One of the most great characteristics of

THE COVENANT OF BAHÁ'U'LLÁH

the Revelation of Bahá'u'lláh, 'Abdu'l-Bahá tells us,

> a specific teaching not given by any of the Prophets of the past . . . is the ordination and appointment of the Centre of the Covenant. By this appointment and provision He has safeguarded and protected the religion of God against differences and schisms, making it impossible for anyone to create a new sect or faction of belief.[28]

In His Most Holy Book, Bahá'u'lláh has also conferred upon the Centre of the Covenant the responsibility to be the Interpreter of His Writings. This further strengthened the Covenant; 'Abdu'l-Bahá writes that 'from the beginning of time until the present day no religious Dispensation hath produced its like'.[29]

Twin Covenants of Bahá'u'lláh and 'Abdu'l-Bahá

Shoghi Effendi in his writings refers to 'twin Covenants', that is, the Covenant of Bahá'u'lláh and that of 'Abdu'l-Bahá. It is to be noted that both these are part of the Lesser Covenant of Bahá'u'lláh which He has made with the followers of the Greatest Name.*

In one of his letters to America, the Guardian states:

> Above all, the paramount duty of deepening the spiritual life of these newly fledged, these precious and highly esteemed co-workers, and of enlightening their minds regarding the essential verities enshrined in their Faith, its fundamental institutions, its history and genesis – the twin Covenants of Bahá'u'lláh and of 'Abdu'l-Bahá . . . must continue to constitute the most vital aspect of the great spiritual Crusade . . .[30]

Although Bahá'ís may not be familiar with the term 'twin Covenants', they are often mentioned in letters of the beloved Guardian or those written on his behalf in which he underlined the significance of understanding them and following their provisions.[31]

Shoghi Effendi particularly emphasized the importance of deepening new believers in the Covenant of Bahá'u'lláh as well as in the Covenant of 'Abdu'l-Bahá; for example:

---

* Thus, when the Covenant of Bahá'u'lláh is discussed in the remaining chapters of this book, this includes the Covenant of 'Abdu'l-Bahá as well.

STEADFASTNESS IN THE COVENANT

> Above all, the utmost endeavour should be exerted by your Assembly to familiarize the newly enrolled believers with the fundamental and spiritual verities of the Faith . . . to instil in them a deeper understanding of the Covenants of both Bahá'u'lláh and 'Abdu'l-Bahá . . .[32]

Furthermore, the Guardian underscores the value of acquiring the knowledge of the twin Covenants in withstanding tests and tribulations:

> . . . the believers need to be deepened in their knowledge and appreciation of the Covenants of both Bahá'u'lláh and 'Abdu'l-Bahá. This is the stronghold of the Faith of every Bahá'í, and that which enables him to withstand every test and the attacks of the enemies outside the Faith, and the far more dangerous, insidious, lukewarm people inside the Faith who have no real attachment to the Covenant, and consequently uphold the intellectual aspect of the teachings while at the same time undermining the spiritual foundation upon which the whole Cause of God rests.[33]

As we shall see later in the this chapter, as part of His Covenant the Master appointed twin Successors: 'The sacred and youthful branch, the guardian of the Cause of God, as well as the Universal House of Justice, to be universally elected and established, are both under the care and protection of the Abha Beauty . . .'[34]

The Covenant of Bahá'u'lláh and 'Abdu'l-Bahá are based on two mighty pillars: the Kitáb-i-'Ahd and the Will and Testament of 'Abdu'l-Bahá. Therefore, study of these historic documents is of great importance. Some of the significant covenantal events that occurred after the passing of Bahá'u'lláh and 'Abdu'l-Bahá, as well as of Shoghi Effendi, relate to the content of these documents, both of them unprecedented in the history of religion.

Never before has a Prophet left a will entirely written in His own hand, clearly and succinctly identifying His successor. As the Guardian of the Faith indicated, the Kitáb-i-'Ahd is a

> unique and epoch-making Document, designated by Bahá'u'lláh as His 'Most Great Tablet' and alluded to by Him as the 'Crimson Book' in His 'Epistle to the Son of the Wolf'" [which] can find no parallel in the Scriptures of any previous Dispensation, not excluding that of the Bab Himself.[35]

THE COVENANT OF BAHÁ'U'LLÁH

In that document Bahá'u'lláh appointed the 'Most Mighty Branch' (in Arabic <u>Gh</u>uṣn-i-A'ẓam) which refers to 'Abdu'l-Bahá not only as His successor but also as the Centre of His Covenant, 'the One Whom God hath purposed'.³⁶ Bahá'u'lláh also ordained the station of the 'Greater Branch (<u>Gh</u>uṣn-i-Akbar) (Mírzá Muḥammad-'Alí, the half-brother of 'Abdu'l-Bahá) to be beneath that of the Most Great Branch ('Abdu'l-Bahá)'.³⁷

The Will and Testament of 'Abdu'l-Bahá consists of three parts, each of which was written at a different time between 1901 and 1908. During those years 'Abdu'l-Bahá's life was often in great danger. Shoghi Effendi described the Will and Testament of 'Abdu'l-Bahá as 'the Charter of the New World Order'³⁸ that 'may be regárded in some of its features as supplementary to no less weighty a Book than the Kitab-i-Aqdas'.³⁹ He stated that the 'the contents of the Will of the Master are far too much for the present generation to comprehend. It needs at least a century of actual working before the treasures of wisdom hidden in it can be revealed . . .'⁴⁰

The Guardian furthermore explained the 'triple impulse generated through the revelation of the Tablet of Carmel by Bahá'u'lláh and the Will and Testament as well as the Tablets of the Divine Plan bequeathed by the Centre of the Covenant – the three Charters which have set in motion three distinct processes'. Although distinct, they are closely interrelated.⁴¹ The fourth one is the Most Holy Book which is the 'Charter of the future world civilization'.⁴²

In His Will and Testament 'Abdu'l-Bahá summarizes the essence of the Covenant of Bahá'u'lláh in the following concise and unique statement:

'. . . This is the foundation of the belief of the people of Bahá (may my life be offered up for them): His Holiness, the Exalted One (the Báb), is the Manifestation of the Unity and Oneness of God and the Forerunner of the Ancient Beauty. His Holiness the Abhá Beauty (may my life be a sacrifice for His steadfast friends) is the Supreme Manifestation of God and the Dayspring of His Most Divine Essence. All others are servants unto Him and do His bidding.' Unto the Most Holy Book every one must turn and all that is not expressly recorded therein must be referred to the Universal House of Justice. That which this body, whether unanimously or by a majority doth carry, that is verily the

Truth and the Purpose of God Himself. Whoso doth deviate therefrom is verily of them that love discord, hath shown forth malice and turned away from the Lord of the Covenant.[43]

Moreover, 'Abdu'l-Bahá exhorted the believers in these emphatic words:

> O ye that stand fast in the Covenant! When the hour cometh that this wronged and broken-winged bird will have taken its flight unto the Celestial Concourse, when it will have hastened to the Realm of the Unseen and its mortal frame will have been either lost or hidden neath the dust, it is incumbent upon the Afnán, that are steadfast in the Covenant of God, and have branched from the Tree of Holiness; the Hands (pillars) of the Cause of God (the glory of the Lord rest upon them), and all the friends and loved ones, one and all to bestir themselves and arise with heart and soul and in one accord, to diffuse the sweet savours of God, to teach His Cause and to promote His Faith. It behoveth them not to rest for a moment, neither to seek repose. They must disperse themselves in every land, pass by every clime and travel throughout all regions. Bestirred, without rest, and steadfast to the end, they must raise in every land the triumphal cry 'O Thou the Glory of Glories!' (Yá Bahá'u'l-Abhá), must achieve renown in the world wherever they go, must burn brightly even as a candle in every meeting and must kindle the flame of Divine love in every assembly; that the light of truth may rise resplendent in the midmost heart of the world, that throughout the East and throughout the West a vast concourse may gather under the shadow of the Word of God, that the sweet savours of holiness may be diffused, that faces may shine radiantly, hearts be filled with the Divine spirit and souls be made heavenly.[44]

With regard to our relationship with the 'peoples and kindreds of the world' we are advised to

> [c]onsort with all the peoples, kindreds and religions of the world with the utmost truthfulness, uprightness, faithfulness, kindliness, good-will and friendliness, that all the world of being may be filled with the holy ecstasy of the grace of Bahá, that ignorance, enmity, hate and rancour may vanish from the world and the darkness of estrangement amidst the peoples and kindreds of the world may give way to the Light of Unity.[45]

The Will and Testament of the Master makes it very clear that the line of succession includes Shoghi Effendi as the Guardian of the Faith, and in due time the Universal House of Justice:

> O my loving friends! After the passing away of this wronged one, it is incumbent upon the Aghsán (Branches), the Afnán (Twigs) of the Sacred Lote-Tree, the Hands (pillars) of the Cause of God and the loved ones of the Abhá Beauty to turn unto Shoghi Effendi – the youthful branch branched from the two hallowed and sacred Lote-Trees and the fruit grown from the union of the two offshoots of the Tree of Holiness, – as he is the sign of God, the chosen branch, the guardian of the Cause of God . . . He is the expounder of the words of God and after him will succeed the first-born of his lineal descendants.[46]

Twin Institutions of the Guardianship and the Universal House of Justice

The passing of 'Abdu'l-Bahá on 28 November 1921 marked the close of the Heroic or Apostolic Age of the Dispensation of Bahá'u'lláh. It was during that glorious age that the Founders of this Dispensation lived, suffered and planted the seeds of their teachings in the hearts of people and watered them with the tears and blood of thousands of heroes, heroines and martyrs of the Cause so that it would germinate, grow and spread its branches throughout the entire planet.

Shoghi Effendi, referring to that historic Heroic Age, wrote:

> a period whose splendours no victories in this or any future age, however brilliant, can rival – had now terminated with the passing of One Whose mission may be regarded as the link binding the Age in which the seed of the newborn Message had been incubating and those which are destined to witness its efflorescence and ultimate fruition.
>
> The Formative Period, the Iron Age, of that Dispensation was now beginning, the Age in which the institutions, local, national and international, of the Faith of Bahá'u'lláh were to take shape, develop and become fully consolidated . . .[47]

The institutions of the Guardianship and the Universal House of Justice are the twin successors of 'Abdu'l-Bahá in the Administrative

World Order of Bahá'u'lláh. '[T]hey supplement each other's authority and functions, and are permanently and fundamentally united in their aims,'[48] writes Shoghi Effendi. However, as well as being appointed the sacred Head of the Faith, Shoghi Effendi was also appointed by 'Abdu'l-Bahá as His successor and as the 'expounder of the Word of God'.[49] The Universal House of Justice was invested by Bahá'u'lláh with 'the function of legislating on matters not expressly revealed in the teachings'.[50] These two institutions have certain functions and responsibilities which are in common with or complement each other. For example, one of their common responsibilities is 'to insure the continuity of that divinely-appointed authority which flows from the Source of our Faith, to safeguard the unity of its followers . . .'[51] On the other hand, each of those two institutions 'operates within a separate and distinct sphere'.[52]

According to the Writings, the 'Supreme House of Justice' should be elected by the National Spiritual Assemblies worldwide. Furthermore, it is to be noted that

> there is nothing in the Texts to indicate that the election of the Universal House of Justice could be called only by the Guardian. On the contrary, 'Abdu'l-Bahá envisaged the calling of its election in His own lifetime. At a time described by the Guardian as 'the darkest moments of His (the Master's) life, under 'Abdu'l-Ḥamíd's regime, when He stood to be deported to the most inhospitable regions of Northern Africa,' and when even His life was threatened, 'Abdu'l-Bahá wrote to Mullá Ḥájí Mírzá Taqí Afnán, the cousin of the Báb and chief builder of the 'Ishqábád Temple, commanding him to arrange for the election of the Universal House of Justice should the threats against the Master materialize. The second part of the Master's Will is also relevant to such a situation and should be studied by the friends.[53]

The Infallibility of the Guardian and the Universal House of Justice

In the Bahá'í Writings infallibility was conferred upon the Guardian and the Universal House of Justice. In His Will and Testament, 'Abdu'l-Bahá made the following emphatic statement:

The sacred and youthful branch, the guardian of the Cause of God, as well as the Universal House of Justice, to be universally elected and established, are both under the care and protection of the Abhá Beauty, under the shelter and unerring guidance of His Holiness, the Exalted One (may my life be offered up for them both). Whatsoever they decide is of God.[54]

Furthermore, the Master underlined the fact that the Universal House of Justice is divinely guided. In another statement, the Centre of the Covenant elaborates more specifically about the scope of the infallibility of the Universal House of Justice with regard to its decisions:

> Let it not be imagined that the House of Justice will take any decision according to its own concepts and opinions. God forbid! The Supreme House of Justice will take decisions and establish laws through the inspiration and confirmation of the Holy Spirit, because it is in the safekeeping and under the shelter and protection of the Ancient Beauty...[55]

From the above statement we understand that the House of Justice is divinely inspired in making decisions other than establishing laws – for example, decisions on solving problems which have caused differences of opinion:

> Should there be differences of opinion, the Supreme House of Justice would immediately resolve the problems. Whatever will be its decision, by majority vote, shall be the real truth, inasmuch as that House is under the protection, unerring guidance, and care of the one true Lord.[56]

Interpretations of the Guardian and Elucidations of the Universal House of Justice

In the Revelation of Bahá'u'lláh, authoritative interpretation of the sacred Writings has been devolved to the Centre of the Covenant and to Shoghi Effendi, the Guardian of the Faith. No one else has the right to do it. This is a fundamental departure from the religions of the past where the apostles and clergy took on the task of interpretation of the holy Writings. As a result, there have been countless divisions and difference among the followers of the diverse religions.

With the passing of Shoghi Effendi the authoritative interpretation of the Writings of the Founders of this Dispensation came to an end. The Universal House of Justice does not have the privilege of interpretation of the Writings. Yet the House of Justice carefully and exhaustively researches and reviews the volumes of the writings of Shoghi Effendi before any decisions are made.

In a letter dated 9 March 1965, the Universal House of Justice wrote:

> There is a profound difference between the interpretations of the Guardian and the elucidations of the House of Justice in exercise of its function to 'deliberate upon all problems which have caused difference, questions that are obscure, and matters that are not expressly recorded in the Book.'[57]

The Guardian reveals what the Scripture means; his interpretation is a statement of truth which cannot be varied. Upon the Universal House of Justice, in the words of the Guardian, 'has been conferred the exclusive right of legislating on matters not expressly revealed in the Bahá'í Writings.'[58] Its pronouncements, which are susceptible to amendment or abrogation by the House of Justice itself, serve to supplement and apply the Law of God. Although not invested with the function of interpretation, the House of Justice is in a position to do everything necessary to establish the World Order of Bahá'u'lláh on this earth. Unity of doctrine is maintained by the existence of the authentic texts of Scripture and the voluminous existing interpretations of 'Abdu'l-Bahá and Shoghi Effendi, together with the absolute prohibition against anyone propounding 'authoritative' or 'inspired' interpretations or usurping the function of the Guardian. Unity of administration is assured by the authority of the Universal House of Justice.

In the words of Shoghi Effendi,

> Such is the immutability of His revealed Word. Such is the elasticity which characterizes the functions of His appointed ministers. The first preserves the identity of His Faith, and guards the integrity of His law. The second enables it, even as a living organism, to expand and adapt itself to the needs and requirements of an ever-changing society.[59]

Furthermore, the Universal House of Justice has stated that

> Every true believer, if he is to deepen in his understanding of the Cause of Bahá'u'lláh, must needs combine profound faith in the unfailing efficacy of His Message and His Covenant, with the humility of recognizing that no one of this generation can claim to have embraced the vastness of His Cause nor to have comprehended the manifold mysteries and potentialities it contains. The words of Shoghi Effendi bear ample testimony to this fact:
> > 'How vast is the Revelation of Bahá'u'lláh! How great the magnitude of His blessings showered upon humanity in this day! And yet, how poor, how inadequate our conception of their significance and glory! This generation stands too close to so colossal a Revelation to appreciate, in their full measure, the infinite possibilities of His Faith, the unprecedented character of His Cause, and the mysterious dispensations of His Providence.'[60]

Can individuals make their own personal interpretation of the Writings?

To respond to this question, the following clarification by the Universal House of Justice is very enlightening.

> A clear distinction is made in our Faith between authoritative interpretation and the interpretation or understanding that each individual arrives at for himself from his study of its teachings. While the former is confined to the Guardian, the latter, according to the guidance given to us by the Guardian himself, should by no means be suppressed. In fact such individual interpretation is considered the fruit of man's rational power and conducive to a better understanding of the teachings, provided that no disputes or arguments arise among the friends and the individual himself understands and makes it clear that his views are merely his own. Individual interpretations continually change as one grows in comprehension of the teachings. As Shoghi Effendi explained: 'To deepen in the Cause means to read the writings of Bahá'u'lláh and the Master so thoroughly as to be able to give it to others in its pure form. There are many who have some superficial idea of what the Cause stands for. They, therefore, present it together with

all sorts of ideas that are their own. As the Cause is still in its early days we must be most careful lest we fall under this error and injure the Movement we so much adore. There is no limit to the study of the Cause. The more we read the Writings, the more truths we can find in them and the more we will see that our previous notions were erroneous.' So, although individual insights can be enlightening and helpful, they can also be misleading. The friends must therefore learn to listen to the views of others without being overawed or allowing their faith to be shaken, and to express their own views without pressing them on their fellow Bahá'ís.[61]

Sometimes Bahá'í speakers and writers, in discussing a subject, mix their own views and interpretations into a matter without clearly indicating what is their own personal view and what is from the Writings. Making this distinction is important, as we live in the so-called digital age when personal thoughts can be widely diffused through the Internet, sometimes causing misunderstanding and confusion.

Metaphors in Understanding the Covenant

In the Bahá'í Writings, the Covenant and firmness in it have been expressed in beautiful metaphors which relate to the nature and significance of this institution. Let's take the metaphor of the Covenant as an **ocean**. The ocean is vast and mysterious. On its surface, it can be calm or agitated, but in its depths it has a magnificent world of its own. The calmness of the surface, however, may change due to high winds and raging storms through which the ocean may surge and cleanse itself from harmful entities which will be thrown to the shore. The ocean also contains countless pearls, but only those who are true seekers will be able to discover them. 'Abdu'l-Bahá compares Covenant-breakers to the foam of the ocean: 'These agitations of the violators are no more than the foam of the ocean . . . but the ocean of the Covenant shall surge and cast ashore the bodies of the dead, for it cannot retain them.' Moreover, He comments that '[t]his foam of the ocean shall not endure and shall soon disperse and vanish, while the ocean of the Covenant shall eternally surge and roar . . . '[62]

Another metaphor is that of the Covenant as a **pulsating artery**. Imagine the Covenant as a heart and the Bahá'í community as the body with various parts and organs within this physical frame. Believers are like the cells of the body, and the institutions of the Cause like the arteries and vessels which connect the heart to all different parts of the body. The teachings and the Writings are likened to the sacred life-blood which is circulated to the entire body, reaching every organ and cell. There is a harmony and reciprocity between the heart and all the other organs of the body, through which life is sustained and physical and mental vitality are nurtured and preserved. In like manner, writes 'Abdu'l-Bahá, the body of the contingent world is vitalized through the power of the Covenant: '. . . the dynamic power of the world of existence is the power of the Covenant which like an artery pulsateth in the body of the contingent world . . .'[63]

In His Will and Testament, 'Abdu'l-Bahá refers to the Covenant as the **shield** protecting the Cause of the God from the assaults of the Covenant-breakers.[64] The purpose of the Covenant is to safeguard the unity of the Bahá'í community and protect it against division. The Covenant is also like a tree: 'The world of the Covenant is like unto the **Blessed Tree** which is growing beside the river of the Water of Life in the utmost delicacy and beauty, and day by day it is developing and adding to its verdancy.'[65] (emphasis added)

In other metaphors that speak of the Covenant's protective power we read: 'The Covenant of God . . . is a **lifeboat** and **ark of salvation**. All true followers of the Blessed Perfection are sheltered and protected in this ark.'[66] 'It is the fortified **fortress** of the Cause of God and the firm **pillar** of the religion of God,' He writes in the Tablets of the Divine Plan.[67] 'Abdu'l-Bahá also tells us that 'the **pivot** of the oneness of mankind is nothing else but the power of the Covenant'.[68] It is 'the **Cord** stretched betwixt the earth and the Abhá Kingdom'[69] and its light 'is the educator of the minds, the spirits, the hearts and souls of men'.[70] The power of the Covenant is likened to the heat of the **sun** 'which quickeneth and promoteth the development of all created things on earth'.[71]

Finally, the Guardian in *God Passes By* writes that 'Abdu'l-Bahá referred to the Covenant as 'the "Conclusive Testimony", the "Universal Balance", the "Magnet of God's grace", the "Upraised Standard", the "Irrefutable Testament" ', and mentions other of its names such as '"the Ark of His (God's) Testament", the "Tree of Anísá" (Tree of Life), the "Ark of Salvation".'[72]

2

Responses to the Covenant

> Today, the Lord of Hosts is the defender of the Covenant, the forces of the Kingdom protect it, heavenly souls tender their services, and heavenly angels promulgate and spread it broadcast. If it is considered with insight, it will be seen that all the forces of the universe, in the last analysis serve the Covenant. In the future it shall be made evident and manifest.
>
> 'Abdu'l-Bahá [1]

One of the most characteristic and amazing developments in the history of each religion is the fact that after the appearance of a new Prophet two strong opposing forces emerge in response to the declaration of His prophethood. Among the people who witness the dawn of the Revelation, many embrace the message of the new Prophet and propagate it with staunch determination and unshakeable resolve. They go so far as to lay down their lives and face the most barbaric persecution and torture in upholding the truth of their beliefs and expressing their faith.

However, there are many more who rise up against these faithful believers and their Prophet, ferociously attacking them with raging fanaticism. These people are incited relentlessly by the clergy to oppose the new believers in order to extinguish the fire of their love and devotion. In fact, inciting hatred against the rise of a new religious belief has been an action characteristic of the clergy throughout history. And, as if this were not enough to bear by the new believers, their faith is also tested through internal opposition by some people who, after accepting the Prophet, break their Covenant with Him and turn against Him. This causes even greater suffering and sorrow to the Divine Manifestation and His followers. Why is this so? The paradox of responses to the birth of a new religion is a mystery. The intensity of the clashes between the forces of light and darkness raises many questions. Is ignorance about the truth of the new revelation to blame, or is the selfishness of humanity, blinded by prejudice, the cause of so much hardship and suffering? What is the role of human ego and the passion for power in unleashing hatred and betrayal?

In one of His prayers Bahá'u'lláh makes this statement:

> No sooner had He proclaimed Thy Cause, and risen up to carry out the things prescribed unto Him in the Tablets of Thy decree, than the Great Terror fell upon Thy creatures. Some turned towards Thee, and detached themselves from all except Thee, and sanctified their souls from the world and all that is therein, and were so enravished by the sweetness of Thy voice that they forsook all Thou hadst created in the kingdom of Thy creation. Others recognized Thee and then hesitated, others allowed the world to come in between them and Thee and to withhold them from recognizing Thee. Others disdained Thee, and turned back from Thee, and wished to prevent Thee from achieving Thy purpose. And yet behold how all of them are calling upon Thee, and are expecting the things they were promised in Thy Tablets. And when the Promised One came unto them, they recognized Him not, and disbelieved in Thy signs, and repudiated Thy clear tokens, and strayed so grievously from Thy path that they slew Thy servants, through the brightness of whose faces the countenances of the Concourse on high have been illumined.[2]

Sometimes tests may come from unexpected sources, which can cause a great deal of anguish and disunity. In the letter on behalf of the Guardian to an individual believer, quoted above in the Introduction, it is stated: 'Perhaps the greatest test Bahá'ís are ever subjected to is from each other; but for the sake of the Master they should be ever ready to overlook each other's mistakes, apologize for harsh words they have uttered, forgive and forget.'[3] As we discuss tests related to the Covenant and steadfastness in the Covenant, it is befitting that we examine the lives of a few individuals who, because of the task to which they were appointed – serving as secretary to Bahá'u'lláh – became some of His closest companions. Such an examination shows how gazing at the sun in its midmost splendour can blur the vision and dazzle the mind of those who are not strong in their faith.

Two Witnesses to Divine Revelation

Writing about the power released in this world by the Revelation of Bahá'u'lláh, the Báb stated:

> Should a tiny ant desire, in this day, to be possessed of such power as to be able to unravel the abstrusest and most bewildering passages of the Qur'án, its wish will no doubt be fulfilled, inasmuch as the mystery of eternal might vibrates within the innermost being of all created things.[4]

This statement shows the power of Bahá'u'lláh to raise the capacity of a person's mind. But possession of such a blessing comes with a test of the sincerity of the person who is engaged in attaining such a capacity. There have been individuals in the history of the Bahá'í community who were raised up in knowledge and capacity, but who were later overcome by self-pride and became victims of their own ego. The stories of the lives and services of two secretaries of Bahá'u'lláh are interesting in this regard. It is important to bear in mind the station of Bahá'u'lláh, a station that the Báb Himself exalted in the Bayán, which is referred to as the 'Mother Book' by Bahá'u'lláh in the Tablet of Aḥmad. We read in the history of the Faith that when Bahá'u'lláh was revealing new Tablets or commentaries, within a single day and night He would reveal a volume of verses equal in length to the whole Bayán. The revelation came down so fast that the secretaries could not keep up with it.

Mírzá Áqá Ján of Kashán

Mírzá Áqá Ján was one of the secretaries of Bahá'u'lláh and served Him for a long time. He has been named as the first person to believe in Bahá'u'lláh as 'Him Whom God shall make manifest'.[5] Bahá'u'lláh gave him the title 'Khádim'u'lláh', which means 'Servant of God'. Mírzá Áqá Ján was a young man when he met Bahá'u'lláh in Iraq, but he didn't have much education. He gained knowledge from Bahá'u'lláh, earned His trust, and began to serve the Blessed Beauty. He served Bahá'u'lláh for 40 years as His secretary, servant and companion. Among the companions of Bahá'u'lláh, writes Adib Taherzadeh, no one was closer to Him than Mírzá Áqá Ján.[6] From Baghdad to 'Akká,

RESPONSES TO THE COVENANT

he constantly accompanied Bahá'u'lláh in exile and imprisonment. He had the unique and priceless privilege of being present when Bahá'u'lláh received and dictated the revealed words of God which at times would come down like a torrent; on many such occasions Mírzá Áqá Ján was probably the only one to be in the presence of Bahá'u'lláh at the time. (Only Bahá'u'lláh's amanuensis was allowed to be present at the time of revelation, however occasionally Bahá'u'lláh would allow some of the believers to remain in His presence for a short time. Those who had this special privilege witnessed the glory and radiance emanating from Him.)[7] To have had the blessing of being in the same room, breathing the same air, hearing the voice of the Manifestation of God while sitting next to Him, must have been extraordinary.

Following the passing of Bahá'u'lláh, Mírzá Áqá Ján faced the biggest test of his life. After 40 years of service, seized by selfish pride he turned against 'Abdu'l-Bahá, the successor to Baha'u'llah and the Centre of His Covenant. Thus was Mírzá Áqá Ján destroyed by his own ego. Five years after the passing of Bahá'u'lláh he joined hands with the Covenant-breakers and rose as a most powerful collaborator of Mírzá Muḥammad-'Alí. By doing so he caused much anguish and suffering to 'Abdu'l-Bahá.[8] It is reported that, before His passing, Bahá'u'lláh was so displeased with Mírzá Áqá Ján's 'unbefitting behaviour' that He dismissed this man from His presence.[9]

Mishkín-Qalam

In contrast, another person among the believers who was also given the great bounty of serving the Blessed Beauty (Bahá'u'lláh) for a period of time was Mishkín-Qalam.

Mishkín-Qalam was a mystic and a leading Persian calligrapher of his time. He was called the 'second Mír 'Imád' (the most eminent calligrapher of Iran who worked at the court of Shah Abbas Safavi (1557–1628)). Mishkín-Qalam was a pen-name meaning 'musk-scented pen' or 'jet black pen' (*mishk* means musk.) He was renowned in Asia Minor and held a special position among the court ministers of Teheran. He was also an astronomer.[10]

After hearing about Bahá'u'lláh, he left Teheran and travelled all the way to Adrianople where he was received by Bahá'u'lláh with much affection. When he embraced the Faith his life was transformed. He became a great, bold and knowledgeable teacher of the Cause and was firm in the Covenant. His creative calligraphy was sought after by Persians of all classes in Asia Minor. However, his name, fame and position did not deter him from becoming a loyal servant of Bahá'u'lláh and he was later named as one of the Apostles of Bahá'u'lláh. He spent many years of his life transcribing His Tablets and creating calligraphies of them. The well-known beautiful calligraphic expressions of 'Yá Bahá'u'l-Abhá' and the Greatest Name (O Thou Glory of the All-Glorious) are his work.[11] In fact, several volumes of the Tablets of Bahá'u'lláh were transcribed by Mishkín-Qalam.[12]

When Bahá'u'lláh was sent to the prison-city of 'Akka, Mishkín-Qalam was one of the few faithful believers who were sent into exile in Cyprus with the arch-enemy of Bahá'u'lláh Mírzá Yaḥyá Azal and his followers. For nine years this pure-hearted Bahá'í lived on the same island as Azal. But in contrast to Mírzá Áqá Ján, who was easily deceived by the Covenant-breakers and actively joined them, Mishkín-Qalam refused to allow his faith and loyalty to the Covenant to be shaken. He likened this time to being in hell, surrounded by the poison of the Covenant-breakers. Eventually, through the help of the Blessed Beauty, Mishkín-Qalam was released and brought to 'Akká where he served Bahá'u'lláh and remained faithful to Him until the end of his life. He was a very humble soul and remained loyal to the Covenant following the passing of Baha'u'llah.[13]

Sufferings of Bahá'u'lláh and 'Abdu'l-Bahá

Bahá'u'lláh bore his countless trials, His exiles from country to country and His imprisonment, with long-suffering and divine patience so that mankind could be 'released from its bondage' and attain 'true liberty', as He declares in the following passage:

> The Ancient Beauty hath consented to be bound with chains that mankind may be released from its bondage, and hath accepted to be made a prisoner within this most mighty Stronghold that the whole world may attain unto true liberty. He hath drained to its dregs the cup of sorrow, that all the peoples of the earth may attain unto abiding joy, and be filled with gladness. This is of the mercy of your Lord, the Compassionate, the Most Merciful. We have accepted to be abased,

O believers in the Unity of God, that ye may be exalted, and have suffered manifold afflictions, that ye might prosper and flourish. He Who hath come to build anew the whole world, behold, how they that have joined partners with God have forced Him to dwell within the most desolate of cities![14]

In the following prayer Bahá'u'lláh at first expresses His sorrow and suffering to God. He laments that His sorrow is not because He is perturbed by calamities but rather by the delay in the fulfilment of what has been ordained.

> Glorified be Thy name, O Lord my God! Thou beholdest my dwelling-place, and the prison into which I am cast, and the woes I suffer. By Thy might! No pen can recount them, nor can any tongue describe or number them. I know not, O my God, for what purpose Thou hast abandoned me to Thine adversaries. Thy glory beareth me witness! I sorrow not for the vexations I endure for love of Thee, nor feel perturbed by the calamities that overtake me in Thy path. My grief is rather because Thou delayest to fulfil what Thou hast determined in the Tablets of Thy Revelation, and ordained in the books of Thy decree and judgment.[15]

In this prayer, after the initial supplication to God regarding the suffering that Bahá'u'lláh is enduring, there is a conversation between Him and His own blood (the vital part of His physical existence) about the length and depth of the pain of suffering. The latter complains to Bahá'u'lláh and asks how long it should remain a captive of the world before it be freed. Bahá'u'lláh replies that it must be patient as He continues to quaff the cup of God's decree. His soul admonishes His physical reality to be content with what God has destined:

> My blood, at all times, addresseth me saying: 'O Thou Who art the Image of the Most Merciful! How long will it be ere Thou riddest me of the captivity of this world, and deliverest me from the bondage of this life? Didst Thou not promise me that Thou shalt dye the earth with me, and sprinkle me on the faces of the inmates of Thy Paradise?' To this I make reply: 'Be thou patient and quiet thyself. The things thou desirest can last but an hour. As to me, however, I quaff continually in

the path of God the cup of His decree, and wish not that the ruling of His will should cease to operate, or that the woes I suffer for the sake of my Lord, the Most Exalted, the All-Glorious, should be ended. Seek thou my wish and forsake thine own. Thy bondage is not for my protection, but to enable me to sustain successive tribulations, and to prepare me for the trials that must needs repeatedly assail me. Perish that lover who discerneth between the pleasant and the poisonous in his love for his beloved! Be thou satisfied with what God hath destined for thee. He, verily, ruleth over thee as He willeth and pleaseth. No God is there but Him, the Inaccessible, the Most High.' [16]

The suffering of the Central Figures of this Revelation has not only been due to the darts inflicted by the external enemies of the Faith. They also grieved over the actions of those who had embraced the Faith and then turned around and attacked Bahá'u'lláh and His successors.

The Guardian tells us that in a Tablet addressed to the American believers a few days before his passing, 'Abdu'l-Bahá wrote,

> 'I have renounced the world and the people thereof . . . In the cage of this world I flutter even as a frightened bird, and yearn every day to take My flight unto Thy Kingdom. Yá Bahá'u'l-Abhá! Make Me drink of the cup of sacrifice, and set Me free.'

Shoghi Effendi goes on to tell us that 'Abdu'l-Bahá

> revealed a prayer less than six months before His ascension in honour of a kinsman of the Báb, and in it wrote: 'O Lord! My bones are weakened, and the hoar hairs glisten on My head . . . and I have now reached old age, failing in My powers.' . . . No strength is there left in Me wherewith to arise and serve Thy loved ones . . . O Lord, My Lord! Hasten My ascension unto Thy sublime Threshold . . . and My arrival at the Door of Thy grace beneath the shadow of Thy most great mercy . . .' [17]

The Guardian comments on 'Abdu'l-Bahá's travels to the West:

> Who knows what thoughts flooded the heart of 'Abdu'l-Bahá as He found Himself the central figure of such memorable scenes as these?

RESPONSES TO THE COVENANT

Who knows what thoughts were uppermost in His mind as He sat at breakfast beside the Lord Mayor of London, or was received with extraordinary deference by the Khedive himself in his palace, or as He listened to the cries of 'Alláh-u-Abhá' and to the hymns of thanksgiving and praise that would herald His approach to the numerous and brilliant assemblages of His enthusiastic followers and friends organized in so many cities of the American continent? Who knows what memories stirred within Him as He stood before the thundering waters of Niagara, breathing the free air of a far distant land, or gazed, in the course of a brief and much-needed rest, upon the green woods and countryside in Glenwood Springs, or moved with a retinue of Oriental believers along the paths of the Trocadero gardens in Paris, or walked alone in the evening beside the majestic Hudson on Riverside Drive in New York, or as He paced the terrace of the Hotel du Parc at Thonon-les-Bains, overlooking the Lake of Geneva, or as He watched from Serpentine Bridge in London the pearly chain of lights beneath the trees stretching as far as the eye could see? Memories of the sorrows, the poverty, the overhanging doom of His earlier years; memories of His mother who sold her gold buttons to provide Him, His brother and His sister with sustenance, and who was forced, in her darkest hours, to place a handful of dry flour in the palm of His hand to appease His hunger; of His own childhood when pursued and derided by a mob of ruffians in the streets of Ṭihrán; of the damp and gloomy room, formerly a morgue, which He occupied in the barracks of 'Akká and of His imprisonment in the dungeon of that city – memories such as these must surely have thronged His mind. Thoughts, too, must have visited Him of the Báb's captivity in the mountain fastnesses of Ádhirbáyján, when at night time He was refused even a lamp, and of His cruel and tragic execution when hundreds of bullets riddled His youthful breast. Above all His thoughts must have centered on Bahá'u'lláh, Whom He loved so passionately and Whose trials He had witnessed and had shared from His boyhood. The vermin-infested Síyáh-Chál of Ṭihrán; the bastinado inflicted upon Him in Ámul; the humble fare which filled His kashkúl while He lived for two years the life of a dervish in the mountains of Kurdístán; the days in Baghdád when He did not even possess a change of linen, and when His followers subsisted on a handful of dates; His confinement behind the prison-walls of 'Akká, when for nine years even the sight of verdure was denied Him; and the public humiliation to which He was subjected at government headquarters in that city – pictures from the tragic past such as these must have many a time overpowered Him with feelings of mingled gratitude and sorrow, as He witnessed the many marks of respect, of esteem, and honour now shown Him and the Faith which He represented. 'O Bahá'u'lláh! What hast Thou done?' He, as reported by the chronicler of His travels, was heard to exclaim one evening as He was being swiftly driven to fulfil His third engagement of the day in Washington, 'O Bahá'u'lláh! May my life be sacrificed for Thee! O Bahá'u'lláh! May my soul be offered up for Thy sake! How full were Thy days with trials and tribulations! How severe the ordeals Thou didst endure! How solid the foundation Thou hast finally laid, and how glorious the banner Thou didst hoist!'[18]

In His last Tablet to America, the Centre of the Covenant expresses heart-rending sorrow and the grief caused by internal and external oppressors of the Cause. In His lamentation He turns to Bahá'u'lláh and supplicates 'to drink the cup of sacrifice' and be relieved from all those afflictions and troubles caused by the Covenant-breakers and others:

> O Lord of the Covenant! O luminous Star of the world! The persecuted 'Abdu'l-Bahá has fallen into the hands of persons who appear as sheep and in reality are ferocious wolves; they exercise every sort of oppression, endeavour to destroy the foundation of the Covenant, and claim to be Bahá'ís. They strike at the root of the Tree of the Covenant, and count themselves persecuted . . .
>
> O thou Bahá'u'lláh! 'Abdu'l-Bahá did not rest a moment until he had raised Thy Cause and the Standard of the Kingdom of Abhá waved over the world. Now some people have arisen with intrigues and evil aspirations to trample this flag in America, but My hope is in Thy confirmations. Leave Me not single, alone and oppressed! As thou didst promise, verbally and in writing, that Thou wouldst protect this gazelle of the pasture of Thy love from the attacks of the hounds of hatred and animosity . . .
>
> O thou Bahá'u'lláh! I have forsaken the world and its people, am heartbroken because of the unfaithful – and am weary. In the cage of this world I flutter like a frightened bird and long for the flight to Thy Kingdom.
>
> O thou Bahá'u'lláh! Make Me to drink the cup of sacrifice, and

RESPONSES TO THE COVENANT

free Me! Relieve Me from these difficulties, hardships, afflictions and troubles! Thou art the Assister, the Helper, the Protector and the Supporter!¹⁹

Many of us may not have realized that the Centre of the Covenant of this mighty Dispensation, this Mystery of God and most beloved of the world Bahá'í community, had suffered so grievously at the hands of the Covenant-breakers and the unfaithful that he felt 'oppressed' and 'heartbroken', beseeching God to be relieved from this world and its 'afflictions and troubles'! But 'Abdu'l-Bahá also remained a staunch and supreme example of the defence of the Covenant which has inspired Bahá'ís around the world.

In a letter written in 1924, the Greatest Holy Leaf reflected upon the sufferings of Bahá'u'lláh and 'Abdu'l-Bahá:

> Let us then, affectionate brothers and sisters, ponder for awhile upon the underlying reason that had made God's divine Messengers prefer a life of torture to one of ease, and those blessed martyrs, so many of them cut off in the springtime and promise of their youth choose death with faces radiant with joy. What did the Báb sacrifice His promising youth for except out of a burning desire to have mankind live in unity and peace; and what was the spirit that animated those bold and heroic martyrs but love and adoration to a Cause they wished to triumph? What made Bahá'u'lláh, born and brought up in opulence, fling away all earthly possessions and choose upon Himself unspeakable hardships and deprivation, save for an earnest appeal to the world at large to turn their hatred for one another into genuine love and to make a world seething with blood a peaceful home for God's children; and why did 'Abdu'l-Bahá, who could have chosen a life of ease and comfort, prefer to lead a crusade against the strongholds of human hearts and make a direct appeal to individuals as well as groups that unless we love one another with all our might and with all our heart we are absolutely doomed. He carried a crusade not with a sword of steel but with a sword of love and affection. And if we dare call ourselves Bahá'ís it simply means that we have to follow in their wake. It means that we must always have the public weal in mind and not give ourselves wholly to our inclinations and desires, and it means that we must picture before us the perseverance and self-sacrifice of those early

volunteers and make a whole-hearted effort to be like unto them; and it shall be only in this way that we can safe-guard the Cause of God.[20]

Mysterious Forces which Expand the Faith

Mysterious forces beyond human comprehension are at work to proclaim and spread the Cause amidst all the turmoil and crises around us. 'It should not be surmised that the events which have taken place in all corners of the globe, including the sacred land of Iran, have occurred as isolated incidents without any aim and purpose,' the Universal House of Justice tells us. They quote the words of our beloved Guardian: 'The invisible hand is at work and the convulsions taking place on earth are a prelude to the proclamation of the Cause of God,' going on to explain that:

> This is but one of the mysterious forces of this supreme Revelation which is causing the limbs of mankind to quake and those who are drunk with pride and negligence to be thunderstruck and shaken . . .
>
> In such an afflicted time, when mankind is bewildered and the wisest of men are perplexed as to the remedy, the people of Bahá, who have confidence in His unfailing grace and divine guidance, are assured that each of these tormenting trials has a cause, a purpose, and a definite result, and all are essential instruments for the establishment of the immutable Will of God on earth . . .[21]

Bahá'ís should be steadfast and have confidence that the suffering and persecution of the believers will not be in vain but rather will strengthen this mighty Cause to forge ahead. 'Every drop of blood shed by the valiant martyrs,' writes the Universal House of Justice,

> every sigh heaved by the silent victims of oppression, every supplication for divine assistance offered by the faithful, has released, and will continue mysteriously to release, forces over which no antagonist of the Faith has any control . . . Indeed, this new wave of persecution sweeping the Cradle of the Faith may well be seen as a blessing in disguise . . .[22]

Bahá'ís have often been subjected to persecution or other hardships in the path of service to Bahá'u'lláh. For example, in Iran the latest waves of persecution and injustice inflicted on Bahá'ís since the Islamic Revolution of 1979 have dragged on and there is a feeling of discouragement and sometimes despair. Heart-breaking as it is, we are reminded by the following statement written in a letter on behalf of Shoghi Effendi that 'There is always an important difference between friends and tested friends. No matter how precious the first type may be, the future of the Cause rests upon the latter . . .'[23]

Are the present-day Bahá'ís of the West immune from tests and calamities? It is easy to have the impression that the trials and tribulations of persecution are the lot only of the Bahá'ís in the cradle of the Faith and in other Muslim countries. But as the Cause grows and expands around the globe, the Bahá'ís of the West will also share in this persecution. 'Abdu'l-Bahá explains:

> . . . the friends in the West will unquestionably have their share of the calamities befalling the friends in the East. It is inevitable that, walking the pathway of Bahá'u'lláh they too will become targets for persecution by the oppressors . . .
>
> Now ye, as well, must certainly become my partners to some slight degree, and accept your share of tests and sorrows. But these episodes shall pass away while that abiding glory and eternal life shall remain unchanged forever. Moreover, these afflictions shall be the cause of great advancement.[24]

Tribulation as 'Horizon to Revelation'

The history of religion bears witness that for each prophet with a divine revelation came severe suffering and persecution. Why does this phenomenon repeat itself in each cycle of a new revelation? What is its result? There is no doubt that the hate and agitation instigated by divines against a new change in the destiny of humanity is an important factor. But what comes after suffering? Are we strong enough to face these calamities or is there another force above and beyond us which will save us in our plight? We get impatient, and that is our limitation in this world, while divine power has no limit and will come to our assistance when its wisdom commands. The Guardian encouraged us not to get 'discouraged or depressed, but rest assured that Bahá'u'lláh will assist you. Every set-back this Cause receives is invariably a means of ensuring a future victory, for God will never permit His Faith to be put out or uprooted.'[25]

Bahá'u'lláh writes,

> Tribulation is a horizon unto My Revelation. The day star of grace shineth above it, and sheddeth a light which neither the clouds of men's idle fancy nor the vain imaginations of the aggressor can obscure.
>
> Follow thou the footsteps of thy Lord, and remember His servants even as He doth remember thee, undeterred by either the clamour of the heedless ones or the sword of the enemy . . . Spread abroad the sweet savours of thy Lord, and hesitate not, though it be for less than a moment, in the service of His Cause. The day is approaching when the victory of thy Lord, the Ever-Forgiving, the Most Bountiful, will be proclaimed.[26]

In the Tablet of Aḥmad, Bahá'u'lláh reminds us of His own suffering when we face our trials and tribulations in the path of God.[27] In each religious dispensation, perseverance in the face of suffering has been the lot of the believers.

There is a great mystery in connecting the persecution of the oppressor with the resilience and steadfastness of believers. What we know from the Writings is that these two opposite forces contribute to the growth of the Faith and its emergence from obscurity. One force is determined to halt and destroy this divinely ordained movement, while the other unwaveringly withstands the storm of hatred and incitement to attack and eradicate. It is a strange combination which ultimately will enhance and reinforce the power of this new Revelation.

Crisis and Victory

Shoghi Effendi unravelled the nature of this paradoxical phenomenon by explaining that in the organic life of the Faith there is a dialectic process at work which consists of crisis and victory.

> Shoghi Effendi perceived in the organic life of the Cause a dialectic of victory and crisis. The unprecedented triumphs, generated by the adamantine steadfastness of the Iranian friends, will inevitably provoke

opposition to test and increase our strength. Let every Baháʼí in the world be assured that whatever may befall this growing Faith of God is but incontrovertible evidence of the loving care with which the King of Glory and His martyred Herald, through the incomparable Centre of His Covenant and our beloved Guardian, are preparing His humble followers for ultimate and magnificent triumph.[28]

For example, in the development and progress of the Cause in Iran, the staunchness and steadfastness of the Baháʼís provoked a reaction characterized by opposition which ultimately strengthened the triumph of the Faith.[29] This dialectic phenomenon of crisis and victory is governed by a spiritual power and a divine plan beyond our understanding. If we reflect on the life and development of social and political movements, we note that not always do the opposing forces of states against a socio-political movement or ideology contribute to the triumph of the movement. The brutality and power of governing forces may crush and obliterate uprising movements. So there must be a different power at work in the evolution of a new religion. The fruits of such a religious movement historically have been that common people without military and technological armaments or support are able to achieve their goal. Indeed their message is for peace and unification of nations and peoples and not destruction. They are what may be called pacific and non-aggressive, using a peace-loving approach to unify people for the good of mankind. Many of them are brutalized, persecuted, tortured or killed. Yet the new religion will ultimately prevail and eventually triumph and usher in a new era with a new world order.

A Blessing in Disguise

We frequently find in the Writings of the Faith reference to trials and tribulations that the loved ones of God are destined to experience. For example, Shoghi Effendi has explained that many calamities will eventually prove to be blessings in disguise, 'designed, by a Wisdom inscrutable to us all, to establish and consolidate the sovereignty of Baháʼu'lláh on this earth'.[30] In fact, the atrocities and adversity he was writing about accomplished the opposite of what the enemies had hoped for, which was to retard and impede the growth of the Cause. Rather these attacks became the means 'to purge and purify its life, to stir it to still greater depths, to galvanize its soul, to prune its institutions, and cement its unity'.[31]

Although during almost 170 years of the history of the Faith the persecution of believers in Iran has never ceased completely, the beginning of the Islamic Revolution in 1979 unleashed one of the most vehement and relentless repressions of the Bahá'ís ever instigated by the theocratic regime of that country. The tribulations that were heaped upon innocent Bahá'ís were no longer only physical, i.e. public lashings, torture, imprisonment and death. This time they were at once physical, psychological, economic, educational and political, with the clergy publicly inciting hate by making false accusations. The attack was also broader and aimed not only at youth and adults but also at children. In such an environment where thousands lost their jobs and were refused government employment, where higher education was denied to tens of thousands of Bahá'í youth, and where children were mistreated, ridiculed and abused in schools or in the street, how was one supposed to remain calm and be steadfast?

How long was one expected to endure exposure to this emotional strain without becoming depressed and suffering breakdown? Iran had become a concentration camp without visible barbed wire. This camp was different. Bahá'ís could move around, travel, and have a house, but were deprived of employment, denied higher education, and refused their civil rights including conducting business as Bahá'ís. In short, it was a life in psychological captivity, with severe oppression, economic deprivation, and social injustice. In spite of all this discrimination, however, the Bahá'ís did stay calm and constant, appealing for justice and surviving under brutal and relentless hardship. They became like living martyrs beset with calamities, hoping that tomorrow might be different. They continued to educate their children, to work in jobs below their qualifications and to remain faithful to their beliefs while letting the world know of their plight. Their crime was being a Bahá'í, a well-wisher of mankind, including their fellow Iranians.

Servitude and Certitude

When one reaches the stage of certitude a new realization develops which can change one's life. The creative Word of God can kindle this deeper realization. Bahá'u'lláh states, 'O My servant! Free thyself from the fetters of this world, and loose thy soul from the prison of self. Seize thy chance, for it will come to thee no more.'³² Servitude at His Threshold is that 'chance' that many of us strive to seize in our lives. But we should also realize that by living in today's materialistic world, many of us may lose this chance and remain oblivious of such an inner and spiritual realization because of the thick veil of fascination with the material world. To attain that state of higher consciousness, therefore, we need to become a channel of love and obedience, submitting our will to the will of God. Juliet Thompson, one of the early American believers, recounts the following personal account that she heard from 'Abdu'l-Bahá:

> I am the servant of the Blessed Perfection. In Baghdad I was a child. Then and there He announced to me the Word, and I believed in Him. As soon as He proclaimed to me the Word, I threw myself at His Holy Feet and implored and supplicated Him to accept my blood as a sacrifice in His Pathway.³³

Juliet Thompson wrote about that statement, 'The sacrifice, of life at least, was accepted, and prolonged for fifty-six years in prison and exile.'³⁴ She drew attention to the saying by Jesus Christ, 'He that is greatest among you shall be your servant.'³⁵

In the Kitáb-i-Íqán, the Book of Certitude, Bahá'u'lláh expounds on the significance of the City of Certitude and how glorious are its splendours and attributes. He explains that

> the attainment of this city quencheth thirst without water, and kindleth the love of God without fire. Within every blade of grass are enshrined the mysteries of an inscrutable wisdom, and upon every rosebush a myriad nightingales pour out, in blissful rapture, their melody. Its wondrous tulips unfold the mystery of the undying Fire in the Burning Bush, and its sweet savours of holiness breathe the perfume of the Messianic Spirit. It bestoweth wealth without gold, and conferreth immortality without death. In every leaf ineffable delights are treasured and within every chamber unnumbered mysteries lie hidden.³⁶

In a marvellous mystical language filled with symbolism, Bahá'u'lláh unravels the mysteries of the City of Certitude. To understand His words one needs to be endowed with spiritual insight and comprehension. Those who labour in their quest to attain the joy of entering this City should have renounced all worldly attachments and be so attracted and attached to this City that even a moment of separation from it would be unthinkable.[37] This is a reference to the Manifestation of God, Whom Bahá'u'lláh characterizes as the 'Rose', and the 'Nightingale' of that City. 'Once in about a thousand years shall this City be renewed and re-adorned.'[38] Attainment unto this City, to which we are exhorted to make a mighty effort, is through nothing but the Word of God which is revealed through the Manifestation of God in every dispensation. 'In these cities', Bahá'u'lláh furthermore states, 'spiritual sustenance is bountifully provided, and incorruptible delights have been ordained.'[39]

Shaykh Salmán, the 'Messenger of the Merciful'

One of the early believers who entered the City of Certitude, attained the presence of the Blessed Beauty and was intoxicated by the fragrance of that 'Rose' was Shaykh Salmán, who became a trusted servant of His threshold.

Shaykh Salmán was a highly devoted and staunch believer who was a disciple of Bahá'u'lláh. He was originally known as Shaykh Khánjár (which means 'dagger'), but Bahá'u'lláh named him Salmán after an eminent believer in the time of the Prophet Muhammad who was also named Salmán. This earlier Salmán was a Persian disciple of the Prophet whose name had been Rúz-bih. Muhammad loved Rúz-bih and changed his name to Salmán.[40]

Shaykh Salmán became a messenger, a channel of communication who would carry Tablets revealed by Bahá'u'lláh to believers in different parts of Persia and bring back to Him their letters and messages. He arrived in Iraq shortly after Bahá'u'lláh was exiled to that land. He served the Blessed Beauty as His messenger for forty years. The designation 'Messenger of the Merciful' was conferred upon him by Bahá'u'lláh and he served in that capacity with utmost dedication and faithfulness. He would travel thousands of miles every year, often on foot, and acted with prudence, fortitude and wisdom in delivering Tablets despite untold hardships.[41]

Although poor and illiterate, he acquired a deep understanding of and insight into the Cause. In contrast to Rúz-bih, who had been very handsome, Shaykh Salmán was not so endowed – in fact, his face was disfigured. There are many delightful anecdotes demonstrating his sound judgment and clear wisdom in different circumstances. The following account is recorded by Adib Taherazadeh; it relates to a journey that Taherzadeh's father, a historian, undertook together with Shaykh Salmán to the city of Shiraz.

Shaykh Salmán was once given the task of carrying a Tablet of Bahá'u'lláh to Mushíru'l-Mulk, a former Governor of Shiraz who had become a Bahá'í. When Mushíru'l-Mulk heard that Shaykh Salmán was in Shiraz, he expressed the wish to meet him personally. Shaykh Salmán declined to meet him, using the excuse that he had no time and was in a hurry to leave Shiraz. His host in Shiraz who was a Bahá'í could not understand the reason why Shaykh Salmán had refused to meet Mushíru'l-Mulk. Later, upon the insistence of his host, he explained his action:

> 'If Mushíru'l-Mulk meets me he will lose his faith and will leave the Cause . . . Mushíru'l-Mulk has heard many traditions and stories about Salmán, the disciple of Muhammad. For instance, he has heard the fantastic story that fire had no effect upon the feet of Salmán, and that he used to put his own feet instead of wood into a fireplace and heat the pots up with them. No doubt, Mushíru'l-Mulk expects to see similar things from me or he thinks that I have a face radiant and beautiful as an angel's. When he sees my ugly face and rough appearance he will leave the Faith.' Later on this story was mentioned to Bahá'u'lláh Who confirmed that Shaykh Salmán had been right and that Mushíru'l-Mulk would have left the Faith had that meeting taken place.[42]

In those early years of the Faith, carrying a Tablet or any document which would identify one as a Bahá'í, and much more so if he was a messenger from Bahá'u'lláh, was a grave and dangerous responsibility. The Tablets which Shaykh Salmán carried would often not indicate the name and address of the recipient for reasons of security, for otherwise he and the recipients could be persecuted. So heavy was Salmán's mission and responsibility.

Warning and Preparation for Challenges Ahead

'That the Cause of God should, in the days to come, witness many a challenging hour and pass through critical stages in preparation for the glories of its promised ascendancy in the new world . . . is abundantly proved to us all by its heroic past and turbulent history,' writes Shoghi Effendi.⁴³

'Abdu'l-Bahá, referring to the greatness of the Cause and challenges that it will face, said,

> How great, how very great is the Cause! How very fierce the onslaught of all the peoples and kindreds of the earth. Ere long shall the clamour of the multitude throughout Africa, throughout America, the cry of the European and of the Turk, the groaning of India and China, be heard from far and near. One and all, they shall arise with all their power to resist His Cause. Then shall the knights of the Lord, assisted by His grace from on high, strengthened by faith, aided by the power of understanding, and reinforced by the legions of the Covenant, arise and make manifest the truth of the verse: 'Behold the confusion that hath befallen the tribes of the defeated!'⁴⁴

Shoghi Effendi predicted that the Faith will pass through 'successive stages of unmitigated obscurity, of active repression and of complete emancipation, leading in turn to its being acknowledged as an independent Faith . . .'⁴⁵

Bahá'u'lláh called to mind the fact that we should be assured that whatever crises we may face, ultimately they will result in the progress of the Cause:

> Whatever hath befallen you, hath been for the sake of God. This is the truth, and in this there is no doubt. You should, therefore, leave all your affairs in His Hands, place your trust in Him, and rely upon Him. He will assuredly not forsake you. In this, likewise, there is no doubt. No father will surrender his sons to devouring beasts; no shepherd will leave his flock to ravening wolves. He will most certainly do his utmost to protect his own.
>
> If, however, for a few days, in compliance with God's all-encompassing wisdom, outward affairs should run their course contrary to

one's cherished desire, this is of no consequence and should not matter. Our intent is that all the friends should fix their gaze on the Supreme Horizon, and cling to that which hath been revealed in the Tablets. They should strictly avoid sedition, and refrain from treading the path of dissension and strife. They should champion their one true God, exalted be He, through the hosts of forbearance, of submission, of an upright character, of goodly deeds, and of the choicest and most refined words.[46]

3
Opposition and the Capacity to Respond

> As opposition to the Faith, from whatever source it may spring, whatever form it may assume, however violent its outbursts, is admittedly the motive-power that galvanizes on the one hand, the souls of its valiant defenders, and taps for them, on the other, fresh springs of that Divine and inexhaustible Energy, we who are called upon to represent, defend and promote its interests, should . . . acclaim it as both a God-sent gift and a God-sent opportunity . . .
> *Shoghi Effendi*[1]

The Nature of Opposition

The Bahá'í Writings are very explicit about opposition and challenges to the Covenant in the Cause of Bahá'u'lláh. Understanding the nature and purposes of attacks against the Faith will help us to be better prepared for challenges in steadfastness. As the Faith achieves prominence in various parts of the world, it is bound to attract attention which will result, in part, in actions aimed to discredit, distort or destroy the fundamental teachings of this new religion.

The words 'opposition' and 'attack' usually evoke a sense of fear and terror and arouse the desire to respond with hostility and aggression in order to exact revenge and destruction. But in the Bahá'í Writings opposition to the Faith imparts a deeper meaning, a constructive one, that leads to change. Opposition is viewed as 'a blessing in disguise' or a 'motive-power' which galvanizes the community to bring about a transformation destined to change a wayward humanity into an enlightened and unified family under the World Order of Bahá'u'lláh.

The Universal House of Justice draws our attention to the importance of the 'inevitability' of the forces of opposition and to be prepared to repel these dark forces 'with confidence':

OPPOSITION AND THE CAPACITY TO RESPOND

We feel strongly that, whatever method is chosen to inform the friends, the time has come for them to clearly grasp the inevitability of the critical contests which lie ahead, give you their full support in repelling with confidence and determination 'the darts' which will be levelled against them by 'their present enemies, as well as those whom Providence will, through His mysterious dispensations, raise up, from within or from without,' and aid and enable the Faith of God to scale loftier heights, win more signal triumphs, and traverse more vital stages in its predestined course to complete victory and worldwide ascendancy.[2]

Shoghi Effendi elucidated the intensity of the critical contests ahead and their nature:

> For let every earnest upholder of the Cause of Bahá'u'lláh realize that the storms which this struggling Faith of God must needs encounter, as the process of the disintegration of society advances, shall be fiercer than any which it has already experienced. Let him be aware that so soon as the full measure of the stupendous claim of the Faith of Bahá'u'lláh comes to be recognized by those time-honoured and powerful strongholds of orthodoxy, whose deliberate aim is to maintain their stranglehold over the thoughts and consciences of men, this infant Faith will have to contend with enemies more powerful and more insidious than the cruellest torture-mongers and the most fanatical clerics who have afflicted it in the past. What foes may not in the course of the convulsions that shall seize a dying civilization be brought into existence, who will reinforce the indignities which have already been heaped upon it![3]

The nature and character of such opposition and attacks have been vividly depicted in the writings of the Guardian. In them he tells us that Bahá'ís, as 'the valiant warriors' amidst these adversaries, will face many challenges foreseen by 'Abdu'l-Bahá:

> . . . the valiant warriors struggling in the name and for the Cause of Bahá'u'lláh must, of necessity, encounter stiff resistance, and suffer many a setback. Their own instincts, no less than the fury of conservative forces, the opposition of vested interests, and the objections of a corrupt and pleasure-seeking generation, must be reckoned with,

resolutely resisted, and completely overcome. As their defensive measures for the impending struggle are organized and extended, storms of abuse and ridicule, and campaigns of condemnation and misrepresentation, may be unloosed against them. Their Faith, they may soon find, has been assaulted, their motives misconstrued, their aims defamed, their aspirations derided, their institutions scorned, their influence belittled, their authority undermined, and their Cause, at times, deserted by a few who will either be incapable of appreciating the nature of their ideals, or unwilling to bear the brunt of the mounting criticisms which such a contest is sure to involve. 'Because of 'Abdu'l-Bahá,' the beloved Master has prophesied, 'many a test will be visited upon you. Troubles will befall you, and suffering afflict you.'[4]

The Forces of Opposition

Opposition to any Revelation in history is instigated and intensified by the clergy of the established older religion, who are threatened by the force of change on the one hand, and the fear of loss of their influence, control and power over people on the other. Blinded by their own passion to rule, they do not search to discover the truth of the new Manifestation. Instead, they appeal to the emotions of their congregations and provoke hatred to resist and defy the force of illumination and enlightenment.

As Shoghi Effendi explains,

> The resistless march of the Faith of Bahá'u'lláh . . . propelled by the stimulating influences which the unwisdom of its enemies and the force latent within itself, both engender, resolves itself into a series of rhythmic pulsations, precipitated, on the one hand, through the explosive outbursts of its foes, and the vibrations of Divine Power, on the other, which speed it, with ever-increasing momentum, along that predestined course traced for it by the Hand of the Almighty.
>
> As opposition to the Faith, from whatever source it may spring, whatever form it may assume, however violent its outbursts, is admittedly the motive-power that galvanizes on the one hand, the souls of its valiant defenders, and taps for them, on the other, fresh springs of that Divine and inexhaustible Energy, we who are called upon to represent, defend and promote its interests, should, far from regarding

OPPOSITION AND THE CAPACITY TO RESPOND

any manifestation of hostility as an evidence of the weakening of the pillars of the Faith, acclaim it as both a God-sent gift and a God-sent opportunity which, if we remain undaunted, we can utilize for the furtherance of His Faith and the routing and complete elimination of its adversaries.

The Heroic Age of the Faith, born in anguish, nursed in adversity, and terminating in trials as woeful as those that greeted its birth, has been succeeded by that Formative Period which is to witness the gradual crystallization of those creative energies which the Faith has released, and the consequent emergence of that World Order for which those forces were made to operate.[5]

Continuing his theme, Shoghi Effendi, with his remarkable clarity of vision and power of foresight, depicts the onslaught of the enemies and ultimate victory of the Cause of Bahá'u'lláh:

Fierce and relentless will be the opposition which this crystallization and emergence must provoke. The alarm it must and will awaken, the envy it will certainly arouse, the misrepresentations to which it will remorselessly be subjected, the setbacks it must, sooner or later, sustain, the commotions to which it must eventually give rise, the fruits it must in the end garner, the blessings it must inevitably bestow and the glorious, the Golden Age, it must irresistibly usher in, are just beginning to be faintly perceived, and will, as the old order crumbles beneath the weight of so stupendous a Revelation, become increasingly apparent and arresting.

Not ours, dear friends, to attempt to survey the distant scene; ours rather the duty to face the trials of the present hour, to ponder its meaning, to discharge its obligations, to meet its challenge and utilize the opportunity it offers to the fullest extent of our ability and power.[6]

In one of His Tablets Bahá'u'lláh admonishes the enemies of the Cause who tried to 'extinguish the lamp which the Hand of Divine power hath lit'.[7] They were utterly unaware of the fact that 'adversity is the oil that feedeth the flame of this lamp!'[8] What is ironic is that the fiercest forces of opposition in Iran came from Muslim clerics and their followers, people who in their daily prayers supplicate God for the coming of the Promised One. Veiled by selfish arrogance and prejudices, they have grandiose ideas and strategies to eradicate the truth of the new religion, but they do not realize the source of its power and majesty. Nor can they appreciate the depth and extent of steadfastness with which the believers are endowed to overcome such adversities.

The clergy's possession of theological knowledge has given this privileged group of people in each religious dispensation a false sense of omnipotence which has bolstered their egos and deprived them from searching and discovering the truth. Only a handful of such divines were able to recognize the Manifestation of God. Bahá'u'lláh affirmed in His Writings that such fierce opposition can never shake 'the foundation upon which the rock-like stability' of His chosen ones rests.[9] It was this 'rock-like stability' that moved believers such as Sulaymán Khán to dance through the streets as he was approaching his martyrdom while the flame of candles consumed his flesh. Such courage amidst the clamour of the mob demonstrates the power of certitude and firmness in the Covenant.

It is due to this unshakeable foundation that thousands upon thousands of Bahá'ís in Iran, subjected to physical and psychological torture, have been able to endure countless incidents of persecution and repression since the beginning of the Islamic Revolution. Many were expelled from their jobs or had their businesses confiscated. Hundreds were arrested, imprisoned, tortured, deprived of their basic rights, and some were executed. Their houses were burned, their shops were closed; even their dead were not spared – many of the Bahá'í graves were broken or destroyed and, in some cases, the bodies of the deceased were removed and burned.

Each one of those who were arrested or imprisoned was given the opportunity of recanting their faith in Bahá'u'lláh and being set free with fanfare and attractive positions and privileges. Why did they refuse to do so? This act of refusal was the essence of their love and belief in the truth of the message of Bahá'u'lláh. They were the inhabitants of the 'City of Certitude' described in Chapter 2 of this book.

Dire Contests, Both Internal and External

As the progress of the Cause of God intensifies and the news of its increasing triumphs spreads worldwide, no doubt there will be reaction to these victories with fresh attacks by internal and external enemies of the Cause to 'dampen the enthusiasm of its supporters',[10] as the Universal House of Justice has indicated:

> Five months before he passed away, the beloved Guardian . . . drew our attention to the fact from both without and within the Faith evidences of 'increasing hostility' and 'persistent machinations' were apparent, and that they foreshadowed the 'dire contest' predicted by 'Abdu'l-Bahá, which was destined to 'range (the) Army (of) light (against the) forces (of) darkness, both secular (and) religious'.[11]

Furthermore, with the progressive unfoldment of the Faith we should expect that the rise of opposition in turn will 'accelerate the expansion of the beloved Cause'.[12] In their letter of 26 November 1974 quoted above, the House of Justice draws our attention to the 'inevitability of the critical contests which lie ahead'.[13]

Shoghi Effendi commented about the trials and tribulations of the Revelation of Bahá'u'lláh as compared to the religions of the past and also about the future of the Faith with respect to the opposition which will assail it. He wrote,

> The tribulations attending the progressive unfoldment of the Faith of Bahá'u'lláh have indeed been such as to exceed in gravity those from which the religions of the past have suffered. Unlike those religions, however, these tribulations have failed utterly to impair its unity . . .[14]

In his closing paragraph of *God Passes By*, the Guardian sums up the future direction and destiny of this mighty Cause, which will advance in spite of relentless attacks of opposition,:

> Whatever may befall this infant Faith of God in future decades or in succeeding centuries, whatever the sorrows, dangers and tribulations which the next stage in its world-wide development may engender, from whatever quarter the assaults to be launched by its present or future adversaries may be unleashed against it, however great the reverses and setbacks it may suffer, we, who have been privileged to apprehend, to the degree our finite minds can fathom, the significance of these marvellous phenomena associated with its rise and establishment, can harbour no doubt that what it has already achieved in the

first hundred years of its life provides sufficient guarantee that it will continue to forge ahead, capturing loftier heights, tearing down every obstacle, opening up new horizons and winning still mightier victories until its glorious mission, stretching into the dim ranges of time that lie ahead, is totally fulfilled.[15]

How Severe Will the Forces of Opposition Be?

The attacks by the enemies of the Faith, whether from within or outside the Bahá'í community, will not only target the Central Figures of the Cause but also its administrative institutions as well as individual believers, who will become the object of ostracism, slander and ridicule. The rise of lawlessness, prejudice, fanatic ideologies and a pervasive sense of mistrust by a growing number of people toward religion in general, together with the widespread denial of the existence of God, especially by young people, will be a worldwide challenge. The Bahá'í Faith, as a new religion with progressive perspectives on spiritual and social issues of humankind, will be particularly targeted as a threat to a wayward humanity.

In Western countries, too, Bahá'ís will undergo their share of adversity and attacks. 'Abdu'l-Bahá warned about persecution in these countries: 'a large multitude of people will arise against you, showing oppression, expressing contumely and derision, shunning your society, and heaping upon you ridicule.'[16]

What Should Our Attitude Be Toward Opposition?

There is a tendency in society for some people to react to hatred and violence with antagonism, agitation and sometimes with outbursts of aggressive behaviour. This is a short-sighted, emotional reaction which can result in the effect of escalated aggression. Instead of reacting with an emotional outburst or verbal condemnation, even for a worthy cause, an attitude of forbearance and patient reasoning which would be conducive to mutual understanding is more likely to be effective. This is particularly the case when we are privileged to defend the interests of the Faith; such an attitude sets a peaceful and non-violent example for all concerned.

There are cultural elements in the way we express our feelings and thoughts during a disagreeable or argumentative attack. In some cultures reaction is more visceral, while in other cultures it is a more intellectual. In the Bahá'í Writings, conflict and contention are strongly discouraged but this does not mean that we cannot defend ourselves or express our ideas to convey the truth. But we need to develop an attitude of magnanimity, love and forbearance, and this may not be easy!

Another factor bearing on our attitude is the fact that the outbursts of violence, hatred and calumny on the part of the enemies of the Cause are bound to occur, and these will, in part, raise public awareness of the existence and true nature of the Faith. It will arouse their interest and curiosity to investigate the truth of the new Manifestation.

How to Respond to Opposition

Human beings have been endowed with the capacity to respond to life challenges, including challenges of opposition whether internal or external. But in order to activate this capacity, we need to become enkindled by our love for Bahá'u'lláh and by His teachings. Sometimes when such enkindlement is lacking, we become complacent and then feel insecure and frustrated. In the Tablet of Aḥmad, Bahá'u'lláh writes:

> Forget not My bounties while I am absent. Remember My days during thy days, and My distress and banishment in this remote prison. And be thou so steadfast in My love that thy heart shall not waver, even if the swords of the enemies rain blows upon thee and all the heavens and the earth arise against thee.[17]

Such words fire us up and increase our capacity to respond. The Word of God is a great kindler of individual capacity, but to receive that inspiration we need to be connected. The Writings are our spiritual life-blood which we need for our sustenance.

There are psychological and spiritual approaches to develop such insight and skills. We don't necessarily have to obtain a university degree in order to develop this virtue. Concentrating on the meaning and purpose of the Revelation of Bahá'u'lláh and seeing ourselves as part of this universal enterprise for the advancement of a new civilization will help us to develop wisdom and forbearance in promoting the Cause. At the core of it all is the Creative Word of God which enables and empowers us to face calamities. Also, it is helpful to remember that each religious era began with persecution and suffering. Shoghi Effendi assures us that

> with every fresh outbreak of hostility to the Faith, whether from within or from without, a corresponding measure of outpouring grace, sustaining its defenders and confounding its adversaries, has been providentially released, communicating a fresh impulse to the onward march of the Faith . . .[18]

Besides the 'outpouring grace' which sustains us in the face of atrocities, and the Word of God, there is another kindler of capacity frequently mentioned in the Writings: the gift of encouragement. This is a most precious motivator. Yet it is the least available of gifts. I have often reflected on why, especially in the Western world, we neglect it. Perhaps it is because at times we tend to be so absorbed in our own needs and interests that we neglect to act with loving generosity and to encourage others. No doubt the corrosion of a materialistic environment has influenced our attitude, and this is something we need to guard against.

The dialectic process of crisis and victory characterizes the pattern of growth and expansion of the Cause in this Dispensation. Shoghi Effendi likens the tumultuous history of development of our Faith to 'rhythmic pulsations' which are 'precipitated, on the one hand, through the explosive outburst of its foes, and the vibrations of Divine Power, on the other . . . '[19] These pulsations enhance and propel the expansion of the Cause toward its destiny as part of the plan of God.

The spread and expansion of any new ideology or social movement are bound to attract attention, resulting in new believers as well as creating opposition. As the Revelation of Bahá'u'lláh has ushered in fundamental change in the social order, with new precepts and principles regarding human conduct and relationships, the opposition will be multidimensional and severe. Modern communications and technology have made it possible for the masses of humanity to become aware of the message of Bahá'u'lláh. The same system of communications may also provide the means for machinations and sedition more pernicious and oppressive than any religion of the past has witnessed. Yet according to the Writings, the flame of hatred and opposition will become the means of the promotion of the Faith and the transformation of the hearts of peoples of the world:

OPPOSITION AND THE CAPACITY TO RESPOND

> Great is the multitude who will rise up to oppose you, who will oppress you, heap blame upon you, rejoice at your misfortunes, account you people to be shunned, and visit injury upon you; yet shall your heavenly Father confer upon you such spiritual illumination that ye shall become even as the rays of the sun which, as they chase away the sombre clouds, break forth to flood the surface of the earth with light. It is incumbent upon you, whensoever these tests may overtake you, to stand firm, and to be patient and enduring. Instead of repaying like with like, ye should requite opposition with the utmost benevolence and loving-kindness, and on no account attach importance to cruelties and injuries, but rather regard them as the wanton acts of children. For ultimately the radiance of the Kingdom will overwhelm the darkness of the world of being, and the holy, exalted character of your aims will become unmistakably apparent. Nothing shall remain concealed: the olive oil, though stored within the deepest vault, shall one day burn in brightness from the lamp atop the beacon.[20]

It is interesting to note how in the above quotation 'Abdu'l-Bahá defines the believers' attitude toward opposition as being 'firm', 'patient', 'enduring' and with 'utmost benevolence and loving kindness'. These are spiritual virtues which defy psychological theories of 'fight or flight', vengeance or aggression.

Bahá'u'lláh exhorts the believers to remain steadfast and constant in the face of adversity and not be perturbed or weakened by the forces of persecution.:

> Say: O people of God! Beware lest the powers of the earth alarm you, or the might of the nations weaken you, or the tumult of the people of discord deter you, or the exponents of earthly glory sadden you. Be ye as a mountain in the Cause of your Lord, the Almighty, the All-Glorious, the Unconstrained.[21]

The first prerequisite for encountering any opposition is being deepened and well-grounded in the teachings and the Covenant of Bahá'u'lláh. Firmness in the Covenant is the most essential element necessary to withstand the assaults of the enemies of the Faith and the Covenant-breakers. It strengthens our faith, and with faith and certitude come blessings and resilience. 'Abdu'l-Bahá explains: 'You must make firm the feet at the time when these trials transpire, and demonstrate forbearance and patience. You must withstand them with the utmost love and kindness; consider their oppression and persecution as the caprice of children, and do not give any importance to whatever they do.'[22] Attention-seeking and promotion of hatred on the part of oppressors will be frustrated when the believers remain calm and steadfast.

Second: be patient and confident in considering the agitation of the enemies as 'the caprice of children'.[23] Children are more likely to be impulsive, agitated and irrational when their wants are not met. They need to recognize that they will not get more attention with a flare-up of temper, nor will they solve the problem.

Third: act with knowledge and wisdom. Don't be deterred by criticism, condemnation and slander. In the heat of persecution and oppression our mind is under stress and we are emotionally susceptible to mistreatment and insults. In such an environment, people are tempted to react with aggression. Avoid any verbal and physical altercation or violence. If we react to the violent behaviour of others by acting in a similar way, we lose our moral integrity and forbearance as Bahá'ís. Respond with patience and goodwill by presenting the facts, and defend our rights in a kindly and non-provocative manner. When we speak from a loving heart, it is likely that the hearts of others will respond. Sometimes this response is not forthcoming straight away, and we have to be patient. Sometimes no matter what we do to mitigate the adversarial behaviour of others, there may be no positive effect and we have to accept this.

Fourth: be resolute and resilient through knowledge of the teachings and reliance on divine assistance in a prayerful manner. Accept the fact that trials and tribulations are 'blessings in disguise' and that ultimately victory will prevail. In the West, the storm of opposition will be fierce. The following are Shoghi Effendi's emphatic words on the matter:

> Let not, however, the invincible army of Bahá'u'lláh, who in the West, and at one of its potential storm-centres is to fight, in His name and for His sake, one of its fiercest and most glorious battles, be afraid of any criticism that might be directed against it. Let it not be deterred by any condemnation with which the tongue of the slanderer may seek to debase its motives. Let it not recoil before the threatening advance of the forces of fanaticism, of orthodoxy, of corruption, and of prejudice

OPPOSITION AND THE CAPACITY TO RESPOND

that may be leagued against it. The voice of criticism is a voice that indirectly reinforces the proclamation of its Cause . . .²⁴

Remember the long-suffering of Bahá'u'lláh and other Central Figures of the Faith, and the thousands of believers who gave their lives in witness of the truth of this Revelation.

Fifth: remain united within the Bahá'í community and consult with institutions of the Faith (i.e. Spiritual Assemblies, Auxiliary Board members or their assistants). Opposition aims to weaken the will of the believers and cause division within the Bahá'í community. Such division would further isolate some Bahá'ís from others and make them more vulnerable to the assaults. The efforts of Covenant-breakers, for example, are directed toward creating doubt in the minds of Bahá'ís and breaking their resolve, following which they try to recruit them to their own camp.

Sixth: be firm in and faithful to the Covenant and obedient to the teachings of the Faith. No matter how dark may be the immediate future, ultimate triumph will prevail, as Bahá"lláh assures us:

> Behold how in this Dispensation the worthless and foolish have fondly imagined that by such instruments as massacre, plunder and banishment they can extinguish the Lamp which the Hand of Divine power hath lit, or eclipse the Day Star of everlasting splendour. How utterly unaware they seem to be of the truth that such adversity is the oil that feedeth the flame of this Lamp! Such is God's transforming power. He changeth whatsoever He willeth; He verily hath power over all things . . .²⁵

Despite antagonism, and the distress and suffering that we may experience for the love of Bahá'u'lláh, there are manifold beneficial effects from them:²⁶

- Attacks on the Bahá'í Faith are bound to attract interest in the Cause of Bahá'u'lláh. For the majority of people, this may be the first time that they become aware of this Revelation. Suffering and tribulation at the beginning of each religion have served as a driving force to raise the consciousness of humanity about the dawn of a new civilization.

- People will recognize that the moral and social principles of this religion meet the requirements of the age in which we live. For example, the emergence of Ṭáhirih at the beginning of the history of the Faith, with her knowledge and heroism, was an astonishing revelation, that from the age-old Islamic society came a woman who proclaimed the teachings of the new Dispensation regarding the equality of man and woman. It sent shock waves through a religious system which for over a thousand years had treated women as second-class citizens. Likewise, there are other tenets of this new-born religion about which the public has become aware.

- As a result of the attacks of the enemies, fair-minded people will be able to make a distinction between what Bahá'ís believe and the outdated beliefs of the religions of the past.

- The Bahá'í community will be solidified and purified. Those who are sincere will be distinguished from those who are doubtful. The former will become more deepened in the teachings of the new Revelation.

Two further points are important to mention in this respect. The first is that any misrepresentation of the Faith or attack on it in the media should be referred to one's National Spiritual Assembly for its consideration, as Shoghi Effendi explained:

> The matter of refuting attacks and criticism directed against the Cause through the press is, he feels, one which devolves on the National Spiritual Assembly to consider. This body, whether directly or through the agency of its committees, should decide as to the advisability of answering any such attacks . . .[27]

The second point is that we should not neglect to pray for those who attack the Faith, that they may be guided. Above all, we need to rely on divine assistance and meditate on the life and suffering of Bahá'u'lláh.

Love and Unity as a Protective Force

The degree of love and unity which connects the heart and the soul of the believers is an indicator of their strength as a vibrant community in the face of persecution and adversity. It was through this love, the 'secret of God's holy Dispensation' – in the words of 'Abdu'l-Bahá – that early believers arose with courage and determination to withstand tests and trials.

> Know thou of a certainty that Love is the secret of God's holy Dispensation, the manifestation of the All-Merciful, the fountain of spiritual outpourings. Love is heaven's kindly light, the Holy Spirit's eternal breath that vivifieth the human soul. Love is the cause of God's revelation unto man, the vital bond inherent, in accordance with the divine creation, in the realities of things. Love is the one means that ensureth true felicity both in this world and the next. Love is the light that guideth in darkness, the living link that uniteth God with man, that assureth the progress of every illumined soul. Love is the most great law that ruleth this mighty and heavenly cycle, the unique power that bindeth together the divers elements of this material world, the supreme magnetic force that directeth the movements of the spheres in the celestial realms. Love revealeth with unfailing and limitless power the mysteries latent in the universe. Love is the spirit of life unto the adorned body of mankind, the establisher of true civilization in this mortal world, and the shedder of imperishable glory upon every high-aiming race and nation.[28]

'Abdu'l-Bahá further elaborates on the power of unity among the believers:

> Whensoever holy souls, drawing on the powers of heaven, shall arise with such qualities of the spirit, and march in unison, rank on rank, every one of those souls will be even as one thousand, and the surging waves of that mighty ocean will be even as the battalions of the Concourse on high. What a blessing that will be – when all shall come together, even as once separate torrents, rivers and streams, running brooks and single drops, when collected together in one place will form a mighty sea. And to such a degree will the inherent unity

of all prevail, that the traditions, rules, customs and distinctions in the fanciful life of these populations will be effaced and vanish away like isolated drops, once the great sea of oneness doth leap and surge and roll.[29]

Internal Opposition

Opposition and attack from within the community of the Most Great Name has existed since the beginning of this Dispensation and caused much sorrow and grief to Bahá'u'lláh, 'Abdu'l-Bahá and the Guardian. As is indicated by the Universal House of Justice, 'The Bahá'í Faith has not lacked for ambitious men who would seize the reins of authority and distort the Faith for their own ends, but in every case they have broken themselves and dashed their hopes on the rock of the Covenant.'[30]

Although Covenant-breaking is a major form of internal opposition, there are other forms of attack which can be insidious in character without openly attacking the Central Figures or blatantly undermining the principles and institutions of the Faith. But they can be divisive, calculated and driven by a passion for power and domination. Some individuals eventually broke the Covenant in their burning desire for prominence and leadership. Notable among them were those who after the ascension of the Báb, Bahá'u'lláh and 'Abdu'l-Bahá arose against the appointed successors of these holy Central Figures and brought suffering and divisiveness to the Bahá'í community.

A number of these individuals were among the 'most powerful and renowned' devoted believers who once were counted as 'trusted and ablest propagators, champions, and administrators' of the Bahá'í Faith, as Shoghi Effendi tells us. Indeed, some were even from 'the kindred of the Manifestation, not excluding the brother, the sons and daughters of Bahá'u'lláh, and the nominee of the Báb Himself'.[31]

The history of the Cause is laden with tales characterized by such 'base betrayal, and is stained with the account of unspeakable atrocities'.[32]

Covenant-breaking: Its meaning and gravity

A covenant is 'a binding agreement'.[33] The Universal House of Justice defines Covenant-breaking in the Bahá'í Faith as follows:

> When a person declares his acceptance of Bahá'u'lláh as a Manifestation of God he becomes a party to the Covenant and accepts the totality of His Revelation. If he then turns round and attacks Bahá'u'lláh or the Central Institution of the Faith he violates the Covenant.[34]

Covenant-breakers are characterized by 'Abdu'l-Bahá as 'souls that are deprived of the Spirit of God and are lost in passion and self and are seeking leadership'.[35]

A contagious spiritual disease

In the Bahá'í Writings Covenant-breaking is considered as a 'spiritual disease'.[36] The Guardian stated that 'the whole view-point and attitude of a Covenant-breaker is so poisonous that the Master likened it to leprosy';[37] it is 'a contagious spiritual disease . . . however . . . [t]hese souls are not lost forever . . . It follows, therefore, that God will forgive any soul *if he repents*. Most of them don't want to repent, unfortunately.'[38]

Although there are sometimes signs which may guide a Covenant-breaker to redeem himself or herself, the mirror of the heart needs to be cleansed from the dust of egotism and lust for leadership. Otherwise that mirror may not be able to reflect the light of the Covenant. In his discussion of Covenant-breaking Adib Taherzadeh writes:

> Covenant-breaking is a spiritual disease and those who are affected by it are victims of their own selfish ambitions. It is only through a real awakening of the soul and recognizing one's transgressions against God that a Covenant-breaker can find the urge to repent, and when the repentant is sincere, God will forgive his past and restore his spiritual health. Indeed, there were a number of Covenant-breakers who were forgiven in this way by 'Abdu'l-Bahá and Shoghi Effendi.[39]

STEADFASTNESS IN THE COVENANT

What dangers do Covenant-breakers present?

The Centre of the Covenant admonished the believers about contact with Covenant-breakers in these emphatic words:

> ... one of the greatest and most fundamental principles of the Cause of God is to shun and avoid entirely the Covenant-breakers, for they will utterly destroy the Cause of God, exterminate His Law and render of no account all efforts exerted in the past.[40]

Furthermore, the Master emphasized that 'Were it not for the protecting power of the Covenant to guard the impregnable fort of the Cause of God, there would arise among the Bahá'ís, in one day, a thousand different sects as was the case in former ages.'[41]

The Universal House of Justice underlines the gravity of individual contact with Covenant-breakers:

> The seriousness of Covenant-breaking is that it strikes at the very centre and foundation of the unity of mankind. If God were to allow the instrument to be divided and impaired, how then would His purpose be achieved?[42]

As to whether the violators of the Covenant are fully aware of the nature and seriousness of their spiritually destructive behaviour, 'Abdu'l-Bahá stated:

> These do not doubt the validity of the Covenant but selfish motives have dragged them to this condition. It is not that they do not know what they do – they are perfectly aware and still they exhibit opposition.[43]

Bahá'í attitude towards Covenant-breakers: How to respond

Each individual believer needs to be prepared and deepened to withstand the danger posed by Covenant-breakers. 'Abdu'l-Bahá exhorts us:

> ... in the beginning one must make his steps firm in the Covenant – so that the confirmations of Bahá'u'lláh may encircle from all sides, the cohorts of the Supreme Concourse may become the supporters and the

helpers, and the exhortations and advices of 'Abdu'l-Bahá, like unto the pictures engraved on stone, may remain permanent and ineffaceable in the tablets of the hearts.[44]

Test of faith: A tale of two siblings

The following is the story of a brother and sister who grew up in a Persian Bahá'í family. The older brother became a Covenant-breaker during the ministry of the beloved Guardian and deprived himself from abiding beneath the shelter of the Covenant. Years later, the sister, ignoring the exhortation to shun Covenant-breakers, began to associate with him, claiming that she wanted to save her brother. Thus she became a Covenant-breaker herself.

In the 1980s, feeling isolated from the Bahá'í community, she wrote to the Universal House of Justice asking to be reinstated. In a meeting with an Auxiliary Board member which followed she was sorrowful and grieving at being shunned by Bahá'ís but she remained very adamant about not relinquishing her association with her Covenant-breaker brother. She maintained that her blood relationship with her brother was more important than obedience to the Covenant of Bahá'u'lláh. That was a test which she failed and sadly she remained a Covenant-breaker.

Some twenty-five years later, when she was in her 70s, it was discovered that she was suffering from an advanced and serious cancer which had spread to many organs of her body. She was hospitalized in a palliative care facility and was very hopeless. There, one day, she met a nurse who came to draw blood for a lab test. As she looked at the nurse, her curiosity was aroused and she asked about the nationality and religion of the nurse. It turned out that this nurse was a Bahá'í. The patient (Miss A) found it a very strange coincidence that after years she had now come face to face with a Bahá'í. She wondered what it meant. Miss A told the nurse that for years she had not met Bahá'ís and that she felt isolated. She expressed her wish to rejoin the Bahá'í community. However, the nurse began to feel uncomfortable about this; she began to wonder if Miss A was a Covenant-breaker. The news reached the National Spiritual Assembly, which knew about Miss A and her Covenant-breaker brother. It turned out that the brother was also hospitalized in the same medical facility, but in a different part of it and that the siblings were in contact with one another. When the wish of Miss A to be reinstated as a Bahá'í and the terminal state of her cancer was conveyed to the Universal House of Justice, a person who knew the case well was appointed to meet with Miss A and discuss the matter.

At the meeting, Miss A spoke of the sudden discovery of an aggressive cancer and the subsequent rapid deterioration of her health. As she talked about the 'coincidence' of meeting a Bahá'í nurse in the midst of her despair regarding the gravity of her illness, she realized that there must be a meaning, a message in that encounter. Yet when it was brought to her attention that the event might have an important bearing with respect to her obedience to the Covenant and with turning toward Bahá'u'lláh rather than toward her brother, she reasserted that her relation with her brother remained as before, although she minimized the importance of her association with him. After some reflection and prayer, a new realization dawned on her: she could see the signs of the test of her faith. She realized that there was a meaning to her grave illness and her unexpected encounter with a Bahá'í nurse in light of this transitory life and her spiritual destiny. She finally acknowledged the mistake she had made in not heeding the exhortation to shun Covenant-breakers; she was now longing to obey the Covenant and to remain steadfast in it. Since she appeared to be sincere in her determination, she was then reinstated as a member of the Bahá'í community. She longed to be active again to serve in the community when she was moved to a nursing home. A few months later she passed away, as a Bahá'í who had submitted her will to the will of Bahá'u'lláh, after having reaffirmed her obedience to the Covenant. With regard to her brother, sadly within a few months he too passed away as a result of illness; he, however, remained unchanged.

Shunning Covenant-breakers

In the Writings of Bahá'u'lláh we read the following exhortation: 'Beware! Walk not with the ungodly and seek not fellowship with him, for such companionship turneth the radiance of the heart into infernal fire.'[45] 'Abdu'l-Bahá too emphasized the importance given by Bahá'u'lláh to shunning Covenant-breakers:

> Again He says: 'Say, O my friend and my pure ones! Listen to the Voice

of this Beloved Prisoner in this Great Prison. If you detect in any man the least perceptible breath of violation, shun him and keep away from him.' Then He says: 'Verily, they are manifestations of Satan.'[46]

Any encounter with a Covenant-breaker is like being in contact with someone who has a serious infectious disease. He may be charming and acting kindly, or be boastful about his knowledge of the Faith, but his infection is contagious and will have an effect on the believer. Being deepened in the Covenant is like a form of spiritual vaccination for protection. However, the Writings warn against coming into contact with Covenant-breakers, just as a wise physician warns us to avoid being in contact with someone who has an infectious disease:

> 'Abdu'l-Bahá is extremely kind, but when the disease is leprosy, what am I to do? Just as in bodily diseases we must prevent intermingling and infection and put into effect sanitary laws – because the infectious physical diseases uproot the foundation of humanity; likewise one must protect and safeguard the blessed souls from the breaths and fatal spiritual diseases; otherwise violation, like the plague, will become a contagion and all will perish.[47]

Thus 'Abdu'l-Bahá compares the 'breath' of the violators of the Covenant to a 'poison' which can be detrimental to our spiritual health.[48]

Although we must shun Covenant-breakers, we are also advised to pray for them, as Shoghi Effendi points out:

> Bahá'u'lláh and the Master in many places and very emphatically have told us to shun entirely all Covenant-breakers as they are afflicted with what we might try and define as a contagious spiritual disease; they have also told us, however, to pray for them. These souls are not lost forever ... It follows, therefore, that God will forgive any soul if he repents.[49]

With regard to materials written by Covenant-breakers, the Guardian advised that '[i]t is better not to read books by Covenant-breakers because they are haters of the Light, sufferers from a spiritual leprosy, so to speak. But books by well meaning yet unenlightened enemies of the Cause can be read so as to refute their charges.'[50] The Universal House of Justice, too, advises that it is to be expected that books will be written against the Faith attempting to distort its teachings, to denigrate its accomplishments, to vilify its Founders and leaders and to destroy its very foundations. The friends should not be unduly exercised when these books appear and certainly no issue should be made of them.[51]

And:

There should certainly be no attempt made to destroy or remove such books from libraries. On the other hand there is no need at all for the friends to acquire them, and indeed, the best plan is to ignore them entirely.[52]

Further, the House of Justice tells us that

[i]t is useful to bear in mind that the Internet is a reflection of the world around us, and we find in its infinitude of pages the same competing forces of integration and disintegration that characterize the tumult in which humanity is caught up. In their use of the Internet, Bahá'ís should stand aloof from the negative forces operating within it, availing themselves of its potential to spread the Word of God and to inspire and uplift others. [53]

Does the removal from the Bahá'í community of someone who is a violator of the Covenant infringe upon the concept of unity, as Covenant-breakers themselves sometimes claim? Shoghi Effendi clarified this matter, stating that

it has nothing to do with unity in the Cause; if a man cuts a cancer out of his body to preserve his health and very life no one would suggest that for the sake of "unity" it should be reintroduced into the otherwise healthy organism! On the contrary, what was once a part of him has so radically changed as to have become a poison.[54]

Questions have been raised about Covenant-breakers and their civil rights. It requires much wisdom to respond to this. The Universal House of Justice in a letter to a believer on this subject wrote:

First, the civil rights of Covenant-breakers must be scrupulously upheld. For example, if a Baháʾí owes a debt to a person who breaks the Covenant he must be sure that it is repaid and that his obligations are met.

Secondly, although the believers are required to avoid, if possible, all contact with Covenant-breakers it sometimes happens that contact on business matters cannot be avoided. For example, in one city the head of the rate collection department was a Covenant-breaker. In such situations the believers should restrict their contact with the Covenant-breaker to a purely formal business level and to an absolute minimum.[55]

Counsellors and their auxiliaries are also responsible for protection of the Faith and should be contacted for advice as needed.

The intention of Covenant-breakers is to create doubt and division among the Baháʾís. Therefore the unity and solidarity of the Baháʾí community is of vital importance.

Internal Opposition: Recent Challenges

Internal opposition has taken different forms in the history of the Faith. As communication technology advances, the forms of expression of opposition and the pace of its spread in a country or around the world have also changed. Some of these attacks may manifest themselves subtly and insidiously, while others will be open; both can have pernicious consequences.

Shoghi Effendi describes certain individual internal enemies (as compared with the external ones) to be 'the far more dangerous, insidious, lukewarm people inside the Faith who have no real attachment to the Covenant, and consequently uphold the intellectual aspect of the teachings while at the same time undermining the spiritual foundation upon which the whole Cause of God rests.'[56]

A recent campaign of internal opposition to the teachings of the Faith carried out by a small number of individuals began in the 1990s.[57] Through the use of the Internet they attempted to cast doubt on the integrity of 'the institutional authority established by His Covenant' and to promote a form of 'interpretive authority' based on the views of 'persons technically trained in Middle East Studies'.[58] This is in conflict with the exhortations of the Central Figures of the Faith on interpretation of the Writings. (The issue of authoritative interpretation of the Writings in the Bahá'í Faith is discussed in another chapter of this book.) Although the individuals concerned purported to accept 'the legitimacy of the Guardianship and the Universal House of Justice as twin successors of Bahá'u'lláh and the Centre of the Covenant', nevertheless they 'cast doubt on the nature and scope of the authority conferred on them in the Writings'.[59]

Further, they sought to 'recast the entire Faith into a socio-political ideology alien to Bahá'u'lláh's intent'.[60] The Universal House of Justice elucidated on this development by stating that 'In general, the strategy being pursued has been to avoid direct attacks on the Faith's Central Figures. The effort, rather, has been to sow the seeds of doubt among believers about the Faith's teachings and institutions . . .'[61]

External Opposition: Enemies of the Faith

Ever since its beginning in the mid-nineteenth century, the Bahá'í Faith and its followers have been subjected to episodic outbursts of violence and persecution. Thousands upon thousands of Bábís and Bahá'ís were martyred in the Cradle of their Faith. Waves of persecution were instigated by the clergy, who incited the mob through false accusations against the Bahá'ís, often supported by the government and civil authorities as well. Although Bahá'ís have been discriminated against or persecuted in other countries, nowhere has their persecution been so severe or as intense as in Iran.

The government of the Islamic Republic of Iran, especially in recent years, has stepped up its anti-Bahá'í propaganda by using a wide range of media to incite hatred. They have called Bahá'ís 'misguided', 'deviant', or 'satanic'; people who belong to a 'sect or cult' and are morally corrupt.[62] In order to isolate and stigmatize Bahá'ís they accuse them of having political affiliation with countries such as Israel and other Western countries. The Bahá'í principle of the equality of men and women is called the 'mingling of men and women', implying that this activity is immoral and criminal.[63] Even schoolchildren have not been spared from attempts at indoctrination. 'In a shameful attempt to instil a lifelong prejudice among the young against Bahá'ís' the government gave schoolchildren a 'gift' of an illustrated story book

OPPOSITION AND THE CAPACITY TO RESPOND

that purposely misrepresents the history of the Bahá'í Faith.[64]

Since 1979 thousands of Bahá'ís have been arrested and imprisoned and over 200 of them have been executed. Not content with attacking the living, officials have attacked and desecrated Bahá'í cemeteries in several towns and cities. Arson attacks and firebombings of Bahá'í-owned shops and homes have also occurred, especially in such cities as Semnan, Rafsanjan and Yazd.

In brief, government-sponsored incitement of hatred, supported by mobs, has created a climate of mistrust, hatred and terror against Bahá'ís. (For more detailed information see Chapter 4.)

Civil and religious leaders have constituted the main source of opposition to the Cause. Bahá'u'lláh identified the divines as enemies: 'The source and origin of tyranny . . . have been the divines. Through the sentences pronounced by these haughty and wayward souls the rulers of the earth have wrought that which ye have heard . . .'[65] The divines are the 'veils of glory' who 'because of their want of discernment and their love and eagerness for leadership, have failed to submit to the Cause of God...'[66]

Motivation for opposition to Divine Revelation may stem from two kinds of inner craving: 'ambition, jealousy and pride, on the one hand, and, on the other, ignorance, error and prejudice'.[67]

Because the divines are regarded by people as 'God's spokesmen on earth', when they turn against the Prophet of God, their congregations follow. When they 'called for efforts to stamp out the new religion, mobs very often arose and did their bidding'.[68] Addressing them, Bahá'u'lláh proclaimed:

> O concourse of divines! Fling away idle fancies and imaginings, and turn, then, towards the Horizon of Certitude. I swear by God! All that ye possess will profit you not, neither all the treasures of the earth, nor the leadership ye have usurped. Fear God, and be not of the lost ones.[69]

Writing about the attacks the Faith would be subject to in the future, Shoghi Effendi warned that

> [p]eoples, nations, adherents of divers faiths, will jointly and successively arise to shatter its unity, to sap its force, and to degrade its holy name. They will assail not only the spirit which it inculcates, but the

administration which is the channel, the instrument, the embodiment of that spirit.⁷⁰

He also warned that the Faith can anticipate criticism not only from the Christian clergy but also from the atheistic movements and philosophies that pervade Western society:

> That the forces of irreligion, of a purely materialistic philosophy, of unconcealed paganism have been unloosed, are now spreading, and, by consolidating themselves, are beginning to invade some of the most powerful Christian institutions of the western world, no unbiased observer can fail to admit.⁷¹

He goes on to explain that as these institutions weaken, and as they begin to become aware of the influence of the Faith, they will attempt to assail it, which will result in their further demise.⁷²

Protection of the Faith

'The greatest of all things is the protection of the True Faith of God, the preservation of His Law, the safeguarding of His Cause and service unto His Word,' writes 'Abdu'l-Bahá.⁷³

Let us reflect on the question of what is the purpose of religion and the role of the Covenant. Bahá'u'lláh writes that 'the fundamental purpose animating the Faith of God and His religion is to safeguard the interests and promote the unity of the human race, and to foster the spirit of love and fellowship amongst men'.⁷⁴

Bahá'u'lláh also created a powerful instrument 'to safeguard and promote the unity' of humankind and that is the institution of the Covenant. It embodies the 'spirit, instrumentality and method' required for preserving the integrity of that unity. It provides 'a wholly new relationship between humanity and its Supreme Creator'.⁷⁵

In *The Advent of Divine Justice* Shoghi Effendi quotes Bahá'u'lláh as follows:

> 'In the beginning of every Revelation adversities have prevailed, which later on have been turned into great prosperity.' 'Say: O people of God! Beware lest the powers of the earth alarm you, or the might of the

OPPOSITION AND THE CAPACITY TO RESPOND

nations weaken you, or the tumult of the people of discord deter you, or the exponents of earthly glory sadden you. Be ye as a mountain in the Cause of your Lord, the Almighty, the All-Glorious, the Unconstrained.' 'Say: Beware, O people of Bahá, lest the strong ones of the earth rob you of your strength, or they who rule the world fill you with fear. Put your trust in God, and commit your affairs to His keeping. He, verily, will, through the power of truth, render you victorious, and He, verily, is powerful to do what He willeth, and in His grasp are the reins of omnipotent might.' 'I swear by My life! Nothing save that which profiteth them can befall My loved ones . . .'[76]

To appreciate the significance of the protection of the Cause from the attacks of internal and external enemies, the Universal House of Justice brings to our attention the following:

> The need to protect the Faith from the attacks of its enemies may not be generally appreciated by the friends, particularly in places where attacks have been infrequent. However, it is certain that such opposition will increase, become concerted, and eventually universal. The writings clearly foreshadow not only an intensification of the machinations of internal enemies, but a rise in the hostility and opposition of its external enemies, whether religious or secular, as the Cause pursues its onward march towards ultimate victory. Therefore, in the light of the warnings of the Guardian, the Auxiliary Boards for Protection should keep 'constantly' a 'watchful eye' on those 'who are known to be enemies, or to have been put out of the Faith', discreetly investigate their activities, alert intelligently the friends to the opposition inevitably to come, explain how each crisis in God's Faith has always proved to be a blessing in disguise, and prepare them for the 'dire contest which is destined to range the Army of Light against the forces of darkness'.[77]

4

Persecution, Resilience and Heroism*

> There is always an important difference between friends and tested friends. No matter how precious the first type may be, the future of the Cause rests upon the latter . . .
>
> *Shoghi Effendi* [1]

Shoghi Effendi stated that 'an essential characteristic of this world is hardship and tribulation and that by overcoming them we achieve our moral and spiritual development . . . sorrow is like furrows, the deeper they go, the more plentiful is the fruit we obtain.'[2]

Many believers in the Bahá'í Faith have demonstrated high levels of tolerance and magnanimity in the face of tests and tribulation. Their resilience stands in contrast to the general tendency – particularly in Western society and often encouraged by the media – to see oneself as 'vulnerable' and 'victimized'.

The Power of Faith

Research has shown that although severe life stressors and adversities may increase the risk of emotional disturbance (such as depression in the face of personal losses), most of those who suffer personal adversities do not necessarily become clinically depressed and incapacitated.[3] Resistance to distressful situations is relative and depends on cultural, social and spiritual aspects of life.

In addition to psychological defence mechanisms for coping, one

---

* Parts of this chapter are adapted from Ghadirian, 'Psychological and Spiritual Dimensions of Persecution and Suffering', in *The Journal of Bahá'í Studies*, vol. 6, no. 3 (1994), pp. 1–26. Courtesy of the Association of Bahá'í Studies – North America.

needs to come to terms with the reality of the stressful life events and their meaning. This is a process of making an internal adjustment to a difficult problem of an external nature. Depending on educational and cultural attitudes, the coping mechanisms may vary greatly from person to person. In a life crisis of serious proportions such as a death in the family, the following phases of mourning may take place: shock, denial, despair, recognition, and acceptance. The individual's attitude toward and belief about death and life after death will have an important bearing on the ability to cope. Therefore, adaptational responses are not elicited universally in an identical fashion; there are considerable variations, depending on individual belief, character, and life experience.

Tolerance and magnanimity have been observed among the early believers of each religion and even among certain pioneers in science who defied opposition with logic and peaceful tolerance. One explanation could be that when the life threat, whether psychological or physical, can be explained and made sense of in the light of scientific or spiritual conviction, that insight will arouse considerable courage, which will, in turn, abate the fear and anxiety created by the critical attack. Moreover, faith itself is a potent force in which human beings find their 'ultimate fulfilment', as the 20th-century philosopher Paul Tillich wrote.[4] With true faith, one sees in an inevitable death a fulfilment of one's spiritual principles.

Thus, faith gives a new meaning to suffering that can transform fear into joy and despair into hope. The heroic lives of the martyrs, their determination and perseverance for their cause in spite of the torture and torments inflicted upon them, testify to the strength of their faith and the loftiness of their belief for which they give their most precious possession: life itself. I believe that this is a triumph of the soul in the pursuit of truth, for which contemporary science is at a loss to find a definitive answer.

The history of religions shows that human tolerance to suffering goes far beyond the psychological formulation of defences and stress adaptation. In such cases suffering is perceived neither as a destructive force of despair, nor as a grievous blow to human defences. Rather, it is welcomed with faith and contentment. This does not imply that victims of religious persecution are always entirely free from pain and sorrow; rather it suggests that their spiritual conviction and faith have changed their perception and attitude toward suffering and have empowered them to accept it with greater tolerance. As to how a profound spiritual faith can raise the physiological threshold of pain and suffering, it is difficult to determine with scientific certainty at present, since neither spirituality nor suffering is an experience that can be measured and quantified biochemically or physiologically.

Psychological reactions compared with spiritual responses in the face of adversity

The following table compares psychological distress reactions to spiritual responses:[5]

Psychological reactions	Spiritual responses
Denial or perplexity	Acknowledgement and forbearance
Amnesia or selective attention	Perceptivity and full attention
Fear	Courage
Avoidance and withdrawal	Affiliation and acceptance
Counterbehaviour, e.g. fight or flight	Expression of love and tolerance
Disillusionment and discontent	Certitude and contentment
Dependence solely on self	Submission to Will of God
Coping through reason	Reaching beyond reason: faith

The Triad of Oppression, Resilience and Faith

The impact of a stressor such as oppression may depend on three factors:[6]

- intensity of oppression;
- personal endurance and resilience; and
- spiritual or ideological conviction and attitude toward oppression.

Based on this model, the severity of oppression (e.g. trauma, torment, persecution) may not significantly disturb the believer if the person is prepared to endure for a cause and finds a meaning in it that would be aligned with his or her understanding of the purpose of life and spiritual perspective.

Although the severity of oppression directed toward an individual is usually beyond his or her control, resilience and personal attitude and belief are important factors. Both resilience and attitude are influenced by spiritual or socio-cultural beliefs. In this process, the attitude will strengthen the will to endure and to resist the oppression. In reports of experiences in concentration camps, those who maintained a hopeful and positive attitude or displayed active resistance and perseverance fared better in survival over those who remained as victims, because the resistance activated self-esteem and contact with the outside world.[7] This experience of resistance, however, took place in a circumscribed environment different from a closed prison environment where active resistance can cause punitive reprisal.

Transformation of Hate into Love

The mystic transformation of hate into love is the result of spiritual education and a deeper understanding of the reality of human destiny; it is these that empower a person to change. It would be very difficult, if not impossible, for one to develop such a capacity for personal transformation without the aid of a higher spiritual insight and faith. A distinguishing feature of responses elicited by the brutal persecution of the Bahá'ís of Iran (described in more detail below) is the non-violent and peaceful attitude of the believers in the face of adversity. The teachings of the Faith transformed their reaction to the hatred of enemies of the Faith into a meaningful response and an expression of love, as it is believed that love is the very purpose of the creation of mankind.

The Bahá'í Writings tell us that the creative words of the Manifestation of God can empower the soul and transform the heart and create a new race of people with a world-embracing vision. This transformation can break down the barriers of hatred and prejudice and give a new meaning and purpose to people. As a result of this world view of greater love and harmony for all, hatred is dissipated along with all fears and anxiety.[8]

'Abdu'l-Bahá illustrates the process of transformation of attributes by giving the example of iron, which ordinarily has the qualities of being solid, black and cold. However, when this metal absorbs heat from fire, its natural attributes are 'sacrificed' and transformed into new qualities: its solidity to fluidity; its darkness to light; and its cold to heat. Thus, as the original qualities of iron disappear, the qualities of fire appear in their place.[9] Likewise, in the fire of ordeals, one sacrifices one's material desires and qualities for spiritual attributes.

In the Bahá'í Writings, sufferings and tribulations are considered as blessings in disguise; through them, Shoghi Effendi writes, 'our inner spiritual forces become stimulated, purified and ennobled'.[10] Moreover, there is a great wisdom in their occurrence: 'whatsoever comes to pass in the Cause of God, however disquieting in its immediate effects, is fraught with infinite Wisdom and tends ultimately to promote its interests in the world'.[11] Submission to the Will of God is an essential attitude for Bahá'ís who are faced with adversities beyond their control.

The Covenant and the Persecution of Bahá'ís in Iran

With the rise of the Islamic Republic of Iran another violent long wave of persecution of Bahá'ís began. 'Between 1978 and 1998, more than 200 Bahá'ís were executed by the Iranian government. Hundreds more Bahá'ís were imprisoned and tortured and tens of thousands were deprived of jobs, pensions, business and educational opportunities.'[12] Bahá'ís responded with courage and an unwavering determination in the face of all measures of harassment, intimidation, and dismissal from employment, the purpose of which was to induce them to recant their allegiance to the Bahá'í Faith.

One of the most common forms of resistance in these persecutions has been the refusal of the believers to recant their faith, and instead to actively proclaim their belief. This refusal angered and frustrated the authorities, who failed to break the resistance of these Bahá'ís and thus intensified their repression. Persecutions were often characterized by physical assaults, torture, imprisonment, starvation and death, or psychological insults and abuses by means of false accusations, humiliation, threats, and deprivation of personal and social rights and privileges.

One example was Professor Manúchihr Hakím, an outstanding and much loved physician, who in 1981 was murdered in his office while caring for patients in Teheran. He was killed by an assailant posing as a patient who needed medical advice after office hours. Professor Hakím was a gentle, loving physician whose only 'crime' was to be a member of the Bahá'í Faith. Five years earlier he had been decorated by the French government with the Legion of Honour for his humanitarian services. Well known for his scientific endeavours, he graduated from the Medical College of Paris and was cited in the prestigious *Le Rouvière*, the French medical encyclopedia, for his anatomical discoveries.[13]

As a physician and an academician, he served thousands of his sick and suffering fellow citizens with the highest degree of dedication and professional integrity. But even his profile of service to humanity did not spare his life from those who could not come to terms with his belief as a Bahá'í – further evidence of the terrible influence of blind prejudice that dissociates human virtues and noble accomplishments from personal belief in another religion or ideology.

Psychological Terror Used in the Persecution of Bahá'ís

In recent times, the Islamic Government of Iran has used various forms of psychological intimidation and mental torture as another approach in their arsenal of methods of repression perpetrated with the prime goal of crushing the will of the believers. Among these different psychological approaches used to torment and subjugate innocent believers, the following are just a few examples; they took place particularly during the first two decades of the Republic.[14]

Terrorizing the mind – dehumanization

- Forced exposure of the Bahá'ís to witness the torture of their family members and friends, or to witness the horrifying scene of the lacerated and injured bodies of these individuals in order to arouse fear.

- Mock execution and other acts of terror in an attempt to manipulate emotions and to force Bahá'ís to recant their faith or admit to false accusations.

- In some cases, after the death sentence of a group of Bahá'í prisoners was issued, the identity of those condemned was withheld by the government, causing enormous psychological stress and anguish among relatives and friends. The relatives were left to speculate constantly and painfully about the fate and whereabouts of their loved ones and the possibility of reunion with them.

Deprivation of human contact

- Total solitary confinement in isolated cells (i.e. 1.72 x 2 meters) without verbal contact with anyone, including prison guards, for weeks or even months.[15] Such sensory deprivation and emotional isolation for a long period of time usually leads to serious psychological consequences. But knowing that this suffering was for Bahá'u'lláh and that it might prove the truth of their belief, Bahá'í prisoners bore it with patience and magnanimity.

Shocking of survivors

- Often, after the execution of Bahá'ís, close family members were not informed of their death, and when this was eventually discovered the authorities would refuse the family any access to the body, thus increasing the sorrow of the grieving survivors. Many of the martyrs whose bodies were not delivered to the family by prison authorities had most likely been subjected to cruel physical torture and injuries prior to death, a fact which the authorities were reluctant to have exposed.

- After the victim was executed, his or her house and belongings were confiscated, leaving the surviving spouse and children homeless. To add insult to injury, the survivors of those who were executed by firing squad were ordered to pay for the cost of the bullets that took the life of their loved ones, a cruelty unmatched in modern history. Family members in some areas were asked to make regular monthly payments for the expenses of the inmates, another example of contempt for the Bahá'ís. In recent years, in an Iranian city, young Bahá'í women were targeted for imprisonment while they were pregnant or had infants, who would be taken to prison with their mothers.

Assault on conscience – demoralization

- Many Bahá'í women or girls were victims of violence and assaults. Some were forced to marry Muslims under Islamic law and were deprived of the right to rear their children as Bahá'ís.

Creating hate among children

- Bahá'í children have also been experiencing psychological pressure in their neighbourhoods by being labelled as the offspring of heretics. They have also been ridiculed in their classrooms and discriminated against at school. In the early days of the Revolution, Bahá'í children were refused admission to school.

Desecration of graves

- Mobs in some towns or cities attacked Bahá'í cemeteries, destroyed and desecrated graves, and dug up and burned bodies. Graves were bulldozed and Bahá'ís were prevented from burying their dead. This reflects the extent of out-of-control violence. The attacks were also directed toward the Bahá'í sacred places and writings.[16]

Steadfastness in the Face of Tribulation

Steadfastness on the part of the believer can evoke an even greater hatred in the persecutors, as this is seen as a sign of the latter's failure. Distortions of truth and manipulation of the public perception of Bahá'ís, stigmatizing them as agents of foreign powers or basically unclean people, as a means of discrediting them and justifying the hatred against them, is quite common. In such circumstances, the public's ignorance and its refusal or fear to search after truth create an ideal climate for accomplishing fanatical objectives. One example in the persecution of the Bahá'ís in Iran is the Bahá'í principle of equality of the rights of men and women in the Bahá'í community and the fact that there is no segregation of sexes in Bahá'í gatherings; these have been attacked by the clergy as immoral deviation in a society where male domination has been the rule for centuries.[17] Not only has the theocratic government of Iran failed to make any progress in countering these accusations, but also the rise of women in the country to voice their claim to equality has caused fear and anxiety in the perpetrators of human rights violations in that country.

Bahá'u'lláh reveals that the suffering his followers experience is preordained to proclaim the Cause of God in this new Dispensation. He thus prays for His followers in their suffering:

> Help them through Thy strengthening grace, I beseech Thee, O my God, to suffer patiently in their love for Thee, and unveil to their eyes what Thou hast decreed for them behind the Tabernacle of Thine unfailing protection, so that they may rush forward to meet what is preordained for them in Thy path, and may vie in hasting after tribulation in their love towards Thee.[18]

Moreover, Bahá'u'lláh elucidates that love for God will enable believers to resist the powers arising against them and to overcome any fear. The result is courage and heroism, as observed in the multitude of Bahá'ís who have experienced torture and atrocities. In the Bahá'í Writings, there is a significant association between true love and pain, as reflected in these words from *The Seven Valleys*:

> The steed of this Valley [Love] is pain; and if there be no pain this journey will never end. In this station the lover hath no thought save the Beloved, and seeketh no refuge save the Friend. At every moment he offereth a hundred lives in the path of the Loved One, at every step he throweth a thousand heads at the feet of the Beloved.[19]

Martyrdom and the Bahá'í Faith

The meaning of the word *martyr* in both English and Arabic is 'witness'. It goes beyond bloodshed and physical suffering, as commonly believed. Martyrs are those who bear witness to the truth of their belief by submitting themselves to death under circumstances beyond their control, rather than renouncing their faith. Hence, Bahá'ís do not seek martyrdom for honour or reward in the afterlife. Death is imposed on them because of their refusal to deny their faith. Based on the spiritual concept of martyrdom and the heavy emphasis placed on teaching religion and serving humanity, it is possible for a person to survive and yet be counted as a martyr in the sight of God.[20] Taherzadeh tells us that:

> [i]n one of His Tablets Bahá'u'lláh states that there are two things pleasing to God: the tears shed in fear of Him and the blood of the martyr spilt in His path. But since Bahá'u'lláh has advised His followers not to volunteer to give their lives, He has replaced it with teaching His Cause.[21]

Keith Ransom-Kehler: First and distinguished Western Bahá'í martyr

The mission of Mrs Keith Ransom-Kehler, an American Bahá'í, to travel to Iran under the guidance of the Guardian in order to intercede with the Persian government to lift the ban on the entry and circulation of Bahá'í literature is an example of how the Western believers responded to the suffering and deprivation of the Bahá'ís of Iran.

In 1932 Mrs Ransom Kehler was chosen by Shoghi Effendi to represent the National Spiritual Assembly of the United States and Canada for this assignment. 'In a land where women were still largely secluded in the home,' write Janet and Peter Khan, 'Mrs Ransom-Kehler was required to relate, at the highest level, to government ministers and members of parliament in her efforts to have the Bahá'í petition presented to the Shah. Reflecting on her experience in a letter she wrote from Teheran to her National Spiritual Assembly, she comments, "How strange the ways of God, that I, a poor, feeble, old woman from the distant west, should be pleading for liberty and justice in the land of Bahá'u'lláh." '[22]

During her almost 16 months of service in Iran from 1932 to 1933, she did her utmost with much determination to resolve the obstacles. She also travelled to many cities and villages across Iran to meet and encourage Bahá'ís, especially women. But the government officials never acted upon the request in her petition, and her tireless efforts and letters of request to remedy the problem did not lead to success. 'Disappointed at the failure of her mission and exhausted from her constant efforts to visit and address Baháʼí gatherings throughout Persia, Mrs Ransom-Kehler fell victim to smallpox and passed away in Isfahan on 23 October 1933.'[23]

On receiving the news of her passing, Shoghi Effendi in a cable dated 30 October 1933 lamented her loss and spoke of the significance of her suffering and her station as the 'first and distinguished martyr' of America. He also raised her station, posthumously, to an 'eminent rank among the Hands of the Cause of Baháʼuʼlláh'. He moreover indicated that Keith's precious life had been offered up 'in sacrifice' to 'the beloved Cause in Baháʼuʼlláh's native land'.[24]

Although Mrs Ramson-Kehler felt that she had failed in her mission on behalf of the Baháʼís of Iran, she left a moving and poignant statement about the value of service and sacrifice:

> Nothing in the world is meaningless, suffering least of all. Sacrifice with its attendant agony is a germ, an organism. Man cannot blight its fruition as he can the seeds of the earth. Once sown it blooms, I think, forever in the sweet fields of eternity. Mine will be a very modest flower, perhaps like the single, tiny forget-me-not, watered by the blood of Quddús that I plucked in the Sabz-i-Maydán of Bárfurúsh; should it ever catch the eye, may one who seems to be struggling in vain garner it in the name of Shoghi Effendi and cherish it for his dear remembrance.[25]

Reactions of martyrs' families to persecutors

In the 1990s I conducted a research study on the first-degree relatives of a number of Baháʼís who had been martyred. Among them were 19 children, two grandchildren and eight spouses (all wives). The goal of the study was to find their reactions to the execution of their loved one. The participants of the main part of the study were 27 Persian Baháʼís whose close relative had been executed by the Islamic Revolutionary Government of Iran between 1979 and 1989. Although the details of the study, published in 1998,[26] are beyond the scope of this chapter, I include here a brief excerpt detailing the responses received to one important question of that research as follows: 'What are your thoughts and feelings about those who were responsible for the execution of your martyred family member?'

Some of the respondents reacted by saying that although initially they had a feeling of hatred and anger, later on, they developed a sense of forgiveness. Others felt that the persecution was a part of a greater plan of God to promote His Cause: 'He doeth what He willeth.' In this plan, the protagonists on the scene of persecution played their role, while submission and acceptance became the lot of those who suffered. One person blamed the cleric system and not the individuals for the tragedy. As a whole, there was no sense of revenge. This is not a denial of underlying anger as much as it is an expression of belief based on tolerance and forgiveness. It also reflects a broader vision of calamity, which is viewed as a disguised blessing that ultimately leads to the expansion of the Faith. For example, a daughter grieving the death of her executed father commented that because of the Divine Plan, 'I do not feel any hatred toward those who contaminated their hand with the blood of my father . . . May God forgive their transgressions. I pray fervently for them.'

What is interesting is that several of the respondents reacted initially with anger and hate, but soon these feelings yielded to more positive effects as compassion and forgiveness prevailed. This is a transformation of hate into love. Some left the aggressors to be judged and dealt with by God. Others pitied them for their ignorance.[27]

Inciting Hatred

As we have seen, the persecution of the Bahá'ís of Iran is not new; it has been going on since the birth of the Bahá'í Revelation. A special report by the Bahá'í International Community in 2011 gives a brief overview of persecution in the 20th century, when

> periodic outbreaks of violence against Bahá'ís continued, with the government often using them as a scapegoat. In 1933, for example, Bahá'í literature was banned, Bahá'í marriages were not recognized, and Bahá'ís in public service were demoted or lost their jobs; in 1955, the government oversaw the demolition of the Bahá'í national center in Teheran and many Bahá'í homes were plundered after a radical cleric began broadcasting anti-Bahá'í rhetoric on national radio.
>
> While most of these previous episodes of persecution were the response of a secular government to pressures of the religious clergy and the political factions they influenced, the coming of a genuine

theocracy in 1979 changed everything for the worse for Baháʼís...

After a series of United Nations resolutions condemning Iran's actions, the Iranian government ceased its killing of Baháʼís, focusing more in the early 1990s on the social, economic and cultural restrictions on the Baháʼí community that were already underway. These measures specifically sought to block the development of Baháʼís, including efforts to deprive them of their livelihood, destroy their cultural heritage, and ensure young Baháʼís could not attend university.[28]

This severe and systematic campaign of persecution by the Islamic Republic has 'openly sought the wholesale destruction of the Baháʼí community'.[29] The change in tactics has been as pernicious and destructive as the earlier form of cruel and inhumane treatment of the Baháʼís through torture and execution. The new approach has impacted believers individually and collectively through deprivation of their basic rights of livelihood, culture and education. It is a mass strangulation of the lifelines of the Baháʼí community, aimed at forcing them to despair or recant. The Islamic Republic has promoted this strategy through a state-sponsored media campaign which demonizes Baha'is and targets them with false accusations, raids, arrest and imprisonment; it is aimed at inciting religious hatred. As compared to the persecution of the believers during the first century of the Faith, the present attacks are not only larger in scale, but also include economic strangulation by refusing to allow civil employment and by closing businesses. Such attacks are also meant to spread terror and create a sense of fear and hatred against Baha'is, young and old.

These measures, however, have been rather more successful in generating resilience and heroism among the Baháʼís than in demoralizing them. The Universal House of Justice writes:

> Despite this prolonged and systematic attack on its integrity and values, Iran's Baháʼí community is not dispirited, demoralized or downtrodden. Nor have they risen up to counter-attack their oppressors with force or any trace of bitterness. Rather they have calmly stated their case and called for their fundamental human rights with dignity and courtesy, winning the admiration of their compatriots, observers and, in some cases, even those who are obligated to oppress them under government policy.

In the midst of oppression aimed at their very eradication, the Bahá'ís of Iran have instead been turning their attention to the contributions they can make to improving society. Fundamental Bahá'í ideas – truthfulness, trustworthiness, the elimination of prejudice, the equality of the sexes – are being explored in conversations that are integral to the wider discourses of society from which the Bahá'ís are debarred...

Far from being cowed by oppression, the Bahá'ís have determined to stand proudly by their principles and continue to live according to the Bahá'í teachings. They are refusing to let the dehumanizing impact of public propaganda against them result in their becoming the very embodiment of such allegations.[30]

Some consequences of inciting hatred: Mothers and babies in prison

'The demonization of Bahá'ís has, however, led to many challenges for the individuals targeted. The suffering of innocents is a special feature of the persecution manifested in the city of Semnan, where most of the Bahá'ís are from neighbouring Sangsar. Because of the staunchness of the believers, government officials have intensified persecution, particularly since 2008, in order to crush the determination of the believers and set an example for other parts of the country. This bleak situation has also occurred in several other cities but has not lasted as long nor been so relentless as in Semnan. Persecution there included 'arbitrary arrests and imprisonments, the shutting down of their businesses, cemetery vandalism, denunciations of their faith in school classrooms, distribution of anti-Bahá'í propaganda and arson attacks on their properties.'[31]

Among these measures, two were particularly despicable. One was the repeated desecration of the Bahá'í cemetery and the bulldozing of graves. This was an exemplary punishment of deceased believers; it is an odious act generally forbidden in most religions. The other was the targeting of young Bahá'í women who were pregnant or new mothers who were sentenced to serve prison terms because of their religion. In these cases it was infants, the most vulnerable and innocent of human beings, who were destined to suffer because of their parents' faith.

At least four young married Bahá'í women were sentenced to

prison terms at various times in 2012–13, entering the oppressive, overcrowded women's prison of Semnan. According to Human Rights Activists News Agency (HRANA), the prison sentences for two of them was announced when they were pregnant. The home of one had been previously raided by guards and she was so emotionally traumatized by this act that afterwards she gave birth to her baby one month prematurely. Her husband and the husband of another Bahá'í woman had already been imprisoned (in the men's section of the Semnan prison) so the women had no choice but to take their infants into prison with them.[32] One woman entered the Semnan women's prison with her newborn son, only one month old. The other young mother was also harshly interrogated and sentenced to prison during her pregnancy. She too began her prison sentence with her infant. The first woman was sentenced to 20 months and the other to 23 months. This meant that by the time they completed their prison terms their children would be approximately two years old. These were the youngest prisoners in the women's prison.[33]

Two other young mothers were imprisoned, accompanied by their children below the age of two. Thus there were at least four of them, plus a few others from Muslim background who had children with them in the women's prison of Semnan for various lengths of time. Two of the Bahá'í infants developed infections, one with symptoms serious enough to require hospital treatment.

The Semnan women's prison (which used to be a stable for horses) is known for the violence of its prisoners, some of whom have committed murder or other serious crimes. Seventy female prisoners were accommodated there with very limited space and facilities.[34] The 'crime' of these young Bahá'í mothers was their allegiance to the Bahá'í Faith and the practice of their religion. The prison environment was noisy and at times agitated, without sufficient beds so that some prisoners, including the Bahá'ís, had to sleep on the floor, even during the winter.

With respect to the infants being brought into such an environment with inadequate and unsanitary facilities for children, one can only wonder at the cruelty and injustice of those who are willing to incarcerate these little ones in such a terrible place. One also may wonder why young mothers had to be made to endure such conditions shortly after the delivery of their babies. Perhaps this was another way of reinforcing pressure in order to shatter their loyalty at a time when they should have been caring for their infants at home rather being subjected to this atrocity in a violent and frightening environment.³⁵

Hardships such as these have been studied in the field of developmental psychology. It is well known that the first two years of a child's life are critical for its development. Being deprived of proper care and nutrition as well as a safe environment are just a few of the hazards of prison life for such young children, especially in Iran where the prison facilities are so deplorable, unlike many countries in the West where women's prisons are equipped with facilities for young children. In addition, the jailed mothers have often been subjected to psychological and physical insults, humiliation and intimidation.

One might think that it would be better to separate the infant from its mother and let a caregiver outside of prison take care of it. However, for these Bahá'í mothers this was not possible. Moreover, children who are separated from their mothers at a young age may be scarred for life by emotional isolation, depression or insomnia and suffer developmental consequences unless they are properly cared for and looked after. The mother–child bonding and relationship take place during the first two critical years of life when infants form a strong attachment to their mother. Through this bond, a sense of security and trust develops and children learn about their need to love and be loved. A forced separation of mothers and babies is a form of violence not only against women but also their children who have the right to maternal care.³⁶

Given such heartbreaking circumstances, it is awe-inspiring to hear of the courage and perseverance of these young mothers. Accepting all the above with forbearance and tolerance is quite a challenge. It is hard to even imagine being a young mother alone with a baby incarcerated in a prison, devoid of justice and mercy. But these prisoners' love for Bahá'u'lláh and His longsuffering are helping them to persevere. They are the new generation of heroes! This is steadfastness in the Covenant. The words of Bahá'u'lláh in the Tablet of Aḥmad are befitting: 'Remember My days during thy days, and My distress and banishment in this remote prison. And be thou so steadfast in My love that thy heart shall not waver, even if the swords of the enemies rain blows upon thee . . .'³⁷

Education under Fire: Heroism of young Bahá'ís

Many young Bahá'ís have suffered discrimination, humiliation and imprisonment and several even martyrdom.

Shortly after the 1979 Islamic Revolution, the government banned education for young Bahá'ís. 'At first, all Bahá'í children were excluded from schooling, but in the 1990s, primary and secondary school children were allowed to re-enroll,' reported the Bahá'í International Community.[38] The Bahá'í youth persevered in spite of these hardships and the government's efforts to prevent them from obtaining higher education.

In 1987 in an effort to meet the educational needs of the young believers who had been deprived of their right to attend university, the Bahá'í community of Iran established its own programme of higher education. This gradually evolved into a full-fledged university known as the Bahá'í Institute of Higher Education (BIHE); it has been characterized by *The New York Times* as 'an elaborate act of communal self-preservation'.[39] It made significant progress in expanding its courses and in increasing the number of its students. However, in October 1998 hundreds of government agents raided about 500 homes of Bahá'ís across Iran and arrested some 36 faculty and staff of BIHE. They confiscated books, computers, records and laboratory equipment in their effort to shut down the university. Over time the Institute resumed its courses, established a few laboratories and operated in privately-owned commercial buildings or private homes in Teheran and its suburbs. Among the faculty were some 25–30 Bahá'í professors who had been fired from their jobs at government universities after the 1979 Islamic Revolution. They all worked at BIHE as unpaid volunteers.[40]

In May 2011 officials raided scores of homes of Baha'i teachers and administrators of BIHE and many prominent figures of that Institute were arrested and imprisoned. They again confiscated computers, laptops and records and terrorized staff and students. This, of course, adversely affected the students struggling to complete their educational programmes.

In pondering the plight of the Bahá'í youth and their goal of higher education it is important to note how the false promise of government officials became a test of steadfastness and perseverance for the students. In 2004, as a result of international pressure on Iran regarding its denial of higher education to Bahá'ís, the government indicated that it would allow Bahá'í students to enrol at Iranian universities.⁴¹ As a result, out of 1,000 students who registered for the entrance exam, some 800 Bahá'í students passed it, many with high scores. However, the government announced only the names of 10 of these students as having been admitted to university. Obviously this was very disheartening and caused disappointment to the hundreds of others who had also passed the exam. 'In the end, out of solidarity with the rest of the 800 students who had been unfairly discriminated against, those ten Bahá'ís declined to register in the university to which they had been accepted.'⁴² Consequently, for the academic year 2004–05 young Baha'is were once again 'utterly deprived of access to higher education'.⁴³ This was a test of faithfulness and solidarity of the Bahá'í students who strove for higher education for all.

All of this took place because the students were Bahá'ís. Further review of the entire episode showed that the initial promise of the government – to drop religious affiliation as a criterion in the admission process – was false and deceptive. In fact, the entire plan seems to have been a scheme to accomplish a number of governmental objectives: ⁴⁴

1) to demoralize Bahá'í students and encourage them to leave the country;

2) to identify by name Bahá'í students with outstanding academic achievements who might be capable of playing an important role in the Bahá'í community of Iran; and

3) to tell the international human rights monitors that Iran had given the Bahá'ís a chance to enrol at universities.

Immediately prior to the initial banning of Bahá'í students from receiving higher education in Iranian universities, the majority were attending courses and some were about to take their final exams to complete a degree for their future careers. It was made clear to them that all their efforts and hopes would be in vain unless they denied their faith. This was a heart-breaking situation, and yet the students stood firm and, by doing so, reaffirmed their Bahá'í identity and their faithfulness to the Covenant, just as the 20,000 martyrs who gave their lifeblood for the truth of this Revelation had done over a century earlier. I have often wondered what thoughts filled the minds of those persecuted Bahá'ís who were about to be taken to be martyred. Many were probably asked or pressured one more time by the officials if they had changed their mind, in which case they would have been released to their families and been able to lead a peaceful life. But for those heroes and heroines who refused, it was like asking a true lover to betray his or her beloved under the false pretence that all would then be well. 'Love accepteth no existence and wisheth no life: He seeth life in death, and in shame seeketh glory,' writes Bahá'u'lláh.[45]

Had the students recanted their allegiance to the Bahá'í Faith, they would have been rewarded with money, jobs, fanfare, higher education and more attractive positions. Some of them could have graduated with degrees as engineers, doctors, lawyers, teachers or other professional qualifications. Imagine them facing officials who are trying to persuade or pressure them to recant their faith or who threaten them if they refuse to do so. A student might be all alone when he or she is told that by just one word or stroke of the pen to deny their belief in Bahá'u'lláh they will have their graduation and degree assured and every obstacle will be immediately and completely resolved. What force can prevent them from going along with that idea? This is a test of the Covenant! This is the critical moment when the believer is facing Bahá'u'lláh and His life of unbearable suffering. To accept or refuse is a personal decision to make. It is that inner conviction of the Covenant which connects one to the immense suffering of the Báb and Bahá'u'lláh and empowers one to remain unshakeable.

This is probably what galvanized the soul of 12-year-old Rúhu'lláh Varqá in that horrifying scene of martyrdom in Teheran over a hundred years ago and made his soul victorious; his story is told later in this chapter. Likewise, it was this kind of staunchness and unwavering faith which led Sulaymán Khán to dance through his martyrdom as the flames of the candles were penetrating his flesh. Bahá'u'lláh writes:

> O Son of Man! If adversity befall thee not in My path, how canst thou walk in the ways of them that are content with My pleasure? If trials afflict thee not in thy longing to meet Me, how wilt thou attain the light in thy love for My beauty?[46]

PERSECUTION, RESILIENCE AND HEROISM

Today martyrdom in physical terms is rare. But spiritual and psychological martyrdom in order to stand up for our values and principles still exists. Suffering may take different forms, none of which will make the headlines, such as sacrificing time, energy and substance to the utmost of one's ability to teach the Cause or to pioneer for the love of Bahá'u'lláh with no expectation of reward. There were some Bahá'ís who were named as martyrs by 'Abdu'l-Bahá and the Guardian who never shed a drop of blood or were subjected to physical death for their belief, but who were towers of dedication, teaching and firmness in the Covenant. May Maxwell, Lua Getsinger and Keith Ransom-Kehler were among them.

The courage and heroism of the past has repeated itself in a unique way among the Bahá'í youth of Iran in recent times. Mona Mahmudnizhad, a young girl from Shiraz, is an outstanding example. In June 1983 she and nine other Bahá'í women were martyred. Mona's father had been executed three months previously. Six of the ten were youth, of whom Mona was the youngest. All but one of these six were aged between 17 and 20 and all ten women were subjected to harsh and demeaning interrogation after their arrests. The officials pressed hard to break their determination by repeated threats alternating with promises of release should they recant their belief in the Bahá'í Faith. All steadfastly refused to do so. Then the judge sentenced them to death, falsely declaring them to be spies for Israel.[47]

Returning to the denial of higher education of young Bahá'ís in Iran and their ceaseless hardships and adversity, a letter to these Bahá'í students from the Universal House of Justice reads:

> In these difficult days laden with tribulation, we are with you in spirit, our hearts heavy at the injustice that continues to rain upon you. The persistent position of Iranian authorities in banning Bahá'í students from access to higher education is deeply saddening...
>
> Recent events call to mind heart-rending episodes in the history of the Faith of cruel deceptions wrought against your forebears. It is only appropriate that you strive to transcend the opposition against you with that same constructive resilience that characterized their response to the duplicity of their detractors. Peering beyond the distress of the difficulties assailing them, those heroic souls attempted to translate the Teachings of the new Faith into actions of spiritual and social development. This, too, is your work.[48]

The Universal House of Justice then encourages the Baháʼí students to see their suffering in a larger context:

> The sufferings you bear, the sacrifices you ceaselessly make, however grievous the circumstances, are only a part of the horrors agonizing millions upon millions in Iran and throughout the world in these times of global ferment. Such acknowledgement does not diminish in the least your adversity, but it is essential that you grasp its context. Baháʼuʼlláh remarked often on the dire state of the world. 'The winds of despair are, alas, blowing from every direction, and the strife that divides and afflicts the human race is daily increasing,' He wrote. 'The world is in great turmoil and the minds of its people are in a state of utter confusion.'[49]

I was privileged to work with BIHE colleagues who were in Iran through teaching a course online for a number of years. Among them the hardships of persecution and harassment were also severe. Many of these devoted educators have been arrested and imprisoned in recent years. One example is the plight of a Baháʼí who, after studying at a Canadian university, returned to Iran to serve at the BIHE as a faculty member. In the spring of 2011 he was arrested as a Baháʼí and detained at the notorious Evin prison in Teheran. After some time he was released, only to be arrested and detained again in September for a short period. In November he was notified of a demand to present himself at Evin prison. Not knowing what would happen to him this time, he sent an email on the morning of 27 November, shortly before leaving his home for the prison. The following is an excerpt, slightly edited, from that letter:

> Evin again. Like many other Baháʼís the long process of going back and forth to the courts and prisons has started for me and Keivan – although we are hoping that there will be a 'coming back' after this 'going' to Evin! . . . I held Elham [his wife] in my arms for a long time and deeply felt her sense of terror and shock. We cried together and hoped together.
>
> Now, it is action time. In the past two days I've had flashbacks of my solitary confinement cell. I remembered how I decided to forget about everything of the outside world when I stepped into my lonely

cell . . . I remembered when, sad and lonely, I entered my cell, I quickly noticed a few lines of one of Bahá'u'lláh's Tablets written on the wall. I couldn't stop my tears and joy! There has been another Bahá'í in that cell! Many Bahá'ís who have been arrested have been slaughtered in those cells. It made me feel at home – even if it was 209 Evin.[50]

The steadfastness and heroism of the Iranian Bahá'ís, especially among the younger generation, since the Islamic Revolution, have opened a new chapter of faithfulness and dedication to the Covenant of Bahá'u'lláh. The pages of the history of the Faith during this period are replete with stories of courage, sacrifice and unfailing resilience that demonstrate the power of the Covenant and submission to the will of God. This calls to mind the heroism and sacrifice of some of the young martyrs of the Heroic Age of the Cause.

Rúḥu'lláh Varqá: A junior youth teacher and martyr

Among the early believers, a shining example of firmness in the Covenant until his very last breath was a child called Rúḥu'lláh. There are many stories about his insight, wisdom and resilience in teaching the Faith. 'Rúḥu'lláh' in Persian means 'the Spirit of God', which is also the title of Christ, according to the Qur'án.[51] Together with his father, 'Alí-Muḥammad, surnamed Varqá by Bahá'u'lláh, Rúḥu'lláh had the bounty of attaining the presence of Bahá'u'lláh and, after the Latter's ascension, the presence of 'Abdu'l-Bahá as well. 'Alí-Muḥammad Varqá was one of the luminaries of the Faith, an inspiring poet, and an Apostle of Bahá'u'lláh. The following is Adib Taherzadeh's account:

> Contact with the Supreme Manifestation of God left an abiding impression on their souls [Rúḥu'lláh and his brother Azízu'lláh]. Though young in age they both became charged with the spirit of faith. Rúḥu'lláh in particular flourished spiritually in those holy surroundings. He may be regarded as one of the spiritual prodigies which the hand of God has raised up in this Dispensation. Although He was only about eight years old when He came into the presence of Bahá'u'lláh, his understanding of the Faith was very profound.
>
> To cite one example: One day Bahá'u'lláh asked Rúḥu'lláh, 'What did you do today?'

He replied, 'I was having lessons from – [a certain teacher].'
Bahá'u'lláh asked, 'What subject were you learning?'
'Concerning the return [of the prophets],' said Rúhu'lláh.
'Will you explain what this means?' Bahá'u'lláh demanded.
He replied: 'By return is meant the return of realities and qualities.'
Bahá'u'lláh, questioning him further, said: 'These are exactly the words of your teacher and you are repeating them like a parrot. Tell me in your own words your own understanding of the subject.'
'It is like cutting a flower from a plant this year,' answered Rúhu'lláh. 'Next year's flower will look exactly like this one, but it is not the same.'
The Blessed Beauty praised the child for his intelligent answer and often called him Jináb-i-Muballigh (His honour, the Bahá'í teacher).
On another occasion Bahá'u'lláh asked Rúhu'lláh how he spent his time at home. He answered, 'We teach the Faith and tell the people that the "Promised One" has come.' Bahá'u'lláh, obviously enjoying this conversation, then asked him what he would do if it were found that the Message of the Báb was not authentic and the true Promised One appeared. 'I would try to teach him the Faith,' was his prompt reply. [52]

The story of the martyrdom of Varqá and his 12-year-old son is indeed heart-wrenching.

> Both of them were engulfed in a series of arrests and imprisonments. They were transferred from prison to prison weighed down with chains, their feet placed in stocks. As a result they suffered much hardship and torture until at the end Varqá was martyred when in a rage . . . the chief steward in charge of the Prison of Teheran pierced his stomach with a dagger. Rúhu'lláh saw his father fall to the ground, and then his body was cut into pieces. A short while later, refusing to recant his faith and earnestly wishing to join his father, that noble and heroic child was strangled to death. This was in May 1896.[53]

Such was the degree of the courage and steadfastness of these and other believers who gave their lives, and their unwavering loyalty to the Cause, that Abdu'l-Bahá, in one of His prayers about martyrs and their families has written: 'O Lord! These souls have tasted bitter agony in this earthly life and have, as a sign of their love for the shining beauty of Thy countenance and in their eagerness to attain Thy celestial kingdom, tolerated every gross indignity that the people of tyranny have inflicted upon them.'⁵⁴

Response to Persecution

A letter from the Universal House of Justice to Iranian believers in 154 B.E. (1997) elaborates on the dialectic of two mighty forces at work for the growth of the tree of the Cause in compliance with the will of God:

> One of these forces is the generating power of this spiritual springtime; tempestuous and soul-stirring in nature, it causes lightning and thunder, high winds, torrential rain, and roaring floods. These in turn cause the orchards and fields to become verdant and fruitful. The other force is the inherent germinating capacity of that blessed seed, which causes it to unfold through the rays of the Sun of Truth and the showers from the clouds of bounty and to become a mighty fruit-bearing tree, providing a celestial retreat for the birds of the prairies of guidance. The overall divine design that leads humanity to spiritual maturity is beyond our comprehension; it is well guarded in God's hidden treasure house and its realization is dependent on His Will.⁵⁵

In the same message the House of Justice describes how the Bahá'ís in the Cradle of the Faith, amidst the fire of trials, rallied around the Promised One and 'life in hand, rank upon rank, hastened to the arena of sacrifice'.⁵⁶ Then the Iranian friends everywhere are challenged to 'emulate the example of those lions of the field of steadfastness and learn from them the lessons of servitude'.⁵⁷ Furthermore, the House of Justice calls upon the Iranian believers worldwide to

> [c]onsider the time when the tempest of ordeals started to blow in Iran again: the spark of faith in the hearts of the members of the community, in some cases dormant under the ashes of worldly attachments, suddenly burst into brilliant flame, wiping away the dust of complacency and heedlessness. The warning sound of the thunderbolt of events awakened them. They became mindful and, in the joyful gathering place of nearness to God, drank the brimming chalice of calamity.⁵⁸

The long-suffering Bahá'ás of Iran have astonished their enemies through their deeds, fortitude and reliance on divine assistance:

> It was such behaviour that turned strangers into friends and supporters of the wronged ones. No doubt, tests are not confined to the friends in Iran; the ordeals that confront the believers in the free world, although different in nature, will be as severe and insidious. If the Bahá'ís throughout the world do not face such tests with the aid of a prayerful attitude and constant engagement in service, they are likely to be submerged in the ocean of bewilderment, confusion, and remorse, wasting away the short days of their lives and leaving this world with empty hands.[59]

The following insightful words of Bahá'u'lláh call to mind the swiftness of the passage of time in this world in which we spend our temporary life:

> Night hath succeeded day, and day hath succeeded night, and the hours and moments of your lives have come and gone, and yet none of you hath, for one instant, consented to detach himself from that which perisheth. Bestir yourselves, that the brief moments that are still yours may not be dissipated and lost. Even as the swiftness of lightning your days shall pass, and your bodies shall be laid to rest beneath a canopy of dust. What can ye then achieve? How can ye atone for your past failure?[60]

The Bahá'ís in the Cradle of the Faith responded with unprecedented steadfastness, courage and sacrifice. One and all, having been forcibly deprived of their administrative institutions, having had the members of their national coordinating body, the Yaran, thrown into prison, and having had their Bahá'í gatherings severely restricted, they have endured all this deprivation without wavering or seeking revenge. They arose to defend their rights in spite of the threats they received, the intensity of the restrictions placed on the economic and business aspects of their lives, and on their freedom to practise their Faith, to educate their children, to conduct official marriages and even bury their dead.

Such persecution has in recent years caused Iranians of Muslim faith to raise their voices in sympathy and to praise the Bahá'ís for their certitude, trustworthiness and endurance as well as for being well-wishers of humanity. Many fair-minded journalists and observers have defended the plight of the innocent Bahá'ís. Articles such as 'We are all Bahá'ís'[61] and films like *Iranian Taboo* and *The Gardener* (in Persian) have raised public awareness of the painful plight of the Bahá'ís of Iran.

The Universal House of Justice has elaborated on two paradoxical realities in the course of the progress of the Cause:

> Within the Faith itself, the gathering strength of the Bahá'í community presages a great surge forward, intimations of which are already everywhere apparent. Inevitably, as Shoghi Effendi several times emphasized, this advance will excite even more intense opposition than the Cause has so far encountered, opposition that will in turn release the greater forces needed for the still more demanding tasks that lie ahead.[62]

Referring to the world-shaking crises which are reflecting the disintegration of an old world order and the rise of a new one, the Universal House of Justice depicts the following panorama:

> Events of the most profound significance are taking place in the world. The river of human history is flowing at a bewildering speed. Age-old institutions are collapsing. Traditional ways are being forgotten, and newly born ideologies which were fondly expected to take their place, are withering and decaying before the eyes of their disillusioned adherents. Amidst this decay and disruption, assailed from every side by the turmoil of the age, the Order of Bahá'u'lláh, unshakeably founded on the Word of God, protected by the shield of the Covenant and assisted by the hosts of the Concourse on High, is rising in every part of the world.[63]

In spite of its hostile and adversarial efforts, the fierce and relentless brutality of persecution has not been able to silence the believers nor obliterate the Cause. Bahá'u'lláh promises that 'Should they attempt to conceal His light on the continent, He will assuredly rear His head in the midmost heart of the ocean and, raising His voice, proclaim, 'I am the lifegiver of the world!'[64]

In one of His Tablets the Blessed Beauty, who Himself endured imprisonment, torture, cruelties and banishment, attests to the countless tests and sufferings of His followers in these words.

> ... We call to remembrance Our loved ones and bring them the joyous tidings of God's unfailing grace and of the things that have been provided for them in My lucid Book. Ye have tolerated the censure of the enemies for the sake of My love and have steadfastly endured in My Path the grievous cruelties which the ungodly have inflicted upon you. Unto this I Myself bear witness, and I am the All-Knowing. How vast the number of places that have been ennobled with your blood for the sake of God. How numerous the cities wherein the voice of your lamentation hath been raised and the wailing of your anguish uplifted. How many the prisons into which ye have been cast by the hosts of tyranny. Know ye of a certainty that He will render you victorious, will exalt you among the peoples of the world and will demonstrate your high rank before the gaze of all nations.[65]

The Bahá'í Writings clearly demonstrate the creative interaction of crisis and victory. They also illumine our perception and understanding of suffering in the path of God and the ultimate triumph which will prevail. Gains or losses that believers experience as a result of tests and trials for the Faith are different kinds of experiences which have a unique and profound meaning and whose deeper wisdom we cannot always comprehend. 'Whatsoever occurreth in the world of being is light for His loved ones and fire for the people of sedition and strife,' writes Bahá'u'lláh:

> Even if all the losses of the world were to be sustained by one of the friends of God, he would still profit thereby, whereas true loss would be borne by such as are wayward, ignorant and contemptuous. Although the author of the following saying had intended it otherwise, yet We find it pertinent to the operation of God's immutable Will: 'Even or odd, thou shalt win the wager.' The friends of God shall win and profit under all conditions, and shall attain true wealth. In fire they remain cold, and from water they emerge dry. Their affairs are at variance with the affairs of men. Gain is their lot, whatever the deal. To this testifieth every wise one with a discerning eye, and every fair-minded one with a hearing ear.[66]

5

Steadfastness in the Covenant

> The first condition is firmness in the Covenant of God. For the power of the Covenant will protect the Cause of Bahá'u'lláh from the doubts of the people of error. It is the fortified fortress of the Cause of God and the firm pillar of the religion of God.
>
> *'Abdu'l-Bahá*[1]

Steadfastness is a process and not an event, although events may highlight one's faithfulness and devotion or, on the contrary, one's disloyalty and treachery. In the arena of the Covenant of Bahá'u'lláh, firmness is a test of trustworthiness through obedience. Thus firmness and obedience are like two partners that usually go together. 'Abdu'l-Bahá writes:

> Therefore, in the beginning the believers must make their steps firm in the Covenant so that the confirmations of Bahá'u'lláh may encircle them from all sides, the cohorts of the Supreme Concourse may become their supporters and helpers, and the exhortations and advices of 'Abdu'l-Bahá, like unto the pictures engraved on stone, may remain permanent and ineffaceable in the tablets of all hearts.[2]

There are certain elements which reinforce and strengthen these dual obligations of steadfastness and obedience. One is the love for God which burns in the hearts of believers; others are trust and detachment, as Bahá'u'lláh writes:

> O My servants! Deprive not yourselves of the unfading and resplendent Light that shineth within the Lamp of Divine glory. Let the flame of the love of God burn brightly within your radiant hearts. Feed it with the oil of Divine guidance, and protect it within the shelter of

your constancy. Guard it within the globe of trust and detachment from all else but God, so that the evil whisperings of the ungodly may not extinguish its light.[3]

'Abdu'l-Bahá in a Tablet to the Spiritual Assembly of Los Angeles describes the manner in which believers should withstand the attacks of the violators of the Covenant. He indicates that the blessed souls in California 'like unto an immovable mountain, are withstanding the gale of violation'. They 'have, like unto blessed trees, been planted in the soil of the Covenant and are most firm and steadfast'. Then the Master expresses the hope that 'through the blessings of the Sun of Truth they may daily increase in their firmness and steadfastness'.[4] He further elucidates:

> The tests of every dispensation are in direct proportion to the greatness of the Cause, and as heretofore such a manifest Covenant, written by the Supreme Pen, hath not been entered upon, the tests are proportionately more severe. These trials cause the feeble souls to waver while those who are firm are not affected. These agitations of the violators are no more than the foam of the ocean, which is one of its inseparable features; but the ocean of the Covenant shall surge and shall cast ashore the bodies of the dead, for it cannot retain them. Thus it is seen that the ocean of the Covenant hath surged and surged until it hath thrown out the dead bodies – souls that are deprived of the Spirit of God and are lost in passion and self and are seeking leadership. This foam of the ocean shall not endure and shall soon disperse and vanish, while the ocean of the Covenant shall eternally surge and roar . . .[5]

It is interesting to note that in this Tablet 'Abdu'l-Bahá uses the metaphor of the 'ocean of the Covenant'. An ocean is by definition vast and contains many mysteries in its depths. There are, however, times during which it can be stormy and it 'shall surge and shall cast ashore' the dead bodies which no longer belong to it. This is a stage of purification to maintain the life within. Violators of the Covenant, like the foam of the ocean, have little endurance to withstand the powerful might of the ocean of the Covenant. They cover a small part of the surface of it for a limited time, then they vanish or are cast aside.

Reflecting on the destiny of those who break the Covenant of

STEADFASTNESS IN THE COVENANT

Bahá'u'lláh, 'Abdu'l-Bahá asserts:

> The violators are trampling upon their own dignity, are uprooting their own foundations and are proud at being upheld by flatterers who exert a great effort to shake the faith of feeble souls. But this action of theirs is of no consequence; it is a mirage and not water, foam and not the sea, mist and not a cloud, illusion and not reality. All this ye shall soon see.[6]

Profiles of Steadfastness in the Covenant

The remainder of this chapter tells the stories of just a few outstanding examples of heroism and steadfastness in the Covenant.

Ḥájí Mírzá Ḥaydar-'Alí, the Angel of Carmel

Ḥájí Mírzá Ḥaydar-'Alí was one of the most illustrious disciples of Bahá'u'lláh and the embodiment of humility and detachment. He travelled extensively throughout Persia at Bahá'u'lláh's bidding. He was a staunch, steadfast and most capable defender of the Covenant, particularly during the ministry of 'Abdu'l-Bahá when the machinations of the Covenant-breakers and their attacks on the Centre of the Covenant were brutal.

He was born into a Shaykhi family in Isfahan where later on, as an adult, he embraced the Bábí religion. This happened a few years after the martyrdom of the Báb when the environment in his home town was very agitated and oppressive toward the followers of the Báb. Adib Taherzadeh writes that Mírzá Ḥaydar-'Alí recounted of meetings with the persecuted Bábí friends at that time, that '[t]o ensure that no one would see him leave his house, he had to climb out through a window and return the same way. At the home of his friend, they used to hide their lamp in a hole inside a room, then hold the Writings of the Báb beside the hole, read the verses of God and receive spiritual sustenance through them.'[7]

As he became confirmed in his faith, he also became aware of the glad-tidings of the coming of 'Him Whom God shall make manifest'. This created in him an ardent desire to attain His presence. This burning desire became a flame when he read the Kitáb-i-Íqán (the Book of Certitude) of Bahá'u'lláh and that further confirmed him in the Cause. After Bahá'u'lláh's declaration, Mírzá Ḥaydar-'Alí travelled to Adrianople and attained the presence of his Lord. He championed service to the Cause and protection of it. While travelling in Egypt to teach the Faith, and later in Sudan, he suffered extensively from persecution, fulfilling Bahá'u'lláh's prophecy in a Tablet to him that he would be afflicted by persecutions and ordeals. Bahá'u'lláh also advised Mírzá Ḥaydar-'Alí to be thankful when subjected to suffering in the path of God, and exhorted him to remain steadfast and to be assured of ultimate deliverance and protection.[8]

During Mírzá Ḥaydar-'Alí's journey in Egypt the Consul General of Persia, who resided there and who was a vicious enemy of the Faith, deceived Mírzá Ḥaydar-'Alí and a few other Persian Bahá'ís by pretending that he was a sincere seeker. They were arrested, their feet were placed in stocks, and chains were put around their necks. The Persian Consul also alarmed the Egyptian authorities, describing the prisoners as 'subversive elements teaching a new religion and working against the security of the state'.[9] He persuaded the government officials to condemn them to an indefinite period of imprisonment in Sudan. The Consul led the Egyptian authorities to believe that these innocent men were 'the most vicious criminals, whose aim was to wipe out the religion of Islam, assassinate the King and overthrow the Government'.[10] From that time on, the prisoners were chained and fettered, experienced excruciating hardship and suffering, and were moved to a remote prison in Sudan.

In brief, after months of heart-rending agony and suffering they eventually arrived in Khartoum to stay in a crowded prison for robbers and criminals. Taherzadeh sums up this barbaric journey in these words:

> One day, the authorities called blacksmiths and carpenters to the jail to chain the prisoners permanently for their journey to the Sudan. Four of the prisoners each had their right foot inserted in a huge iron collar and the other four their left foot ... Then they were tied in pairs ... Then came the turn of the carpenters. They were to make stocks for the prisoners' hands ...
>
> ... Ḥájí Mírzá Ḥaydar-'Alí and his companions bore the weight of these gruesome tools of torture. They suffered agony and hardship beyond description. Tied in pairs in this appalling fashion, they sat, slept, and were forced to walk for miles together. During this period,

the rigours of the journey, the agony of being in chains and fetters, the effects of starvation, malnutrition and gross ill-treatment, the pains of associating with the vilest of men, criminals and murderers, and the crushing force of many other unspeakable sufferings which were inflicted upon them, reduced them to such physical frailty that several times they were brought to the verge of death.[11]

This heartrending story of torture and brutality shows how fierce and cruel the persecution of innocent believers could be and what courage was displayed by Mírzá Ḥaydar-'Alí, who remained strong and unmovable as a mountain. We are reminded of the following words of 'Abdu'l-Bahá who indicated how such virtuous souls are aided by 'the unfailing help of the Company on high':

> If in this day a soul shall act according to the precepts and the counsels of God, he will serve as a divine physician to mankind, and like the trump of Israfíl,[12] he will call the dead of this contingent world to life; for the confirmations of the Abhá Realm are never interrupted, and such a virtuous soul hath, to befriend him, the unfailing help of the Company on high. Thus shall a sorry gnat become an eagle in the fullness of his strength, and a feeble sparrow change to a royal falcon in the heights of ancient glory.[13]

Stories of Mírzá Ḥaydar-'Alí's service, dedication and suffering can be found in his book, *Bihjatu's-Ṣudúr* (Delight of the Hearts).

The Greatest Holy Leaf: A pillar of steadfastness

The most exemplary and outstanding heroine in the path of firmness in the Covenant, the Greatest Holy Leaf (Bahíyyih Khánum), occupied a unique role in buttressing the Covenant of Bahá'u'lláh and shouldered heavy responsibilities in the Holy Land during the years of 'Abdu'l-Bahá's absence while He was travelling in the West. She also gave invaluable assistance and support to the Guardian during the first few years of his ministry. Among her many noble virtues, the one that stands out and characterizes her long-suffering life the most is steadfastness. In one of her letters to a believer she wrote:

> All the virtues of humankind are summed up in the one word 'steadfastness', if we but act according to its laws. It draws to us as by a magnet the blessings and bestowals of Heaven, if we but rise up according to the obligations it implies . . . Steadfastness is a treasure that makes a man so rich as to have no need of the world or any person or any thing that is therein. Constancy is a special joy, that leads us mortals on to lofty heights, great progress, and the winning of the perfections of Heaven. All praise be to the Beloved's holy court, for granting this most wondrous grace to His faithful people, and to His favoured ones, this best of gifts.[14]

The ascension of her beloved Brother and Centre of the Covenant of the Bahá'í Dispensation, to which she referred as 'that most dire of calamities, that most great disaster', left her and other believers with burning hearts and deep grief. 'Darkness settled on our souls, of blood were our tears,'[15] she wrote of those gloomy days after the departure of 'Abdu'l-Bahá when Covenant-breakers led by Mírzá Muḥammad-'Alí were preparing to take advantage of the situation and propagate his false claim that now he was the eligible successor of Bahá'u'lláh.

In spite of all the calamities, pain and grief, she remained as a 'river of life' (Tablet of Aḥmad) to His loved ones, inspired to defend the mighty Covenant with determination. In one of her letters to the friends she wrote, 'The news of your firmness in the Covenant, of your endeavour to work in unity and harmony, and of your untiring zeal and devotion in the Path of Service, has been a source of untold joy to me. For now my sole comfort lies in the loyalty and faithfulness of the friends, and my one joy in the progress of the Cause.'[16] She addresses the friends with the following words:

> Dear friends! At this critical time through which the Cause is passing the responsibility that has fallen on every individual Bahá'í is great, and his duties are pressing and manifold . . . Now the time has come for the faithful friends of 'Abdu'l-Bahá, who have been the recipients of the Glorious Light, to shine forth even as brilliant stars. The radiance of our Faith must be such as to dispel the clouds of doubt and guide the world to the Day-spring of Truth . . .
>
> For inspiration and guidance let us turn unto His life-imparting exhortations: 'O friends, show forth your fidelity! O my loved ones, manifest your steadfastness and your constancy! O ye who invoke His

name, turn ye and hold fast unto Him! O ye who lift up your hearts and implore His aid, cling to Him and walk in His ways! It is incumbent upon every one of us to encourage each other, to exert our utmost endeavour to diffuse His divine fragrances and engage in exalting His Word. We must, at all times, be stirred by the breeze that bloweth from the rose-garden of His loving kindness, and be perfumed with the fragrances of the mystic flowers of His grace.'[17]

Shoghi Effendi elaborated on the life and character of the Greatest Holy Leaf, this tower of strength and certitude, in these words: 'How staunch was her faith, how calm her demeanour, how forgiving her attitude, how severe her trials, at a time when the forces of schism had rent asunder the ties that united the little band of exiles . . .'[18]

Throughout her life she suffered the most cruel hardships and experienced afflictions, poverty and loneliness in exile. She was the eldest daughter of Bahá'u'lláh and a very close companion to 'Abdu'l-Bahá, sharing their long tribulations, sorrow and suffering. Yet, writes Shoghi Effendi,

> no calamity, however intense, could obscure the brightness of her saintly face, and no agitation, no matter how severe, could disturb the composure of her gracious and dignified behaviour . . .
>
> In the school of adversity she, already endowed by Providence with the virtues of meekness and fortitude, learned through the example and exhortations of the Great Sufferer, Who was her Father, the lesson she was destined to teach the great mass of His followers for so long after Him.[19]

'Abdu'l-Bahá held Bahíyyih Khánum in deep affection. During His absences such as His travel to the West, He delegated to her the responsibility of carrying out His correspondence. The extent of 'Abdu'l-Bahá's love for His sister can be discerned in some of His letters written when He was away, letters that show his affection for her and how much he cared for her well-being. In one of these letters he conveyed this message to her:

> To My honoured and distinguished sister do thou convey the expression of my heartfelt, my intense longing. Day and night she liveth

in my remembrance. I dare make no mention of the feelings which separation from her has aroused in mine heart; for whatever I should attempt to express in writing will assuredly be effaced by the tears which such sentiments must bring to mine eyes . . .'[20]

Beneath her gentle, serene, graceful demeanour lay a mountain of resilience, determination and wisdom. In the Holy Land, besides the relentless machinations and troubles caused by the Covenant-breakers, she had to face other oppressive trials such as the persecution of the Bahá'ís of Iran. The following is a letter she wrote to that community:

> O steadfast ones, gathered beneath the Abhá Beauty's standard of oneness, O faithful lovers of 'Abdu'l-Bahá! Sad news has come to us out of Iran in recent days, and it has intensely grieved the entire Bahá'í world: they have, in most parts of that land, set bonfires of envy and malevolence, and hoisted the banner of aggression against this much-wronged community; they have left no means untried, no plot or strategy neglected, and have arisen with extreme hostility and spite to pull out by their very roots the trees of this garden of God.
>
> From every side, they are aiming their arrows at hearts that rejoice in the knowledge of God and are filled with the love of Him. From every ambush, they are hunting down gazelles that pasture in the meadows of His unity. They are taking the men and women believers captive, and making orphans of the children. They are plundering the believers' property, sacking their hearths and homes.[21]

In the same letter she states that in contrast to the brutal aggression among the enemies of the Faith, Bahá'ís are to be seen as 'rivers of pure mercy and peace' who avoid any kind of striking back with verbal or physical violence. She helps the Bahá'ís to understand the dynamics of crisis and victory, and that often after the appearance of each Manifestation of God, ignorant people turn against the divine Teachers. But with the progress of time, afflictions become like the oil which feeds the lamp of God and adds to its radiance. She offers practical advice and insightful encouragement as to how to proceed toward a solution: 'During occurrences of this kind, it is incumbent upon the believers in other countries to immediately adopt prudent and reasonable measures, that through wise methods such fires may be put out.'[22] Her words inspire us to learn how Bahá'ís should be defended and guarded against ferocious enemies.

Encountering trials and tribulation in the path of God, harsh and troubling as they may be, can usher in a new transformation of self and society if we fathom the true meaning of such trials and follow the guidance of creative perseverance and proclaim this mighty Cause. Bahá'u'lláh calls this to our attention:

> Say: Tribulation is a horizon unto My Revelation. The day star of grace shineth above it, and sheddeth a light which neither the clouds of men's idle fancy nor the vain imaginations of the aggressor can obscure.
> Follow thou the footsteps of thy Lord . . . undeterred by either the clamour of the heedless ones or the sword of the enemy . . . Spread abroad the sweet savours of thy Lord, and hesitate not, though it be for less than a moment, in the service of His Cause. The day is approaching when the victory of thy Lord, the Ever-Forgiving, the Most Bountiful, will be proclaimed.[23]

'Abdu'l-Vahháb, a youth from Shiraz

Mírzá 'Abdu'l-Vahháb was a young man from Shiraz when he first met Bahá'u'lláh in Kazimayn, Iraq, in 1851 and became one of his 'intoxicated lovers'. He later followed Him to Teheran, but his arrival there coincided with the misguided attempt on the life of the Shah and the arrest of Bahá'u'lláh. 'Abdu'l-Vahháb, who was searching for his Lord and the Bábís in the capital amidst the prevailing turmoil, was arrested and thrown into the Síyáh-Chál while Bahá'u'lláh was imprisoned there.[24] Finding his Lord at last, and even being chained to Him, brought peace of mind and an answer to his longing.

The Blessed Beauty told Nabíl-i-A'zam the following story of this youth's courage and steadfastness:

> We were awakened one night, ere break of day, by Mírzá 'Abdu'l-Vahháb-i-Shírází, who was bound with Us to the same chains. He had left Kazimayn and followed Us to Ṭihrán, where he was arrested and thrown into prison. He asked Us whether We were awake, and proceeded to relate to Us his dream. 'I have this night,' he said, 'been soaring into a space of infinite vastness and beauty. I seemed to be

uplifted on wings that carried me wherever I desired to go. A feeling of rapturous delight filled my soul. I flew in the midst of that immensity with a swiftness and ease that I cannot describe. 'Today,' We replied, 'it will be your turn to sacrifice yourself for this Cause. May you remain firm and steadfast to the end. You will then find yourself soaring in that same limitless space of which you dreamed, traversing with the same ease and swiftness the realm of immortal sovereignty, and gazing with that same rapture upon the Infinite Horizon.'

That morning saw the gaoler again enter Our cell and call out the name of 'Abdu'l-Vahháb. Throwing off his chains, he sprang to his feet, embraced each of his fellow-prisoners, and, taking Us into his arms, pressed Us lovingly to his heart. That moment We discovered that he had no shoes to wear. We gave him Our own, and, speaking a last word of encouragement and cheer, sent him forth to the scene of his martyrdom. Later on, his executioner came to Us, praising in glowing language the spirit which that youth had shown. How thankful We were to God for this testimony which the executioner himself had given![25]

Before leaving the Siyáh-<u>Ch</u>ál prison, 'Abdu'l-Vahháb kissed the knees of Bahá'u'lláh and then he 'sang and danced all the way into the embrace of death'.[26]

Sixty years after the martyrdom of that glorious youth, 'Abdu'l-Bahá while travelling in the United States related his story to some American believers at a gathering. Juliet Thompson wrote that as He reached that moving moment in the story when 'Abdu'l-Vahháb left Bahá'u'lláh to go to the field of martyrdom,

> Suddenly 'Abdu'l-Bahá's whole aspect changed. It was as though the spirit of the martyr had entered into Him . . . With His head thrillingly erect, snapping His fingers high in the air, beating on the porch with His foot till we could scarcely endure the vibrations set up –such electric power radiated from Him – He sang the martyr's song, ecstatic and tragic beyond anything I had ever heard . . . Another realm opened to me – the realm of Divine Tragedy . . .[27]

Lua Aurora Getsinger, 'Herald of the Covenant'

Lua Getsinger was one of the very earliest Bahá'ís in America who, shortly after embracing the Faith, arose to travel extensively to teach and infuse the believers with firmness in the Covenant during the tumultuous and early years of growth of the Cause in the United States. 'Abdu'l-Bahá named her 'Livá', which in Persian means "the Banner" and told her to spread the message of the Faith in His name.[28]

Lua was just twenty-two years old when she came across the name of Bahá'u'lláh as she was reading a newspaper report about the 1893 World Parliament of Religions in Chicago.[29] Subsequently she met and attended the classes of Ibrahim Khayru'lláh to learn about the Bahá'í Faith. Both she and her husband, Edward Getsinger, in the ensuing few years and especially after their pilgrimage of 1898, began to be increasingly concerned about the machinations of Khayru'lláh, who 'secretly harboured the notion that 'Abdu'l-Bahá could captain the Bahá'ís of the orient, while he would take charge of the Bahá'ís of the occident'.[30] Lua and Edward realized that it was important to protect the Bahá'í community from the divisive behaviour of Khayru'lláh. 'Abdu'l-Bahá, through His constant guidance and letters, encouraged the friends to focus on unity within the Bahá'í community. He also sent teachers such as the scholar Mírzá Abu'l-Faḍl to deepen the American Bahá'ís.[31]

As the Cause continued to grow, so did the challenge to protect the newly emerging American Bahá'í community from the darts of Covenant-breaking and division. On the other hand, in the Cradle of the Faith a brutal wave of persecution and bloodshed was being inflicted on the long-suffering Bahá'ís of Iran, who were scapegoated after the assassination of the father of the reigning Shah in 1896.[32] In 1902, on the occasion of the visit of the new Shah to France, Lua was asked by 'Abdu'l-Bahá to travel to Paris and present a petition to the Shah, requesting that the Muslim clerics be restrained from persecuting the Persian Bahá'ís and that he extend his protection to them. Lua, accompanied by Hippolyte Dreyfus, proceeded with determination to encounter the Shah, who was staying at the Elysée Palace Hotel in Paris.[33] This was a very difficult task and Lua was obliged to approach the Shah through his Prime Minister, who was also his advisor during that trip. The latter refused to see her and at one point stated that it was because his son was sick and dying. Nevertheless, Lua persisted, asking

through his secretary, 'if he would consent to see her tomorrow should his son be healed...'
Janet Ruhe Schoen describes what happened next:

> The Prime Minister agreed to Lua's conditions. That night the Bahá'ís of Paris held a prayer vigil till dawn. Lua learned in the morning that the boy was recovering. When she and Monsieur Dreyfus returned to the hotel the Prime Minister promised that measures would be taken to grant the petitions. But Lua wanted to hear that from the Shah himself and she managed to get past the Prime Minister, put the petitions into the Shah's hand, and hear him say he would do all that was within his power.[34]

Lua had succeeded in her mission, but in spite of her efforts the Prime Minister, for political reasons, did not intervene to mitigate the severe persecution against the Bahá'ís. He resigned in 1903 and persecution eased, enabling the Bahá'í community to consolidate its progress.[35]

One of Lua's deep longings was an intense desire to give her life as a martyr of the Cause. When she was in the Holy Land, and also during 'Abdu'l-Bahá's visit to North America, she would constantly plead that the Master grant her martyrdom. As Velda Metelmann writes:

> She longed to give her life for the Faith and, Yúnis Khán recounts with some humour, enlisted everyone in her attempts to persuade 'Abdu'l-Bahá to grant that she might become a martyr. She would prostrate herself at the Master's feet and beg him tearfully to allow her to go to Persia and proclaim the Faith as Ṭáhirih had done; but 'Abdu'l-Bahá did not agree. However, Lua did not give up. Sometimes she would pray all night for martyrdom, searching out special prayers of the Báb. Once the 1903 martyrdoms began in Yazd and Isfahan she could not control her tearful longing. The intensity of her emotion so affected the Bahá'ís that she soon had them praying for her too.[36]

During His visit to New York, on 19 June 1912 'Abdu'l-Bahá at one point looked directly into Lua's eyes and proclaimed, 'I appoint you, Lua, as a Herald of the Covenant. Go forth and proclaim this truth!'[37] That was a transforming and historic moment in Lua's life. As Juliet Thompson told the story, 'Like metal put into the fire, all that had been

STEADFASTNESS IN THE COVENANT

the Lua of the past was burned away, and she had now taken on the characteristics of the fire. "Recreate me, O beloved Master," she cried, 'that I may truly herald Thy Faith." '38

'Abdu'l-Bahá asked Lua to visit India. Before she began her journey, the Master told her:

> Thou must be firm and unshakeable in thy purpose, and never, never let any outward circumstances worry thee . . . Look at me! Thou dost not know a thousandth part of the difficulties and seemingly insurmountable passes that rise daily before my eyes. I do not heed them; I am walking in my chosen highway; I know the destination.[39]

After her return from India to the Holy Land, World War I began and Lua as an American had to leave Haifa for the United States in August 1915 because her security was at risk. The ship docked at Port Said, Egypt and Lua disembarked. However, due to her being seriously ill she was unable to re-board the ship and had to remain in Egypt. There, in spite of failing health, poverty and suffering she increased the tempo of her service and teaching activities for the Cause. Sometimes homeless and sometimes lodged at the home of Bahá'í friends, lonely and frail, she did not rest. She said this was because 'The Master does not rest.'[40] On 2 May 1916, while in Cairo, her soul suddenly winged its flight to the Abhá Kingdom. She was only 45 years old. When the sad news of Lua's passing reached 'Abdu'l-Bahá, it caused him deep sorrow. One of His secretaries wrote that the Master would so many times repeat with emotion, 'What a loss! What a loss! What a loss!'[41]

The following moving conversation which took place between the Master and Lua prior to her departure for India was preserved by Lua herself in her pilgrim notes. In that conversation 'Abdu'l-Bahá, looked at Lua with tender love and asked the following questions, to which Lua gave answer:

> 'What will you do if they persecute you?'
> 'I shall know it is a heavenly gift, and that the love of God is descending upon me.'
> 'What will you do if they put you in prison?'
> 'I shall thank God that I have walked in His path, and have at last been permitted to share what 'Abdu'l-Bahá has suffered for years.'

'Abdu'l-Bahá was silent for a moment. He asked:

'And what will you do if they kill you?'

'I shall know that the first wish that I ever asked of 'Abdu'l-Bahá had been granted, and that I have been privileged to give my life that men may hear the Word of God.'

Lua's eyes were filled with tears. She looked at her Beloved and said, 'And the minute my soul is freed from my body, I shall fly to God from Whom I hope I shall never be separated through all eternity.'

There was a long silence. The Master's eyes were closed. At length He said: 'When one goes forth to teach, he should think of all these things. He must be prepared at all times, for whatever comes in the path of God.'[42]

Amelia E. Collins, 'Lady of the Kingdom'

Amelia Collins, or 'Milly' as she was called, became a Bahá'í in 1919, just three years after the passing of Lua Getsinger. Bahá'ís encouraged her to write a letter to 'Abdu'l-Bahá asking for confirmation and strength. Barron Harper continues the story:

> She reluctantly penned the letter, but afterwards spent an uneasy night. In the morning, when she opened the curtains of her room and saw the sun shining in, she asked herself whether the sun in all its grandeur needed a letter. She then tore up her note, confident that the spirit of the Master would understand. He did not, she was convinced, need to be bothered by her unworthy requests.
>
> Shortly afterwards a Tablet from 'Abdu'l-Bahá arrived, the contents of which Milly kept secret for some time – she would only say that 'Abdu'l-Bahá had addressed her as 'lady of the kingdom'.[43]

After the passing of the Master in 1921, Milly Collins had an enduring desire and longing to make the Guardian happy. She wrote,

> 'Out of the immense treasury of all the Writings, I memorized one sentence and did my utmost to follow that one injunction. It served as a lamp of guidance, shedding light on the dark and obscure paths of my life. That phrase is from the Will and Testament of the Master, where He says that the friends should make Shoghi Effendi happy. Whatever

STEADFASTNESS IN THE COVENANT

step I took in my life, any vote cast in the Assemblies, any trip taken, even any thought, I would first ask myself whether my vote, words, trip or thought would make him happy. When I was sure, then I would take action without fear.'[44]

This illustrates her earnest desire to fulfil one of the wishes of 'Abdu'l-Bahá about the attitude of the friends toward Shoghi Effendi. It may also show that the beloved Master probably had an intuitive insight about the future suffering and anguish which the Guardian would experience from the internal and external enemies of the Cause.

Milly Collins was named a Hand of the Cause of God by Shoghi Effendi. Her immense services to the Cause are recounted in the published memorial article to her.[45]

Catherine H. Huxtable, Knight of Bahá'u'lláh

We now meet another 20th-century heroine of the Cause. Catherine H. Huxtable exemplified another glorious but different kind of steadfastness and sacrifice, not through martyrdom but, like Milly Collins, through living a life of indefatigable service to the Cause of Bahá'u'lláh. She was a shining inspiration for teaching and pioneering in spite of extreme physical disability and hardship.

Catherine was born in England in 1932 and later, together with her family, moved to Canada. When she was 10 years old she was struck by a severe attack of scarlet fever, following which it was discovered that she was suffering from a rare type of muscular dystrophy with a grave prognosis. Because of the illness it was predicted that her life span would be greatly shortened, that she probably wouldn't survive beyond the age of 20. Moreover, she was to be confined to a wheelchair for the remainder of her life.[46]

She entered Havergal College at the age of 7, but at 16, due to her worsening medical condition, she could not continue her formal schooling. But her physical limitations did not break her determination as she grew self-reliant, with diversified interests and a large circle of friends. In 1951, she and her friend Clifford Huxtable embraced the Bahá'í Faith and in 1955 they married.

Catherine served with much dedication on the Spiritual Assembly of Toronto. She had profound insights into the teachings of the Cause which enabled her to actively teach the Faith to others. 'She lived to an unusual degree in a condition of consciousness of the presence of God, equally committed to the victory of the spirit and the joy of a full human life,' writes Roger White.[47] She loved pioneers and frequently corresponded with those in distant areas. The passing of Shoghi Effendi, whom she loved wholeheartedly, in 1957 crystallized her longing to pioneer. Catherine and Clifford pioneered to Regina in Saskatchewan (Canada) and assisted in rebuilding the Spiritual Assembly there in 1957. Then the Huxtables aimed to move to a more distant area. They pioneered to a remote outpost, one of the less hospitable goals in the Gulf Islands in the North Pacific Ocean. There they founded the first Spiritual Assembly of that virgin territory of the Plan and by opening these Islands through sacrificial efforts they joined the ranks of the Knights of Bahá'u'lláh.

When the Universal House of Justice launched the Nine Year Plan and called for pioneers in 1965, once again the Huxtables arose and responded to this call. They offered to go and settle on the volcanic island of St Helena, where Napoleon Bonaparte had been imprisoned.

The fire of the love of Bahá'u'lláh galvanized Catherine to such an extent that her disability and all her physical limitations could not deter her from serving the Cause. Some of those who met her felt that she was like a saint or a heroine, but she said,

> I don't aspire to be a saint; I would rather be one of God's teddybears. I am really no different from anyone else. It is just that I know I shall have less time than others; I cannot be like the unwary bird Bahá'u'lláh speaks of in *The Hidden Words*. Only by centering myself in the Covenant of God can my life or death have any significance. If I have a private prayer, it's this: Let my life and death count in the Faith![48]

Nineteen months after arriving as pioneers in St Helena, Catherine passed away on 25 October 1967. 'The frail vessel which contained her triumphant spirit rests in the bosom of a soft green hill high in the centre of St. Helena looking out to the South Atlantic . . .'[49]

* * *

As we have seen through the stories in this chapter, the creative interaction between crisis and victory can at times be overwhelming and complicated, but we need to be patient with the process and keep our eyes on the horizon of the purpose of this Revelation. We need to be mindful of the fact that each crisis may bring new opportunities for teaching the Cause. In the words of the Universal House of Justice:

> . . . we call upon the believers everywhere not to allow themselves, even for one moment, to be perturbed by any increase in opposition to the Cause. Rather let them deepen their understanding of the creative interaction between crisis and victory in the evolution of the Faith, and increase their awareness of the power inherent in the Cause to surmount all obstacles that threaten its progress. Armed with this knowledge, let them seize the opportunities that arise and embrace the God-given challenges, confident in the invincibility of the Faith and the steady onward march of its Institutions.[50]

6

Scholarship and the Covenant

> The Hand of Omnipotence hath established His Revelation upon an unassailable, an enduring foundation. Storms of human strife are powerless to undermine its basis, nor will men's fanciful theories succeed in damaging its structure.
>
> *Bahá'u'lláh* [1]

Referring to His Revelation, Bahá'u'lláh states that He has 'proclaimed before the face of all the peoples of the world that which will serve as the key for unlocking the doors of sciences, of arts, of knowledge, of well-being, of prosperity and wealth'.[2] This significant statement reflects the power of the Creative Word of the divine Manifestation in influencing the progress of science, arts and other areas of endeavour. It also helps us to understand the nature of Bahá'í scholarship, the source of which is based on the sacred text and the Word of God.

As the mind and intellect of human beings continuously evolve, progressive revelation – which in each of the prophetic cycles showers upon humanity new wisdom and enlightenment – brings a fresh springtime of divine inspiration to revive humanity and renew civilization. In the Bahá'í Dispensation, the mind and its relationship with divine revelation has a new meaning. Likewise, the Bahá'í Writings elucidate the concept of scholarship and the characteristics of Bahá'í scholars in relation to the Faith and the Bahá'í community. Human intellect, although central to the understanding and discovery of truth, has its own limits. But knowledge expressed through divine Revelation has no limit. 'Abdu'l-Bahá elucidates that 'human intellects themselves must change'[3] because the old and outdated beliefs and traditions which are at variance with the foundation of divine reality must disappear and be reformed. This change of intellect involves a change in belief, and a change in belief will entail a change in behaviour. This principle also applies to the notion of scholarship. The traditional concept of scholarship needs to be re-evaluated and redefined in the light of the teachings of Bahá'u'lláh. Bahá'í scholarship is not set apart from the organic process of the purpose of this mighty Revelation, nor is it a fixed and frozen concept, independent of the progress of knowledge and development of human civilization. The Universal House of Justice writes:

> Access to knowledge is the right of every human being, and participation in its generation, application and diffusion a responsibility that all must shoulder in the great enterprise of building a prosperous world civilization . . .[4]

The evolution of the concept of scholarship in the Bahá'í Revelation also makes demands of steadfastness in the Covenant. In this chapter we examine the nature of this new concept of scholarship, while in Chapter 7 we will look at some of the tests that can challenge those who undertake it.

Revelation, Knowledge and Scholarship

Shoghi Effendi articulated the blueprint of the Revelation of Bahá'u'lláh and its goals as follows:

> The Revelation of Bahá'u'lláh, whose supreme mission is none other but the achievement of this organic and spiritual unity of the whole body of nations, should, if we be faithful to its implications, be regarded as signalizing through its advent the *coming of age of the entire human race*. It should be viewed not merely as yet another spiritual revival in the ever-changing fortunes of mankind, not only as a further stage in a chain of progressive Revelations, nor even as the culmination of one of a series of recurrent prophetic cycles, but rather as marking the last and highest stage in the stupendous evolution of man's collective life on this planet.[5]

The immensity of divine wisdom and the regenerative power of the Word of God in reconstructing a new civilization are depicted in the following words of the Blessed Beauty: 'Every single letter proceeding from Our mouth is endowed with such regenerative power as to enable it to bring into existence a new creation – a creation the magnitude of which is inscrutable to all save God. He verily hath knowledge of all things.'[6]

There is no limit to the ocean of the knowledge of the Manifestation of God, but what has been shared with humanity is limited to the extent of the capacity of the people of the world during this Dispensation. Bahá'u'lláh affirms:

> Within the treasury of Our Wisdom there lieth unrevealed a knowledge, one word of which, if we chose to divulge it to mankind, would cause every human being to recognize the Manifestation of God and to acknowledge His omniscience, would enable every one to discover the secrets of all the sciences . . .[7]

'Abdu'l-Bahá explains four methods of acquiring knowledge:

- First, through the senses
- Second, through the power of reason
- Third, through tradition – the text of the Holy Scriptures
- Fourth, through the power of the Holy Spirit[8]

The first three – knowledge through the senses, through the power of reason, logical arguments and deduction, and through tradition – are all fallible and open to error. But the fourth one – that is, knowledge through the power of the Holy Spirit – is infallible and is free from error.[9] 'Abdu'l-Bahá does not discount the value nor forbid the use of the first three methods of acquiring knowledge. Rather, He underlines the fact that the only one which is authoritative and infallible is knowledge through the power of the Holy Spirit.[10]

In this chapter the spiritual attributes required of those who practise Bahá'í scholarship will be discussed and their relationship with the Covenant and the Bahá'í community elaborated. I will also discuss the life and attitudes of two scholars of the first century of the Bahá'í Faith as well as one from the 20th century. This analysis is based on the statement of 'Abdu'l-Bahá in which He indicates that conduct and behaviour should take precedence over knowledge in Bahá'í scholarship: 'Good behaviour and high moral character must come first, for unless the character be trained, acquiring knowledge will only prove injurious. Knowledge is praiseworthy when it is coupled with ethical conduct and virtuous character, otherwise it is a deadly poison . . .'[11]

Among the virtues that a learned person is expected to possess, the first is to 'guard one's own self', writes 'Abdu'l-Bahá.[12] This reflects the fact that such a person should be imbued with humility. Guarding oneself does not mean protecting oneself from calamities and material tests, for even the Prophets were subjected to great afflictions:

> The primary meaning of this guarding of oneself is to acquire the attributes of spiritual and material perfections.
>
> The first attribute of perfection is learning and the cultural attainments of the mind, and this eminent station is achieved when the individual combines in himself a thorough knowledge of those complex and transcendental realities pertaining to God . . . and of those regulations and procedures which would contribute to the progress and civilization of this distinguished country.[13]

Understanding Bahá'í Scholarship

To appreciate the significance of the 'learned in Bahá' and Bahá'í scholarship, we turn to Bahá'u'lláh Who addresses them thus:

> Happy are ye, O ye the learned ones in Bahá. By the Lord! Ye are the billows of the Most Mighty Ocean, the stars of the firmament of Glory, the standards of triumph waving betwixt earth and heaven. Ye are the manifestations of steadfastness amidst men and the daysprings of Divine Utterance to all that dwell on earth.[14]

These words make it clear not only how lofty is the position of the Bahá'í scholar but also how heavy is the responsibility of those who aspire toward such an honour.

The purpose of education is to develop the capacity to serve humanity and to recognize God and the purpose of creation. If the aim of education were merely to accumulate information and knowledge without recognizing the purpose of creation, then education would lose its true meaning. 'Abdu'l-Bahá emphasizes that although the acquisition of science and arts is 'the greatest glory of mankind' this distinction is conferred on the condition that 'man's river flow into the mighty sea'.[15] That is, it should be connected to the source of all knowledge, which is the knowledge of God.

In the same Tablet, 'Abdu'l-Bahá writes that '[t]he sciences of today are bridges to reality; if then they lead not to reality, naught remains but fruitless illusion.'[16] This connection between learning and knowledge of the divine truth preserves the integrity of knowledge and its purpose. Otherwise education becomes simply a system of accumulation of information and will be out of touch with the true purpose of life. Such 'learning' brings with it 'arrogance and pride, and it bringeth on error and indifference to God'.[17] The first sign of the coming of age of humanity referred to in the Writings of Bahá'u'lláh is the emergence of a science which is described as that '"divine philosophy" which will include the discovery of a radical approach to the transmutation of elements. This is an indication of the splendours of the future stupendous expansion of knowledge.'[18]

Bahá'í scholarship is a valuable service encouraged and accessible to all Bahá'ís around the world; it is not confined to a particular population. The task of these individuals is to strive to relate the teachings of the Bahá'í Faith to contemporary issues and all matters of concern and to explore the application of the Bahá'í principles to the requirements and needs of society at large, of any religious or cultural background. The extent of learning and educational achievements is important but it does not necessarily constitute a definitive indication of scholarship. We may encounter individuals with little or no formal education who are endowed with wisdom and experiential knowledge beyond others who have received formal education. Moreover, intelligence does not always bring wisdom, which requires many attributes and cannot be measured by the amount of knowledge acquired; nor is it dependent solely on the level of one's IQ. This should not be construed as minimizing the importance of intellectual excellence, nor should it be seen as underestimating the need for each individual to achieve his or her potential. The Universal House of Justice delineates the connections:

> As the Bahá'í community grows it will acquire experts in numerous fields – both by Bahá'ís becoming experts and by experts becoming Bahá'ís. As these experts bring their knowledge and skill to the service

of the community and, even more, as they transform their various disciplines by bringing to bear upon them the light of the Divine Teachings, problem after problem now disrupting society will be answered ... Paralleling this process, Bahá'í institutional life will also be developing, and as it does so the Assemblies will draw increasingly upon scientific and expert knowledge – whether of Bahá'ís or of non-Bahá'ís – to assist in solving the problems of their communities.

In time great Bahá'í institutions of learning, great international and national projects for the betterment of human life will be inaugurated and flourish.[19]

In the Bahá'í Writings we find a number of attributes related to Bahá'í scholarship. Foremost among them are recognition of this Divine Revelation and partaking of the ocean of His knowledge and embracing His love. A person with these attributes is viewed by Bahá'u'lláh as 'an eye unto mankind' and 'the spirit of life' for the body of all creation.[20] In the Kitáb-i-Íqán He explains that a person who may have spent aeons of time in the pursuit of knowledge but failed to recognize the Divine Manifestation cannot justly be recognized as learned. On the other hand, an unlettered person who has the pure distinction of recognition of the Manifestation of God is honoured as a 'divinely-learned' person whose knowledge is of God and has reached the 'furthermost summit of learning ...'[21] This shows that the mere acquisition of knowledge is not an indication of scholarship.

In elucidating the praiseworthy behaviour and knowledge of learned individuals, 'Abdu'l-Bahá states that 'the lamp of their inner vision derives its light from the sun of universal knowledge'.[22] Such persons are content and 'like the birds, they give thanks for a handful of seeds, and the song of their wisdom dazzles the minds of the world's most wise...'[23] In other Writings, humility is encouraged while pride is discouraged.

Firmness in the Covenant and the Defence of the Faith

Bahá'u'lláh writes:

> Warn, O Salmán, the beloved of the one true God, not to view with too critical an eye the sayings and writings of men. Let them rather

approach such sayings and writings in a spirit of open-mindedness and loving sympathy. Those men, however, who, in this Day, have been led to assail, in their inflammatory writings, the tenets of the Cause of God, are to be treated differently. It is incumbent upon all men, each according to his ability, to refute the arguments of those that have attacked the Faith of God. Thus hath it been decreed by Him Who is the All-Powerful, the Almighty.[24]

Bahá'í scholars and academics also play an important role in research, analysis and publication of the 'present-day requirements of the people', finding relevant applications of Bahá'í teachings in fulfilment of these requirements. 'Abdu'l-Bahá emphasized that

> It is therefore urgent that beneficial articles and books be written, clearly and definitely establishing what the present-day requirements of the people are, and what will conduce to the happiness and advancement of society. These should be published and spread throughout the nation, so that at least the leaders among the people should become, to some degree, awakened, and arise to exert themselves along those lines which will lead to their abiding honour. The publication of high thoughts is the dynamic power in the arteries of life; it is the very soul of the world.[25]

But in this regard we need to be mindful that, in our study of the requirements of the day and of human affairs, we do not bend the Bahá'í Writings in order to please the academic community or to satisfy certain popular needs and desires which would be in conflict with the moral and spiritual principles of the Bahá'í teachings.

One of the characteristics of Bahá'í scholarship is firmness in the Covenant and defence of the Faith. Bahá'u'lláh's emphatic statement underlines the significance of this point:

> If any man were to arise to defend, in his writings, the Cause of God against its assailants, such a man, however, inconsiderable his share, shall be so honoured in the world to come that the Concourse on high would envy his glory. No Pen can depict the loftiness of his station neither can any tongue describe its splendour . . . [26]

Bahá'í professionals, academics and scholars play a vital role in the protection and defence of the Covenant. As the Cause of God emerges from obscurity, no doubt the Faith will be attacked from every direction. Deepening of the Bahá'í community in the Covenant will become increasingly important. The greatest enemy, however, is human ego and the 'temptation of intellectual pride'.[27] 'Sharp must be thy sight, O Dhábih, and, adamant thy soul, and brass-like thy feet, if thou wishest to be unshaken by the assaults of the selfish desires that whisper in men's breasts.'[28]

Priesthood and the Bahá'í Faith

In the Bahá'í Faith the institution of priesthood has been abrogated. This is a ground-breaking departure from the past in the history of religions. Following the promotion of this principle some of the teachers and scholars of the new Dispensation turned against the Covenant; but the teachings of Bahá'u'lláh do not leave room for establishing a clergy-like privileged class of erudite individuals who would assume a position above others in the Bahá'í community.[29] 'Once we begin to ask questions we become scholars, of sorts, and as soon as we think of ourselves as scholars we are in danger of acting like priests,' writes Bahiyyih Nakhjavani.[30] She continues:

> The most distinctive feature of this Revelation, however, and one which bears directly upon the warning against 'priestcraft' as well as the prohibition of priesthood, is the unequivocal nature of Bahá'u'lláh's Covenant, established in His Will and Testament. Through it the burden of interpretation is removed from the shoulders of priests and scholars and given to 'Abdu'l-Bahá. Through it the unity of the Faith is at once secured and protected against any conflicting counter interpretations. With the Word thus removed from any single person's control, and simultaneously made available to all, through the parallel exhortations to meditate, to study, to investigate the truth independently, the traditional role of the priest is annulled. He is no longer the keeper of the Word, the interpreter of its mysteries to the illiterate multitudes.[31]

In the past religious dispensations, the clergy and religious leaders would make authoritative interpretations of divine revelation which became the source of many misconceptions, errors and divisions. They endeavoured to 'encompass the Divine Message within the framework of their limited understanding to define doctrines where definition was beyond their power . . .'[32] As they did not possess the knowledge of divine wisdom and experience, nor were they infallible, their arguments did not lead to essential truth.

Divines and their passion for leadership

Bahá'u'lláh describes those religious leaders and divines who instigated the hardship and suffering undergone by the Prophets of God in these strong words: 'they that worship no God but their own desire, who bear allegiance to naught but gold, who are wrapt in the densest veils of learning, and who, enmeshed by its obscurities, are lost in the wilds of error.'[33] These 'veils of learning' not only prevented many people from accepting the Báb as a new Manifestation of God, but also obscured the inner vision of many of those who embraced the Bábí religion but failed to recognize the Cause of Bahá'u'lláh.

Bahá'u'lláh furthermore addresses as 'veils of glory' those divines who in the days of the Manifestation of God not only failed to embrace the Message of God but 'refused to incline their ears unto the divine Melody'. This was due to their 'want of discernment and their love and eagerness for leadership'.[34] As a result of their attitude and their rejection of the truth, the people who were following these masters remained ignorant and deprived of the life-giving teachings of God for the new era. These people, as a result, acted as though they had no sight, no hearing and no conscience to be able to discern truth from error.

Bahá'u'lláh identifies some of the motives for opposition by the ecclesiastics. He tells us that

> Some for the lust of leadership, others through want of knowledge and understanding, have been the cause of the deprivation of the people. By their sanction and authority, every Prophet of God hath drunk from the chalice of sacrifice, and winged His flight unto the heights of glory. What unspeakable cruelties they that have occupied the seats of authority and learning have inflicted upon the true Monarchs of the world, those Gems of divine virtue! Content with a transitory dominion, they have deprived themselves of an everlasting sovereignty.[35]

He warned them in these emphatic words: 'O concourse of divines! Lay aside all your veils and coverings. Give ear unto that whereunto calleth you the Most Sublime Pen, in this wondrous Day . . . The world is laden with dust, by reason of your vain imaginings . . .'[36]

On the other hand, there were many pure-hearted but little-known people of learning, or sometimes even great scholars and luminaries of their time, who were sincere in their search after the truth. When they recognized it, they rent asunder the 'veil of glory', and accepted the Manifestation of God.

So, as mentioned above, in the Dispensation of Bahá'u'lláh there is no clerical class; all authoritative interpretations of the Writings have been made by the Centre of the Covenant and successor of Bahá'u'lláh and after Him by Shoghi Effendi, the Guardian of the Bahá'í Faith. Following them, there is no authoritative interpreter of the Bahá'í Writings. Individual interpretations of the Writings are permitted, for the purpose of one's own understanding, but have no authoritative significance; they remain as personal opinion only. The Bahá'í Writings are very explicit on this matter and safeguarding this principle is an integral part of the Covenant and a distinguishing feature of the Bahá'í Dispensation.

Throughout the history of religions knowledge about and interpretation of the sacred writings were in the domain of the clergy, as Nakhjavani writes: 'The fundamental purpose of scholarship in early religious societies was closely linked to the institution of priesthood. It was the role of the scholars, that keeper of the Word, to elucidate on matters that the priest, that interpreter of the Word, might teach the multitude.'[37] She then goes on to state that

> The greatest challenge to this generation of Bahá'ís, and one of the first questions raised by those who eagerly turn to this Faith, searching for evidence of hope, rests in this enigmatic relationship between scholars and priests. We say we have no priesthood; why then the emphasis on scholarship? How can we purge the scholar of the old power-hungry desire to interpret the Word? How can we ensure that we are not merely creating a kind of 'priestcraft' under the guise of 'Bahá'í scholarship'?[38]

This call to mindfulness with regard to the history of scholarship and the priesthood is very timely. We must remember that while the Bahá'í

Faith encourages scholarship for this new Dispensation, it radically abolishes the priesthood of the past, as the Universal House of Justice writes:

> Collateral with His summons to the pursuit of knowledge, Bahá'u'lláh has abolished entirely that feature of all past religions by which a special caste of persons such as the Christian priesthood or the Islamic 'ulama came to exercise authority over the religious understanding and practice of their fellow believers.[39]

And the Guardian, in a letter written on his behalf in 1927 to a Spiritual Assembly, underlined this significant departure from the past:

> But praise be to God that the Pen of Glory has done away with the unyielding and dictatorial views of the learned and the wise, dismissed the assertions of individuals as an authoritative criterion, even though they were recognized as the most accomplished and learned among men, and ordained that all matters be referred to authorized centers and specified assemblies.[40]

The Universal House of Justice has made the following comments about academics within the Bahá'í community:

> . . . it is no doubt helpful to keep in mind that Bahá'ís who are trained in various academic disciplines do not constitute a discrete body within the community. While the Bahá'í institutions benefit on an ongoing basis from the advice of believers in many fields of specialization, there is obviously no group of academics who can claim to speak on behalf of Bahá'í scholars generally. Scholarly qualifications enable individuals to make greatly valued contributions to the work of the Cause, but do not set those possessing them apart from the general body of the believers. The House of Justice feels confident that, with patience, self-discipline, and unity of faith, Bahá'í academics will be able to contribute to a gradual forging of the more integrative paradigms of scholarship for which thoughtful minds in the international community are increasingly calling.[41]

Bahá'u'lláh exhorted the friends about the danger of feeling a sense of superiority and distinction over others:

SCHOLARSHIP AND THE COVENANT

Ever since the seeking of preference and distinction came into play, the world hath been laid waste. It hath become desolate . . . Indeed, man is noble, inasmuch as each one is a repository of the sign of God. Nevertheless, to regard oneself as superior in knowledge, learning or virtue, or to exalt oneself or seek preference, is a grievous transgression.[42]

Indeed, in this Dispensation humility and servitude are the crowning glory of true lovers of Bahá'u'lláh.

Síyyid Yaḥyáy-i-Dárábí

Siyyid Yaḥyáy-i-Dárábí, surnamed Vaḥíd (Peerless), was a highly distinguished divine of Islam, well known for his learning, erudition and scholarship. He knew 'almost the whole of the Qur'án by heart and had committed to memory no less than thirty thousand traditions of Islam'.[43]

As the news of the appearance of the Báb as Qá'im captivated the minds and hearts of the people of Iran, Muhammad Shah, the King of Iran, was moved to investigate the truth of the Báb's claim. For this purpose he designated Vaḥíd, 'the most learned, the most eloquent, and the most influential of his subjects' to interview the Báb and send the report of that investigation to the king.[44] During Vaḥíd's meeting with the Báb in Shiraz he was so amazed and moved that he recognized and embraced the Cause of the Báb and became 'one of the greatest luminaries of His Dispensation'.[45]

In *Memorials of the Faithful*, 'Abdu'l-Bahá recounts the following story in which Vaḥíd's scholarship is implicated:

One day the great Siyyid Yaḥyá, surnamed Vaḥíd, was present there. As he sat without, Ṭáhirih listened to him from behind the veil. I was then a child, and was sitting on her lap. With eloquence and fervour, Vaḥíd was discoursing on the signs and verses that bore witness to the advent of the new Manifestation. She suddenly interrupted him and, raising her voice, vehemently declared: 'O Yaḥyá! Let deeds, not words, testify to thy faith, if thou art a man of true learning. Cease idly repeating the traditions of the past, for the day of service, of steadfast action, is come. Now is the time to show forth the true signs of God, to rend asunder the veils of idle fancy, to promote the Word of God, and to sacrifice ourselves in His path. Let deeds, not words, be our adorning!'[46]

This story shows how those two glorious and most learned scholars of the Báb's Dispensation encountered one another and with what power Ṭáhirih challenged Vaḥíd: deeds and not words were to be the emblem of his faith.

The Spiritually Learned

In the Bahá'í Writings there are references to the 'spiritually learned', underlining the importance of the spiritual character of Bahá'ís who are engaged in various scholarly activities.

> The spiritually learned must be characterized by both inward and outward perfections; they must possess a good character, an enlightened nature, a pure intent, as well as intellectual power, brilliance and discernment, intuition, discretion and foresight, temperance, reverence, and a heartfelt fear of God. For an unlit candle, however great in diameter and tall, is no better than a barren palm tree or a pile of dead wood.[47]

'Knowledge is praiseworthy when it is coupled with ethical conduct and virtuous character,' writes 'Abdu'l-Bahá. [48] In acquiring knowledge it is important to harmonize material knowledge with spiritual insight and perspective wherever possible. 'Abdu'l-Bahá elucidated some of the characteristics of the spiritually learned, indicating that acquiring knowledge can bring joy or challenges, depending on how we utilize knowledge for the betterment of mankind. He tells us:

> The spiritually learned are lamps of guidance among the nations, and stars of good fortune shining from the horizons of humankind. They are fountains of life for such as lie in the death of ignorance and unawareness, and clear springs of perfections for those who thirst and wander in the wasteland of their defects and errors . . . It is they who are the strong citadel guarding humanity, and the impregnable sanctuary for the sorely distressed, the anxious and tormented, victims of ignorance.[49]

Furthermore, the Master admonishes the learned, citing a tradition of Islam that '"he must guard himself, defend his faith, oppose his passions and obey the commandments of his Lord" . . . Whoever is lacking in these divine qualifications and does not demonstrate these inescapable requirements in his own life, should not be referred to as learned.'[50]

In brief, 'The man of consummate learning and the sage endowed with penetrating wisdom are the two eyes to the body of mankind.'[51]

Attributes and Attitudes of the Learned

The primacy of high moral conduct over knowledge is an important feature of the academic pursuit of Bahá'ís. This is the opposite of what we observe in society at large, where the behaviour and conduct of a scholar is often of secondary importance.

Furthermore, the Master explains that

> the happiness and greatness, the rank and station, the pleasure and peace, of an individual have never consisted in his personal wealth, but rather in his excellent character, his high resolve, the breadth of his learning and his ability to resolve difficult problems . . .[52]

Bahá'u'lláh brought not only a set of principles and laws but also a new culture which encourages human beings to develop a profound sense of humility and self-effacement in the service of mankind. This runs against the materialistic mindset of the contemporary academic environment. The life of a great scholar of the Faith, Mírzá Abu'l-Faḍl, described later in this chapter, is an example of such a transformation of character in the light of the Revelation of Bahá'u'lláh. This transformation is bound to be a spiritual phenomenon and not purely an intellectual exercise. Bahá'í scholars, with their wealth of knowledge and insight, also need to be 'thoroughly imbued with love for the Faith and its teachings'.[53]

Bahá'í scholars are also called upon to beware of the self-importance which is so prevalent in society. Moreover, the House of Justice explains that there are many aspects of Western thinking in society which, although they have been raised to a status of 'unassailable principle', time may show that they were either wrong or only partially true. This temptation is very strong in the culture of the Western academic community. Bahá'í teachers and budding scholars who rise to eminence in academic circles are frequently exposed to the powerful influence of a sense of pride and entitlement which they need to be on guard against.[54]

Bahá'í scholars will play an important role in the Baha'i community and the advancement of the Cause. The praise and distinction which the Bahá'í Writings accord them also brings formidable responsibility in a world immersed in materialism and self-glorification:

> The sundering of science and religion is but one example of the tendency of the human mind (which is necessarily limited in its capacity) to concentrate on one virtue, one aspect of truth, one goal, to the exclusion of others. This leads, in extreme cases, to fanaticism and the utter distortion of truth, and in all cases to some degree of imbalance and inaccuracy. A scholar who is imbued with an understanding of the broad teachings of the Faith will always remember that being a scholar does not exempt him from the primal duties and purposes for which all human beings are created. All men, not scholars alone, are exhorted to seek out and uphold the truth, no matter how uncomfortable it may be. But they are also exhorted to be wise in their utterance, to be tolerant of the views of others, to be courteous in their behaviour and speech, not to sow the seeds of doubt in faithful hearts, to look at the good rather than at the bad, to avoid conflict and contention, to be reverent, to be faithful to the Covenant of God, to promote His Faith and safeguard its honour, and to educate their fellowmen, giving milk to babes and meat to those who are stronger.
>
> Scholarship has a high station in the Bahá'í teachings, and Bahá'í scholars have a great responsibility. We believe that they would do well to concentrate upon the ascertainment of truth – of a fuller understanding of the subject of their scholarship, whatever its field – not upon exposing and attacking the errors of others, whether they be of non-Bahá'ís or of their fellow believers. Inevitably the demonstration of truth exposes the falsity of error, but the emphasis and motive are important.[55]

Modesty and self-effacement

Another issue which is part of refinement of character for scholars is self-effacement and submission to the will of God. Lowliness and modesty are virtues which are very hard to come by in a materialistic society. North American culture has the dubious distinction of being rooted in the culture of materialism and individualism. These two are closely related to a competitive lifestyle in which 'to have' takes precedence over 'to be'. Hence, possession of knowledge, important as it is, if bereft of humility and submission to divine Will, can only reinforce the temptation to indulge in intellectual pride.

In academic circles, social status and position are a common preoccupation. For some, knowledge brings a sense of selfish ownership and entitlement which can feed into a feeling of superiority. Yet possession of knowledge can be handled in such a way as not to feed into self-promotion and arrogance.

There is a beautiful story in the *Bustan* (the Orchard) of Sa'di, the Persian poet, about the raindrop and the sea. This 'monologue' demonstrates the virtue of humility:

> . . . a drop of rain falling down from the clouds . . . knew itself to be the water of life, the most precious element that God had created, and so it was proud of itself. Boasting all the way down it suddenly saw that it was falling into an ocean beneath. Suddenly it recognized its own insignificance and exclaimed: 'If this exists then what am I?!' When the ocean heard this expression of humility it attracted the drop to itself and, as a reward, made it a companion of the pearl.[56]

In the past, the high respect and prestige accorded to religious scholars and the clergy led many of them to develop a sense of superiority and dominance. But not all scholars harboured this sentiment. Indeed, there have been many examples of humility, whom others have sought to emulate. In the Kitáb-i-Aqdas Bahá'u'lláh writes:

> Amongst the people is he whose learning hath made him proud, and who hath been debarred thereby from recognizing My Name, the Self-Subsisting; who, when he heareth the tread of sandals following behind him, waxeth greater in his own esteem than Nimrod. Say: O rejected one! Where now is his abode? By God, it is the nethermost fire. [57]

With regard to the 'truly learned', however, the following words of Bahá'u'lláh are enlightening:

> Know thou that he is truly learned who hath acknowledged My Revelation, and drunk from the Ocean of My knowledge, and soared in the atmosphere of My love, and cast away all else besides Me . . .[58]

This, then, is the hallmark of the 'truly learned' in this Dispensation. With the Revelation of Bahá'u'lláh a new knowledge is born and mankind is endowed with a new capacity for learning and the ability to unravel the mysteries of the universe. The Word of God, like the rays of the sun, empowers individuals to attain a higher plane of understanding of the purpose of life.

Love and magnanimity

These virtues, in relation to academic and intellectual endeavours, humanize scholarly contributions to society and lessen the likelihood of the development of attitudes of arrogance and self-centredness. 'Show forbearance and benevolence and love to one another,' writes Bahá'u'lláh. 'Should any one among you be incapable of grasping a certain truth, or be striving to comprehend it, show forth, when conversing with him, a spirit of extreme kindliness and good-will.'[59] This is vital, especially in our time when people are very busy. There are so many books and articles published every day on the virtues of happiness, benevolence and forbearance, but in reality even some of those who write about these wonderful attributes fail to follow what they preach! '. . . the believers must recognize the importance of intellectual honesty and humility'.[60]

In a letter 'To the Bahá'í Youth in every Land', the Universal House of Justice wrote in 1966:

> . . . Bahá'ís must increasingly stand out as pillars of righteousness and forbearance. The life of a Bahá'í will be characterized by truthfulness and decency; he will walk uprightly among his fellowmen, dependent upon none save God, yet linked by bonds of love and brotherhood with mankind; he will be entirely detached from the loose standards, the decadent theories, the frenetic experimentation, the desperation of present-day society, will look upon his neighbours with a bright and friendly face, and be a beacon light and haven for all those who would emulate his strength of character and assurance of soul.[61]

Obedience to and fear of God

Shoghi Effendi once wrote that there are two main principles which he wished the believers to always keep in mind and faithfully follow:

> First is the principle of unqualified and wholehearted loyalty to the revealed Word . . . Next is the principle of complete, and immediate obedience to the Assemblies, both local and national . . . [62]

One of the qualities of a spiritually learned person is what 'Abdu'l-Bahá defines as 'heartfelt fear of God'.[63] This fear is different from other kinds of fear, in the sense that it is connected to 'inward perfection'. In the *Epistle to the Son of the Wolf*, Bahá'u'lláh explains that Bahá'ís are committed to 'reconstruct the world'. Then He states that '(t)heir hosts are the hosts of goodly deeds, and their arms the arms of upright conduct, and their commander the fear of God'.[64] Fear of God is a protective factor against self-pride and arrogance. In contrast, egotism is a risk factor with respect to loyalty and obedience. 'Abdu'l-Bahá mentions

> those famed and accomplished men of learning, possessed of praiseworthy qualities and vast erudition, who lay hold on the strong handle of the fear of God and keep to the ways of salvation.[65]

Contrary to common opinion, not every kind of fear is harmful. In some circumstances it plays a protective role against destructive consequences. This is not a romantic perception of fear, but rather a deeper understanding of the wisdom of this dark emotion. Fear of God can prevent many unwise or destructive behaviours. But first one needs to be a believer! When there is certitude and faith, fear is replaced by courage and love, as we see in the heroic acts of religious martyrs.

While fear in emotional terms can sometimes be morbid and a sign of a psychological disturbance that requires treatment, fear of God has a different implication and a meaning which is spiritual. It is a feeling which indicates a deep love for the Creator and a concern over one's actual or potential failure to obey God. It reinforces compliance to laws and ordinances. Materialistic psychology has a reductionistic view of fear. It claims that God is perceived as a father figure, punitive and controlling; therefore, it holds, religious beliefs are created to control the masses through fear. Such a theory denies the existence of God as a loving and merciful Creator. His Teachings, through His Prophets, have been the source of progress of civilization and have established the law of order in the world.

Tact and wisdom

In the Lawḥ-i-Hikmat (Tablet of Wisdom), addressed to a distinguished believer and scholar surnamed Nabíl-i-Akbar, Bahá'u'lláh wrote,

> The beginning of Wisdom and the origin thereof is to acknowledge whatsoever God hath clearly set forth, for through its potency the foundation of statesmanship, which is a shield for the preservation of the body of mankind, hath been firmly established.[66]

And also,

> Whatever is written should not transgress the bounds of tact and wisdom, and in the words used there should lie hid the property of milk, so that the children of the world may be nurtured therewith, and attain maturity. We have said in the past that one word hath the influence of spring and causeth hearts to become fresh and verdant, while another is like unto blight which causeth the blossoms and flowers to wither. God grant that authors among the friends will write in such a way as would be acceptable to fair-minded souls, and not lead to cavilling by the people.[67]

Mírzá Abu'l-Faḍl: A great example for Bahá'í scholars

Abu'l-Faḍl Gulpáygání was one of the foremost scholars of the Faith during the first century of the Bahá'í era. Not only was he renowned for his knowledge of history, divine philosophy and other subjects, but he was also a master of Arabic and Persian literature. In Egypt he was once referred to as 'a pillar of history and the corner stone of knowledge and virtue'.[68]

He was also a luminary of knowledge and humility in the Bahá'í Faith. Besides his prodigious erudition and scholarship, he was 'a model of humility, detachment, service to the Cause, and servitude to his fellow-believers'.⁶⁹ Although his name was Muḥammad, and his given appellation Abu'l-Faḍl or Father of Excellence, 'Abdu'l-Bahá always called him Abu'l-Faḍa'il (plural, meaning Father of All Excellence).⁷⁰ He was so dear to 'Abdu'l-Bahá that when the Master was in the United States and heard that Mírzá Abu'l-Faḍl was ill, He sent a cable to the friends in Cairo asking them to provide for Mírzá Abu'l-Faḍl's comfort, stating that 'he consists of my own self'.⁷¹

After becoming a Bahá'í in 1876, on the advice of Bahá'u'lláh he travelled for ten years through Iran for the purpose of teaching the Faith and was imprisoned several times. He was encouraged by Bahá'u'lláh to devote his pen as well as his tongue to the promotion of the Cause and to use his scholarship for the defence of the Faith. In Egypt, after the passing of Bahá'u'lláh, he became a magnet for Bahá'í activities and an exponent of the Baha'i Faith. Later 'Abdu'l-Bahá gave him another assignment which included travelling to the United States, where he rendered crucial services to the Cause and deepened the friends in the Covenant of Bahá'u'lláh. Mírzá Abu'l-Faḍl once said, 'Before attaining to the gift of faith, human beings are like the dead; and after attainment of faith, all achieve nothingness at the sacred threshold of the Divine.'⁷²

He wrote extensively on the history of the Faith, on the Covenant of Bahá'u'lláh and the proofs and prophecies in the Qur'án and the Bible. His masterpiece is the book *Farā'id*, written in response to a Muslim cleric's attack on the Bahá'í Faith and published in 1898 in Cairo. While in the United States from 1901 to 1904 he wrote *The Bahá'í Proofs*, which was translated into English and published. His collection of essays entitled *Miracles and Metaphors* also reflects the depth of his scholarship and insight.

The hallmarks of his character were selflessness, devotion, and detachment. Besides his scholarly work, he dedicated his time to service to God and to the believers and the community, and to participation in teaching and deepening. He was designated a Hand of the Cause posthumously by 'Abdu'l-Bahá, who wrote about him:

> Pure souls, such as Mírzá Abu'l-Faḍl, upon him be the Glory of God, spend their nights and days in demonstrating the truth of the Revelation, by adducing conclusive and brilliant proofs and expanding the verities of the Faith, by lifting the veils, promoting the religion of God and spreading His fragrances.⁷³

In his introduction to the book *Miracles and Metaphors*, Amin Banani writes that Abu'l-Faḍl believed that 'knowledge is nothing but comprehension of the reality of things and the reality of things can only be reflected in the hearts which are pure. That purity is attainable through prayer and spiritual concentration.'[74]

The following account was written by Ḥabíb Mu'ayyad, who knew Mírzá Abu'l-Faḍl personally.

> Once people asked him how he had acquired this vast erudition and how he had become the recipient of this God-given knowledge. He became so displeased with his questioners that he angrily remarked 'Who is Abu'l-Faḍl! What is Abu'l-Faḍl! I am only a drop from the vast ocean of Bahá'u'lláh's school. If you also enter the same school, you will become the master of Abu'l-Faḍl.[75]

Adib Taherzadeh has written about the scholarship and virtuous character of Mírzá Abu'l-Faḍl. He recounts the following story:

> In the early years of this century [20th], 'Abdu'l-Bahá sent Mírzá Abu'l-Faḍl to the United States of America to teach and help the believers deepen in the Faith. After his return, he and a number of American pilgrims were seated in the presence of 'Abdu'l-Bahá in 'Akká. The pilgrims began to praise Mírzá Abu'l-Faḍl for the help he had given them, saying that he had taught many souls, defended the Cause most ably against its adversaries, and had helped to build a strong and dedicated Bahá'í community in America. As they continued to pour lavish praise upon him, Mírzá Abu'l-Faḍl became increasingly depressed and dejected, until he burst into tears and wept loudly. The believers were surprised and could not understand this, even thinking that they had not praised him enough!
>
> Then 'Abdu'l-Bahá explained that by praising him they had bitterly hurt him, for he considered himself as utter nothingness in the Cause and believed with absolute sincerity that he was not worthy of any mention or praise.[76]

Mírzá Abu'l-Faḍl's deep sense of humility in the Bahá'í community is expressed in a statement through which he acknowledges his ignorance of the vast world of the Almighty and emphasizes how we should prioritize our focus while in this earthly life.

There are some scholars who claim to know all the mysteries of creation and all the truths of its genesis. But I do not know the number of the stars or how many grains of sand are in the sea. I have not learned the names of the created things on the moon, or counted how many souls are on Mars, nor do I ask why God did not give human beings wings or eyes in the back of their heads. I cannot fathom the wisdom that led Him to single out the dove for pleasant warbling and the crow for raucous cawing. I have no idea what mothers will be naming their daughters in the future or what fathers will call their sons.

Does the status of these matters as unknown mean that they so deserve to attract our attention that we should spend our lives trying to understand them while neglecting the divine promises whose time of fulfilment has arrived?[77]

Hasan M. Balyuzi: A scholar and defender of the Faith in the 20th century

Hand of the Cause of God Hasan Balyuzi, an Afnán and an outstanding scholar and historian of the Faith, was characterized with a profound sense of modesty and humility.[78] Born in Shiraz in 1908, he spent most of his early childhood in Bushihr, learning English from an early age and later studying history at the American University of Beirut. During a visit to Haifa at this time, he met the youthful Guardian, a meeting that completely transformed him. He became then an energetic and brilliant servant of the Cause and one of the top students at the American University.

After he moved to London he continued his education in diplomatic history, and in 1934 published an article in an Iranian newspaper about the current political situation of Europe. In view of the political nature of his article, the Guardian drew to his attention that he should refrain from direct or indirect participation in political activity. After receiving this guidance, Mr Balyuzi immediately ceased those activities and decided not to enter any diplomatic or political field, sacrificing a possibly brilliant career. Shoghi Effendi was much impressed by Mr Balyuzi's immediate action performed in a spirit of obedience.[81] The fact that both he and the Guardian shared an illustrious lineage (a great-grandfather of both was Ḥájí Mírzá Abu'l-Qásim) did not prevent Mr Balyuzi from remaining faithful and obedient. After serving for many years as a member (and often Chairman) of the National Spiritual Assembly of the British Isles, he was appointed a Hand of the Cause by Shoghi Effendi. The Guardian had advised him to write on the history of the Faith and especially on the lives of the Báb, Bahá'u'lláh and 'Abdu'l-Bahá. Beginning in the early 1960s, he wrote not only these but other outstanding contributions to Bahá'í historical research and literature. His fellow Hand of the Cause Ugo Giachery has characterized his books as 'gem-like'; he believed that they 'will remain among the most outstanding writings to enlighten the paths of seekers for centuries to come'.[79] Moojan Momen, who worked closely with Mr Balyuzi, has commented:

> Much of his writings ran counter to present-day styles of scholarly prose. But his work is imbued with two qualities which will cause it to be remembered long after much other material written to such standards has been forgotten. First, was his assiduous pursuit of truth. He would take endless trouble to track down even the most minor fact or date. He would write several letters in pursuit of just one piece of information which might take up only one line in his book. He did not hesitate to discard large sections of his manuscript if his researches left any doubt as to the truth of what he had written...Second, was his integrity . . . He wrote nothing for fame or self-advancement. He wrote only what he thought correct after due consideration. He always maintained that it was best to tell it 'warts and all'.[80]

In the announcement of his passing in February 1980, the Universal House of Justice referred to Mr Balyuzi as one of the 'powerful defenders' of the Cause and one of its 'most resourceful historians'.[82]

7

Tests of the Covenant among Scholars and Teachers of the Faith

> Sharp must be thy sight, O <u>Dh</u>abíh, and, adamant thy soul, and brass-like thy feet, if thou wishest to be unshaken by the assaults of the selfish desires that whisper in men's breasts.
>
> Bahá'u'lláh[1]

During His visit to North America in 1912–13, 'Abdu'l-Bahá frequently spoke about the paramount importance of unity and firmness in the Covenant. The young American Bahá'í community of that time had already been tested by covenantal issues related to the activities of Ibrahim <u>Kh</u>ayru'lláh who, after remarkable teaching success which resulted in a large number of new believers in that country beginning in 1894, later on violated the Covenant and turned against 'Abdu'l-Bahá.

<u>Kh</u>ayru'lláh was a Lebanese Christian who become a Bahá'í in Egypt and then moved to the United States in 1892. From February 1894 he began to teach the Cause with much success in Chicago, New York and a few other cities. Because of his extraordinary teaching achievements, 'Abdu'l-Bahá gave him the titles 'the second Columbus' and 'Conqueror of America'. These titles served as tests of ego to a man who, after all his teaching services, allowed his passion for power to lead to his downfall. In the fall of 1898 <u>Kh</u>ayru'lláh and his wife went to the Holy Land as guests of Phoebe Hearst, a prominent American Bahá'í. Upon his return to the United States in December 1899 he turned against the Centre of the Covenant and began openly seeking leadership of the Bahá'í community. While he was in the Holy Land he was influenced by the pernicious machinations of the Arch-Covenant-breaker Mírzá Muḥammad-'Alí. The symptoms of that toxic relationship appeared

when he began to entertain the thought of 'dividing the Bahá'í world into two parts, he becoming the leader of the Bahá'ís of the West and 'Abdu'l-Bahá of the East!'² Such an egotistical suggestion is indicative of a break with the reality of faithfulness to the Centre of the Covenant.

19 June 1912 was a historic day for the American Bahá'ís and in particular the Bahá'ís of New York; on that day 'Abdu'l-Bahá named New York City the 'City of the Covenant'. In a gathering of the friends He spoke publicly for the first time about the Tablet of the Branch, revealed by Bahá'u'lláh in Adrianople, which names Him as the Centre of the Covenant. This emphatic and authoritative statement of the Master invested New York with a special distinction.³ This public historic declaration on the Covenant was important for the United States, whose believers would be distinguished in the West as the spiritual descendants of the Dawn-Breakers, those early heroic followers of the Báb in Persia. Moreover, it was in North America that the Administrative Order of Bahá'u'lláh was first to rise, so that that continent would become known as the 'cradle' of that Order.⁴ The North American continent was also destined to encounter and overcome many tests and troubles which would befall it as one of the 'potential storm centres' in the West on its path to its glorious future.⁵

'Abdu'l-Bahá's declaration in New York was to be taken as a means of fortifying the foundations of unity, fidelity and holding fast to the power of the Covenant. 'Abdu'l-Bahá took to heart the issue of faithfulness and fidelity, as in the following Tablet, which also expresses His innermost longing for servitude and martyrdom:

> True fidelity is attained when a wanderer, nameless and traceless, I become. O Lord! Ordain for Thy servant the realization of his utmost wish, this bounty which shines resplendent upon the horizon of fidelity, like unto the sun arisen at dawn. One request I have to put to the loved ones of Bahá, that they prostrate themselves before the holy threshold, lay their heads on the ground and ask that the sinful 'Abdu'l-Bahá be granted the cup of immolation, so that he may, in servitude to the threshold of Bahá taste the sweet savour of a drop from the ocean of fidelity.⁶

Intellectual Pride and Arrogance

The majority of Bahá'í academics and scholars sincerely strive to have a clear understanding of the dynamics of the Revelation of Bahá'u'lláh. Among them are many who are 'adorned with the robe of humility' and renounce self-glorification and attention-seeking behaviours. Large numbers of them have enriched the Bahá'í community and society at large with their brilliant and scholarly contributions through the application of Bahá'í teachings to academic and social issues and the betterment of humanity.

The materialistic way of life in today's society encourages competitive superiority in ownership of wealth or knowledge. When possession of knowledge is to satisfy selfish pride, devoid of servitude to humanity, such a possession can be divisive. The Universal House of Justice writes:

> Bahá'í scholars must beware of the temptation of intellectual pride. 'Abdu'l-Bahá has warned the friends in the West that they would be subjected to intellectual tests . . . Any Bahá'í who rises to eminence in academic circles will be exposed to the powerful influence of such thinking . . . [7]

'Abdu'l-Bahá has written that 'there is no veil more obstructive than the self'.[8] It is well-known that in medicine there are herbs and chemicals, some of which can cure and lead to well-being, while others have terrible adverse effects. Among the most crippling toxic effects of chemicals is neurotoxicity, which can paralyse the normal functioning of the brain and nervous system and cripple cognitive and decision-making processes. In the Bahá'í community, egotism has its own toxic effects: it can penetrate mind and soul, cripple one's grasp of the power of unity and distort one's perception of the true meaning of the Covenant. The sad thing about the toxicity of egotism is that it may grow in a very insidious way and go unnoticed by family and friends as well as by the person who harbours it. 'Abdu'l-Bahá spoke about 'the subtlety of the ego' and stated that 'it is the Tempter (the subtle serpent of the mind)'.[9] Egotism makes captive the perception of the self more than anything else and kindles a passion for self-exaltation. One sees one's own needs and interests as standing above all else. One seeks the spotlight and is discouraged when that spotlight turns away. Bahá'u'lláh stated that some individuals are 'captive to their own evil passions and corrupt desires'.[10] In this way some people become prisoners of their own selves, guided by their own egos.

One of the functions of the learned in the Bahá'í community – in this case the Hands of the Cause – is to 'edify the souls of men'.[11] How can this be possible if a soul is captivated by its own ego and is willingly blinded to the beauty of others who are equal to him or her? 'Life is a constant struggle,' writes Shoghi Effendi, 'not only against the forces around us but above all against our own ego.'[12] This struggle, however, is part of growth and should not be dismissed as abnormal. Teaching the Cause and serving the poor, the sick and the helpless drive our attention away from undue self-centredness.

With regard to the question of self, Shoghi Effendi explained that it can have different meanings:

> Self has really two meanings, or is used in two senses, in the Bahá'í writings; one is self, the identity of the individual created by God. This is the self mentioned in such passages as 'he hath known God who hath known himself,' etc. The other self is the ego, the dark, animalistic heritage each one of us has, the lower nature that can develop into a monster of selfishness, brutality, lust and so on. It is this self we must struggle against, or this side of our natures, in order to strengthen and free the spirit within us and help it to attain perfection.[13]

Throughout the Bahá'í Writings, self-sacrifice has been defined as subordination of the lower nature with its desires, to the higher nature, the godly and noble side of human nature.

Materialistic culture values the role of ego, based on the assumption that the interrelationship of ego and human desires and instinct contribute to human satisfaction and happiness. Freud believed that 'What decides the purpose of life is simply the programme of the pleasure principle,' and that 'satisfaction of instinct spells happiness for us'.[14] This materialistic concept reinforces the dominance of the lower nature over the higher nature in a human being. Contrary to this concept, the Bahá'í teachings explain that our lower nature should be subordinated by our higher or spiritual nature rather than dominated by it. 'Abdu'l-Bahá affirms that 'True happiness depends on spiritual good and having the heart ever open to receive the Divine Bounty.'[15]

TESTS OF THE COVENANT AMONG SCHOLARS AND TEACHERS OF THE FAITH

In North American society the cult of individualism is a popular phenomenon and it is promoted constantly. This gives a false perception of self and a thirst for narcissism. In such a society, where obedience loses its meaning, raising up scholars to be the embodiment of humility and self-effacement is a miracle! But miracles can happen.

In modern society, an 'incessant promotion of individualism' is frequently observed which reinforces narcissism and glorification of self.[16] Although reflecting on our inner reality is important in order to know ourselves, an egotistical preoccupation with self can have the opposite effect, as Shoghi Effendi writes:

> The more we search for ourselves, the less likely we are to find ourselves; and the more we search for God, and to serve our fellow-men, the more profoundly will we become acquainted with ourselves, and the more inwardly assured. This is one of the great spiritual laws of life.[17]

An analogy of the serious effect of egotism is as follows. A glass of pure milk is a source of nutrition and energy. However, if a drop of poison is added to it, the essential quality of the milk changes, loses its usefulness – it is no longer pure.[18] Likewise, egotism can poison one's life and character. There were many whose lives were blessed with great services to the Cause, but because they broke the Covenant their spiritual lives were destroyed.

Humans are endowed with the potential to develop capacities. Through education and life experience, choices are made that nurture qualities such as love, justice, service and other spiritual virtues, or develop those of cruelty, injustice and egotistical behaviour. The nature and quality of education will have a bearing on such decision-making and to those processes which are beneficial and conducive to the betterment of mankind and the strengthening of love and unity.

What are the tools available to human beings to make a value judgement and distinguish between virtuous or cruel and oppressive behaviour?

There are resources with which every individual is endowed; one is the intellect. According to the Bahá'í Writings, human intellect is one of the greatest gifts of God. Through the power of intellect we can discern good from evil. But intellect can be hijacked by ego and selfish pride.

The other tool is the human heart (not the physical heart), which does not have the power of the intellect but rather possesses intuition. According to the Baháʾí teachings, the heart is the source of the emanation of another capacity, and that is the capacity to love, to be compassionate. The heart is the seat which receives the descent of God's inspiration. The Baháʾí teachings are very emphatic about the spiritual significance of the heart; for example, Baháʾuʾlláh states, 'O Son of Being! Thy heart is My home; sanctify it for My descent.'[19] Scholars of science and psychology have yet to understand the spiritual significance of the heart. Scientific discoveries during the past two centuries have been largely directed toward the brain and its physiological and neurological functions and has lagged behind in explaining and understanding the station and power of the heart (human conscience, inner reality). The brain, with its 106 billion neurons or nerve cells, each of which has a large number of axons, has become a universe in itself, attracting much attention. But the meaning of the inner reality of the heart is just beginning to be recognized. Baháʾuʾlláh writes:

> The heart must needs therefore be cleansed from the idle sayings of men, and sanctified from every earthly affection, so that it may discover the hidden meaning of divine inspiration, and become the treasury of the mysteries of divine knowledge.[20]

As mentioned above, in Islam there is a statement confirmed by Baháʾuʾlláh which says, 'Knowledge is a light which God casteth into the heart of whomsoever He willeth.'[21] The meaning of this statement indicating that the heart is the dawning-place of the knowledge of God is profoundly mystical. The acquisition of knowledge is usually attributed to the mind, not the heart. But knowledge of God, like faith, is like seeds that are planted in the heart, and the mind then begins to understand it. In the current state of health sciences, our neurobiological knowledge is unable to unravel and illustrate such a connection of a deeper reality; our technologies and methodologies are not prepared for this phenomenon.

My personal understanding of the word 'heart' in this context is the human conscience. It is also frequently alluded to as a place of love and affection, a place that, as we have seen, needs to be kept pure and clean. Let us look again at Baháʾuʾlláh's statement quoted above: 'O Son of Being! Thy heart is My home, sanctify it for My descent. Thy spirit is

My place of revelation, cleanse it for My manifestation.'[22] Here, heart and spirit seem to have a similar meaning. Yet human spirit has no place, as it is not a material entity and thus is free from the limitations of time and space.

'Abdu'l-Bahá underlines the importance of purifying personal intent from 'self-love': 'The heart is a divine trust; cleanse it from the stain of self-love, adorn it with the coronal of pure intent . . .'[23] This self-love or narcissistic interest in personal benefits is often a by-product of the materialistic mindset so pervasive in the world. It can be captivating – literally so, as it leads one to become a prisoner of self. The Master praises a person who can free himself/herself from this captivity: 'Happy the soul that shall forget his own good, and like the chosen ones of God, vie with his fellows in service to the good of all . . .'[24]

There are many references in the Writings which underline the significance of purity of intent and sincerity in day-to-day life. 'Abdu'l-Bahá refers to sincerity as 'the foundation stone of the faith' and continues:

> That is, a religious individual must disregard his personal desires and seek in whatever way he can wholeheartedly to serve the public interest; and it is impossible for a human being to turn aside from his own selfish advantages and sacrifice his own good for the good of the community except through true religious faith. For self-love is kneaded into the very clay of man, and it is not possible that, without any hope of a substantial reward, he should neglect his own present material good. That individual, however, who puts his faith in God and believes in the words of God . . . will for the sake of God abandon his own peace and profit and will freely consecrate his heart and soul to the common good.[25]

One of the many benefits of religious teaching is to draw the natural human inclinations away from narcissism and self-love toward the love of a greater source of love – God Almighty – and to come to the realization that creation is based on love of humanity and service to humankind.

Both the intellect (mind) and the heart, vital as they are, are susceptible to dark forces of evil and destructive behaviour. For the heart and the intellect to remain healthy, first and foremost they need to be moderately detached from the world of being, and this is very hard, especially in a materialistic world. The temptations of the ego and attraction to the material world around us may form barriers which could impede the development of noble capacities. The mind and heart complement one another, but are not the same. If the mind is bereft of the influence of the heart, it may not attain faith and discover spiritual reality. Likewise, if the heart is deprived of the power of the mind, it may not be able to explore knowledge of the world or scientific discoveries. Science relies entirely on the intellect, while divine revelation goes beyond the intellect and speaks the language of the heart. It unravels the many mysteries which the intellect fails to comprehend.[26]

Can knowledge and recognition of the Manifestation of God harness the power of the ego? Not necessarily, unless ego and passion for power are subordinated by detachment and humility. Otherwise knowledge can actually feed the ego. Consider the plight of Mírzá Áqá Ján, the long-time secretary of Bahá'u'lláh whose story is told in Chapter 2. This man was one of the very few individuals during the Ministry of Bahá'u'lláh who had the rare and precious bounty of witnessing and writing down the utterances of Bahá'u'lláh at the time of divine revelation. He gained much knowledge from his 40 years of experience as secretary and attendant of the Blessed Beauty. Yet after the passing of Bahá'u'lláh he was overtaken by the passion for power and the temptation of ego and he broke the Covenant. This sad ending was not out of ignorance but rather due to submission to the promptings of the ego and being deceived by the Covenant-breakers.

Siyyid Mihdíy-i-Dahají

The stories of two great teachers of the Faith during the lifetime of Bahá'u'lláh who were well-known in the Persian Bahá'í community but who succumbed to egotism are told by Adib Taherzadeh.[27] These were Jamál-i-Burújirdí and Siyyid Mihdíy-i-Dahají, to both of whom Bahá'u'lláh had given the title 'Ismu'lláh' (The Name of God). Siyyid Mihdí was called Ismu'lláhu'l-Mihdí (The Name of God, He Who is Guided). These two men were arrogant and ambitious. Both broke the Covenant of Bahá'u'lláh and rebelled against the Centre of the Covenant. They had at least one thing in common and that was 'an insatiable lust for leadership'.

TESTS OF THE COVENANT AMONG SCHOLARS AND TEACHERS OF THE FAITH

Siyyid Mihdí was a native of a village in the province of Yazd. He met Bahá'u'lláh in Baghdad, Adrianople and 'Akká, Who showered him with loving-kindness and at the same time exhorted him to strive for sincerity, purity and detachment. He received several Tablets and when Bahá'u'lláh left Baghdad for Constantinople, He asked Siyyid Mihdí to move into His house (known as the 'Most Great House') and become its caretaker. During his residence there, a small incident occurred which revealed Siyyid Mihdí's weakness and over-attachment to material things. Some thieves broke into the house and stole some of his personal belongings. This caused him such grief that he wrote to Bahá'u'lláh and complained about it. Bahá'u'lláh revealed a Tablet to him bidding him to be detached; his loss was nothing as compared to Bahá'u'lláh's own suffering.

Although Siyyid Mihdí was famous and popular among the Bahá'ís, some of them had noted his insincerity, egotism and deep attachment to material things. As a great teacher of the Cause he travelled extensively throughout Iran. He had an air of superiority when he was in Bahá'í gatherings. He loved to see a retinue of the believers walking behind him. At night, he was preceded by several Bahá'ís who carried lanterns for him. In those days people needed to carry lanterns at night because there was no public street lighting. One night, it was reported, no fewer than 14 men holding lanterns in their hand were seen to be escorting him. This suggests the extent of his selfish pride.

Indeed, 'Abdu'l-Bahá exhorts the friends, 'man must become evanescent in God. Must forget his own selfish conditions that he may thus arise to the station of sacrifice.'[28]

Bahá'u'lláh frequently writes of the influence of human utterance and the need for moderation in speech. For instance, he explains that the influence of utterance is 'conditional upon refinement, which in turn is dependent upon hearts which are detached and pure'.[29] He also indicates in the Tablet to Siyyid Mihdíy-i-Dahají that utterance must possess 'penetrating power', without which it will fail to exert influence. This 'penetrating influence dependeth on the spirit being pure and the heart stainless. Likewise, it needeth moderation . . .'[30]

In the matter of 'moderation', Bahá'u'lláh points out in the Lawḥ-i-Ḥikmat that moderation has to be combined with 'tact and wisdom as prescribed in the Holy Scriptures and Tablets'.[31] With the two qualities of penetrating power and moderation, utterance 'will prove highly effective and will be the prime factor in transforming the souls of men'.[32]

There is an important Tablet of Bahá'u'lláh called the Súriy-i-'Ibád (Surih of the Servants) in which Bahá'u'lláh urges Siyyid Mihdí to live a pious life with purity of heart and freedom from the defilement of the world.[33] And in the Tablet to Siyyid Mihdíy-i-Dahají, Bahá'u'lláh urges him to ponder and meditate upon the methods of teaching and to memorize phrases and passages of the holy Scriptures for various occasions as 'these holy verses are the most potent elixir, the greatest and mightiest talisman'[34]

In the same Tablet Bahá'u'lláh makes the following statement which Siyyid Mihdí could have perceived as a warning regarding his own unseemly behaviour, had he been a man of wisdom: 'They that have passed beyond the bounds of wisdom fail to understand the meaning of assisting God as set forth in the Book. Say: Fear ye God and sow not the seeds of dissension amongst men.'[35]

In discussing the behaviour of this and other eminent teachers of the Faith during the Ministry of Bahá'u'lláh, Taherzadeh states that Bahá'u'lláh concealed the wrongdoings of Siyyid Mihdí. Although He showered upon this man His loving-kindness, He also exhorted him to 'sincerity, purity and detachment', as is also emphasized in other Tablets of Bahá'u'lláh revealed to Siyyid Mihdí.[36] In spite of all those exhortations and all that advice, Siyyid Mihdí was unable to control his passion for power and was eventually expelled as a Covenant-breaker.

Taming the Ego, Learning Humility

'Ever since the seeking of preference and distinction came into play,' writes Bahá'u'lláh, 'the world hath been laid waste. It hath become desolate . . .'[37]

Taming ego and selfish pride is a lifelong struggle. The more we wholeheartedly submit ourselves to the will of God the easier it becomes to carry out this task. But it becomes harder when we indulge in self-love rather than love of God. We live in a world dominated by a cult of consumerism and a marketing industry whose extensive and widespread publicity influences people's minds. In such an environment, self-satisfaction, self-centredness and competition for self-promotion and entitlement are portrayed as 'virtues'. Breaking away from this social attitude, which is becoming increasingly corrupt, is a formidable task. Fear of God, a most important protective force, is largely ignored or denied.

TESTS OF THE COVENANT AMONG SCHOLARS AND TEACHERS OF THE FAITH

Shoghi Effendi pointed out that among the life struggles for which we should be prepared, one of those challenges is the ego within ourselves.

> Life is a constant struggle, not only against forces around us, but above all against our own 'ego'. We can never afford to rest on our own oars, for if we do, we soon see ourselves carried down stream again. Many of those who drift away from the Cause do so for the reason that they had ceased to go on developing. They became complacent or indifferent, and consequently ceased to draw the spiritual strength and vitality from the Cause which they should have.[38]

Bahá'ís, including those working in the fields of teaching, research and scholarship, are not immune to these dark forces that tempt them to view themselves as superior to others. On the other hand, Bahá'ís are profoundly blessed by having access to the teachings of the Faith which provide them with the most illuminating inspiration and guidance.

In order to subdue our ego, we need first to recognize that

> [t]he ego is the animal in us, the heritage of the flesh which is full of selfish desires. By obeying the laws of God, seeking to live the life laid down in our teachings, and prayer and struggle, we can subdue our egos. We call people 'saints' who have achieved the highest degree of mastery over their ego.[39]

Can we succeed in eliminating egocentricity? Shoghi Effendi addresses this question: 'the complete and entire elimination of the ego would imply perfection – which man can never completely attain – but the ego can and should be ever-increasingly subordinated to the enlightened soul of man. This is what spiritual progress implies.'[40]

A deeper realization of our innermost reality, the life of our soul and its journey in the worlds of God, can help to protect us from the decadence of the world. Bahá'u'lláh is very explicit in His statement that 'the heart wherein the least remnant of envy yet lingers, shall never attain My everlasting dominion . . .'[41] Furthermore, He warns: 'Take heed lest pride deter you from recognizing the Source of Revelation, lest the things of this world shut you out as by a veil from Him Who is the Creator of heaven.'[42]

Today's popular literature are replete with the praise and promotion of the self and self-love. Yet 'Abdu'l-Bahá wrote that self-love 'is a strange trait and the means of the destruction of many important souls in the world. If man be imbued with all good qualities but be selfish, all the other virtues will fade or pass away and eventually he will grow worse.'[43]

Bahá'u'lláh in one of His Tablets is categorical that 'the most burning fire is to question the signs of God, to dispute idly that which He hath revealed, to deny Him and carry one's self proudly before Him.'[44] He also reminds us of the manner in which we should voice our opinions: 'the tongue is a smouldering fire, and excess of speech a deadly poison. Material fire consumeth the body, whereas the fire of the tongue devoureth both heart and soul. The force of the former lasteth but for a time, whilst the effects of the latter endureth a century.'[45]

And there is a statement by 'Abdu'l-Bahá about the attitude of a teacher: 'The teacher should not see in himself any superiority; he should speak with the utmost kindliness, lowliness and humility, for such speech exerteth influence and educateth the souls.'[46]

A review of the history of the lives of violators of the Covenant reveals a common thread in all of them, that is, passion for power and authority and seeking leadership to divide and dominate the Bahá'í community. Such burning desire for domination and fame often reached a point at which there was no room for humility, servitude and submissiveness. Like addicts, they craved satisfaction through entitlement. Yet Bahá'u'lláh has redefined leadership in this Dispensation, transforming it into servitude with humility. Lusting for power, a believer may have no fear of breaking the Covenant even though he or she knows that this is wrong. Covenant-breakers know that what they are doing is wrong, but their ambition for leadership over the community leads them to follow this path.

To counteract egotism one must detach oneself from self-centredness and cling to the cord of humble servitude and magnanimity in all aspects of life. Taherzadeh provides the following analogy about the relationship between the creature and the Creator:

> . . . opposites attract each other like the poles of a magnet. God and man may be said to be positioned on the two opposite poles. God is the Sovereign Lord of all, and man a humble servant, hence there is a force of attraction between the two . . . God is the possessor of

all divine attributes. But by reason of His Sovereignty, He cannot be humble. The best gift, then, which man can offer to God is the only one which He does not already possess, namely, humility and servitude. These are the most befitting attributes for man. The lordship of God and the servitude of man are opposites bound together by the force of love. On the other hand, we note in the analogy of the magnet that similar poles repel each other. Therefore, should an individual, having recognized a Manifestation of God, aspire to reach His station or attempt to appear equal with Him, such an act will provoke the wrath of God and there will be a force of repulsion between the two parties. This is Covenant-breaking.[47]

Underlining the significance of being imbued with lowliness and humility, we find this statement by Bahá'u'lláh: 'Humility exalteth man to the heaven of glory and power, whilst pride abaseth him to the depths of wretchedness and degradation.'[48] Moreover, He writes: 'Every soul that walketh humbly with its God, in this Day, and cleaveth unto Him, shall find itself invested with the honor and glory of all goodly names and stations.'[49] In one of His Tablets He illustrates the importance of humility and submissiveness by drawing the following beautiful metaphor in which there is a conversation between an individual and the dust beneath his feet:

> They who are the beloved of God, in whatever place they gather and whomsoever they may meet, must evince, in their attitude towards God, and in the manner of their celebration of His praise and glory, such humility and submissiveness that every atom of the dust beneath their feet may attest the depth of their devotion. The conversation carried by these holy souls should be informed with such power that these same atoms of dust will be thrilled by its influence. They should conduct themselves in such manner that the earth upon which they tread may never be allowed to address to them such words as these: 'I am to be preferred above you. For witness, how patient I am in bearing the burden which the husbandman layeth upon me. I am the instrument that continually imparteth unto all beings the blessings with which He Who is the Source of all grace hath entrusted me. Notwithstanding the honour conferred upon me, and the unnumbered evidences of my wealth – a wealth that supplieth the needs of all creation – behold the

measure of my humility, witness with what absolute submissiveness I allow myself to be trodden beneath the feet of men . . .'⁵⁰

The implications for Bahá'í scholarship are clear, as the International Teaching Centre has pointed out:

> A vital element of Bahá'í scholarship is humility in recognising the limitations of the human mind in its attempts to encompass the Divine Message. Bahá'u'lláh addresses the Creator in a prayer, using these terms:
> 'Exalted, immeasurably exalted art Thou, O my Beloved, above the strivings of any of Thy creatures, however learned, to know Thee; exalted, immensely exalted art Thou above every human attempt, no matter how searching, to describe Thee! For the highest thought of men, however deep their contemplation, can never hope to outsoar the limitations imposed upon Thy creation, nor ascend beyond the state of the contingent world, nor break the bounds irrevocably set for it by Thee.'⁵¹

Pursuit and Purpose of Scholarship

Bahá'ís are encouraged to advance their academic studies in current fields of science and philosophy and to break new ground in the light of Bahá'í teaching and scientific knowledge. A letter from the Universal House of Justice makes this clear in reviewing a number of statements on the subject by Shoghi Effendi:

> It is hoped that all the Bahá'í students will follow the noble example you have set before them and will, henceforth, be led to investigate and analyse the principles of the Faith and to correlate them with the modern aspects of philosophy and science. Every intelligent and thoughtful young Bahá'í should always approach the Cause in this way, for therein lies the very essence of the principle of independent investigation of truth.
> We need very much the sound, sane, element of thinking which a scientifically trained mind has to offer. When such intellectual powers are linked to deep faith a tremendous teaching potential is created . . .
> Shoghi Effendi has for years urged the Bahá'ís (who asked his advice, and in general also) to study history, economics, sociology,

etc., in order to be au courant with all the progressive movements and thoughts being put forth today, and so that they could correlate these to the Bahá'í teachings. What he wants the Bahá'ís to do is to study more, not to study less. The more general knowledge, scientific and otherwise, they possess, the better. Likewise he is constantly urging them to really study the Bahá'í teachings more deeply.[52]

In the same letter the Universal House of Justice writes:

In the simultaneous endeavour to pursue their studies and to delve deeply into the Bahá'í Teachings, believers are enjoined to maintain a keen awareness that the Revelation of Bahá'u'lláh is the standard of truth against which all other views and conclusions are to be measured. They are urged to be modest about their accomplishments, and to bear in mind always the statement of Bahá'u'lláh that: 'The heart must needs therefore be cleansed from the idle sayings of men, and sanctified from every earthly affection, so that it may discover the hidden meaning of divine inspiration, and become the treasury of the mysteries of divine knowledge.'[53]

In principle, the Universal House of Justice advises, Bahá'í scholarship should not be defined too narrowly and Bahá'í academics should strive to develop respect for a wide range of scholarly approaches and endeavours.[54] A letter written on its behalf to an Association for Bahá'í Studies states: 'Your aim should be to promote an atmosphere of mutual respect and tolerance within which will be included scholars whose principal interest is in theological issues as well as those scholars whose interests lie in relating the insights provided by the Baha'i teachings to contemporary thought in the arts and sciences.'[55] Bahá'í scholars thus have broad opportunities to relate the Bahá'í teachings to their diverse fields of professional and academic interest. Moreover, 'Bahá'í scholars have a vital role to play in the defence of the Faith through their contribution to anticipatory measures and their response to defamatory accusations levelled against the Faith.'[56]

With regard to the terminology of scholarship, the Universal House of Justice expressed its wish to avoid use of the terms 'Bahá'í scholarship' and 'Baha'í scholars' in an exclusive sense which would effectively establish a demarcation between those admitted into this category and those denied entrance to it . . . The House of Justice seeks the creation of a Bahá'í community in which the members encourage each other, where there is respect for accomplishment, and a common realization that everyone is in his or her own way, seeking to acquire a deeper understanding of the Revelation of Bahá'u'lláh and to contribute to the advancement of the Faith.[57]

Freedom and Responsibility

'From a Bahá'í point of view,' writes the Universal House of Justice, 'the exercise of freedom of speech must necessarily be disciplined by a profound appreciation of both the positive and negative dimensions of freedom, on the one hand, and of speech, on the other.'[58]

Freedom is one of the most sought-after and least understood concepts in contemporary society. In the Bahá'í Faith, it is perceived as in the following statement by 'Abdu'l-Bahá:

> There are three types of freedom. The first is divine freedom, which is one of the inherent attributes of the Creator for He is unconstrained in His will, and no one can force Him to change His decree in any matter whatsoever . . .
>
> The second is the political freedom of Europeans, which leaves the individual free to do whatsoever he desires as long as his action does not harm his neighbour. This is natural freedom, and its greatest expression is seen in the animal world. Observe these birds and notice with what freedom they live. However much man may try, he can never be as free as an animal, because the existence of order acts as an impediment to freedom.
>
> The third freedom is that which is born of obedience to the laws and ordinances of the Almighty. This is the freedom of the human world, where man severs his affections from all things. When he does so, he becomes immune to all hardship and sorrow. Wealth or material power will not deflect him from moderation and fairness, neither will poverty or need inhibit him from showing forth happiness and tranquillity. The more the conscience of man develops, the more will his heart be free and his soul attain unto happiness . . .[59]

Not all freedom of speech can go on without limits or borders. Society has laws which limit freedom of speech, such as laws against sedition and hate-mongering which would lead to action.[60] Certain arguments which are aimed at undermining the Bahá'í Faith, using antagonistic ideas which are spread by the Internet, can be burdensome and even 'spiritually corrosive'.[61]

Freedom, then, so much talked about and sought after especially in the West, has its own meaning in the Revelation of Bahá'u'lláh. Bahá'u'lláh defines liberty in these words: 'True liberty consisteth in man's submission unto My commandments,' and writes: 'We approve of liberty in certain circumstances and refuse to sanction it in others . . . Were men to observe that which We have sent down unto them from the Heaven of Revelation, they would, of a certainty, attain unto perfect liberty.'[62]

And 'Abdu'l-Bahá lists 'man's freedom' as 'among the teachings of Bahá'u'lláh . . . that through the ideal Power he should be free and emancipated from the captivity of the world of nature; for as long as man is captive to nature he is a ferocious animal, as the struggle for existence is one of the exigencies of the world of nature.'[63] Furthermore, he explains, 'the moderate freedom which guarantees the welfare of the world of mankind and maintains and preserves the universal relationships, is found in its fullest power and extension in the teachings of Bahá'u'lláh.'[64]

Scholarship and Authoritative Interpretation of the Writings

As we have already discussed earlier in this book, in the Bahá'í Faith interpretation of the Writings differs from that of past religions. In previous dispensations the divines, scholars and leaders of religion made their own interpretations, and this was one of the sources of division and disunity among the followers of that religion. In the Bahá'í Faith, authority to interpret the Writings was given only to the successors of Bahá'u'lláh, that is, to 'Abdu'l-Bahá and then to Shoghi Effendi, the Guardian of the Bahá'í Faith. Only their interpretations of the Word of God are authoritative and infallible. Any deductions and statements by individual believers based on their own interpretations are not authentic or acceptable as authoritative interpretation. This guidance on the use of interpretation has safeguarded the unity of the Faith and prevented differences and divisions in the Bahá'í community, in contrast to what has been observed in former dispensations.

About individual interpretation by Bahá'ís, as compared to that by 'Abdu'l-Bahá and the Guardian, the Universal House of Justice has stated:

> A clear distinction is made in our Faith between authoritative interpretation and the interpretation or understanding that each individual arrives at for himself from his study of its teachings. While the former is confined to the Guardian, the latter, according to the guidance given to us by the Guardian himself, should by no means be suppressed. In fact such individual interpretation is considered the fruit of man's rational power and conducive to a better understanding of the teachings, provided that no disputes or arguments arise among the friends and the individual himself understands and makes it clear that his views are merely his own. Individual interpretations continually change as one grows in comprehension of the teachings. As Shoghi Effendi wrote: 'To deepen in the Cause means to read the Writings of Bahá'u'lláh and the Master so thoroughly as to be able to give it to others in its pure form. There are many who have some superficial idea of what the Cause stands for. They, therefore, present it together with all sorts of ideas that are their own. As the Cause is still in its early days we must be most careful lest we fall into this error and injure the Movement we so much adore. There is no limit to the study of the Cause. The more we read the Writings, the more truths we can find in them, the more we will see that our previous notions were erroneous.'[65]

Elucidating further the issue of authoritative interpretation of the Writings, the House of Justice quotes the Master:

> 'Abdu'l-Bahá wrote, 'Beware lest anyone falsely interpret these words, and like unto them that have broken the Covenant after the Day of Ascension (of Bahá'u'lláh) advance a pretext, raise the standards of revolt, wax stubborn, and open wide the door of false interpretation.' In this context, He continues: 'To none is given the right to put forth his own opinion or express his particular conviction. All must seek guidance and turn unto the Centre of the Cause and the House of

Justice. And he that turneth unto whatsoever else is indeed in grievous error.'⁶⁶

With regard to scholarship and the institutions of the Faith, a letter written on behalf of the Universal House of Justice states:

> Scholarship has a high rank in the Cause of God, and the Universal House of Justice continually consults the views of scholars and experts in the course of its work. However, as you appreciate, scholars and experts have no authority over the Institutions of the Cause. In a letter written on behalf of the Guardian, on 14 March 1927, to the Spiritual Assembly of the Bahá'ís of Istanbul, it is pointed out how, in the past, it was certain individuals who 'accounted themselves as superior in knowledge and elevated in position' who caused division, and that it was those 'who pretended to be the most distinguished of all' who 'always proved themselves to be the source of contention'. 'But praise be to God' he continued, 'that the Pen of Glory has done away with the unyielding and dictatorial views of the learned and the wise, dismissed the assertions of individuals as an authoritative criterion, even though they were recognized as the most accomplished and learned among men and ordained that all matters be referred to authorized centres and specified assemblies . . . '⁶⁷

Since the passing of the Guardian of the Bahá'í Faith in 1957, there is only one divinely appointed centre of authority and that is the Universal House of Justice. The Guardian, as well as the Universal House of Justice, are both 'under the care and protection of the Abhá Beauty, under the shelter and unerring guidance of His Holiness, the Exalted One'.⁶⁸

The Role of Religion in Acquiring Knowledge

The Bahá'í Writings emphasize that 'the fundamental purpose of all religion is the spiritual development of the souls of human beings',⁶⁹ as the Universal House of Justice writes; and they quote a letter from Shoghi Effendi: 'The universal crisis affecting mankind is, therefore, essentially spiritual in its causes. The spirit of the age, taken on the whole, is irreligious. Man's outlook upon life is too crude and materialistic to enable him to elevate himself into the higher realms of the spirit.'⁷⁰

The Baháʼí teachings are very explicit in elucidating this indispensable role of divine education in the development of the human mind and soul and the progress of civilization. As ʻAbduʼl-Bahá explained:

> But education is of three kinds: material, human and spiritual. Material education is concerned with the progress and development of the body, through gaining its sustenance, its material comfort and ease. This education is common to animals and man.
>
> Human education signifies civilization and progress – that is to say, government, administration, charitable works, trades, arts and handicrafts, sciences, great inventions and discoveries and elaborate institutions, which are the activities essential to man as distinguished from the animal.
>
> Divine education is that of the Kingdom of God: it consists in acquiring divine perfections, and this is true education; for in this state man becomes the focus of divine blessings, the manifestation of the words, ʻLet Us make man in Our image, and after Our likenessʼ [Gen. 1:26.]. This is the goal of the world of humanity.
>
> Now we need an educator who will be at the same time a material, human and spiritual educator, and whose authority will be effective in all conditions . . . Then it is plain and evident that man needs an educator, and this educator must be unquestionably and indubitably perfect in all respects and distinguished above all men.[71]

And elaborating on the significance of the station of the Divine Educator, He said,

> He must also impart spiritual education, so that intelligence and comprehension may penetrate the metaphysical world, and may receive benefit from the sanctifying breeze of the Holy Spirit, and may enter into relationship with the Supreme Concourse. He must so educate the human reality that it may become the centre of the divine appearance, to such a degree that the attributes and the names of God shall be resplendent in the mirror of the reality of man . . . [72]

Sages and scholars throughout history have benefited from religious education and knowledge of the prophets:

TESTS OF THE COVENANT AMONG SCHOLARS AND TEACHERS OF THE FAITH

> Even Socrates visited the Jewish doctors in the Holy Land, consorting with them and discussing the principles and basis of their religious belief. After his return to Greece he formulated his philosophical teaching of divine unity and advanced his belief in the immortality of the spirit beyond the dissolution of the body. Without doubt Socrates absorbed these verities from the wise men of the Jews with whom he came in contact. Hippocrates and other philosophers of the Greeks likewise visited Palestine and acquired wisdom from the Jewish prophets, studying the basis of ethics and morality, returning to their country with contributions which have made Greece famous.[73]

The mission of prophets is to edify the souls and renew divine civilization:

> All the Prophets have come to promote divine bestowals, to found the spiritual civilization and teach the principles of morality. Therefore, we must strive with all our powers so that spiritual influences may gain the victory. For material forces have attacked mankind. The world of humanity is submerged in a sea of materialism. The rays of the Sun of Reality are seen but dimly and darkly through opaque glasses. The penetrative power of the divine bounty is not fully manifest.[74]

Divine religions, including the Bahá'í Faith are fundamentally mystic in character. "Religion...is not a series of beliefs, a set of customs; religion is the teachings of the Lord God, teachings which constitute the very life of humankind, which urge high thoughts upon the mind, refine the character, and lay the groundwork for man's everlasting honour.'[75]

Shoghi Effendi comments that it is 'not sufficient for a believer to merely accept and observe the teachings. He should, in addition, cultivate the sense of spirituality which he can acquire chiefly by the means of prayer.'[76] The development and fulfilment of human beings he wrote depends not only on education, knowledge and scientific progress but also on prayer as it is 'absolutely indispensable to their inner spiritual development'.[77]

'Abdu'l-Bahá draws our attention to the fact that there are 'certain pillars which have been established as the unshakeable supports of the Faith of God. The mightiest of these is learning and the use of the mind, the expansion of consciousness, and insight into the realities of the universe and the hidden mysteries of Almighty God . . .'⁷⁸

In the Dispensation of Bahá'u'lláh, then, we are encouraged to explore the immense opportunities afforded by the harmony between religion, science and reason: 'The harmony of religious belief with reason is a new vista which Bahá'u'lláh has opened for the soul of man.'⁷⁹

We also need to be mindful of Bahá'u'lláh's teaching that '[t]he understanding of His words and the comprehension of the utterances of the Birds of Heaven are in no wise dependent upon human learning. They depend solely upon purity of heart, chastity of soul, and freedom of spirit.' ⁸⁰

The source of all knowledge, according to the teachings of Bahá'u'lláh, is divine education, which inspires souls and minds to achieve new understandings of the mysteries of the universe:

> Therefore, hath it been said: 'Knowledge is a light which God casteth into the heart of whomsoever He willeth.' It is this kind of knowledge which is and hath ever been praiseworthy, and not the limited knowledge that hath sprung forth from veiled and obscured minds. This limited knowledge they even stealthily borrow one from the other, and vainly pride themselves therein!⁸¹

And,

> He bestoweth His wisdom upon whomsoever He chooseth amongst men, and withholdeth it from whomsoever He desireth. He, in truth, is the Bestower and the Withholder, and He, verily, is the All-Bountiful, the All-Wise.⁸²

Knowledge and Firmness in the Covenant

Knowledge is a precious gift and a bounty, but it can also become a veil under the influence of ego. Knowledge and selfishness can become a destructive combination. In the opening verse of the Kitáb-i-Aqdas Bahá'u'lláh states that 'The first duty prescribed by God for His servants is recognition of Him Who is the Dayspring of His Revelation . . . '⁸³ Then He emphasizes that such recognition should be followed by obedience to the ordinances of God. It is interesting that Bahá'u'lláh elevates

TESTS OF THE COVENANT AMONG SCHOLARS AND TEACHERS OF THE FAITH

the first duty, that of recognition of the Manifestation of God, to the 'most sublime station' and 'the summit of transcendent glory'.[84] But such elevation is conditioned upon obedience. Without that obedience and submission to the divine authority, recognition of the Sun of Reality could be manipulated and destroyed by egotism and passion for power. The dynamic relationship which exists between these two highlights the importance of the Covenant. 'Today the pulsating power in the arteries of the body of the world is the spirit of the Covenant – the spirit which is the cause of life,' wrote 'Abdu'l-Bahá.[85]

Firmness in the Covenant is a gold standard to insuring our spiritual health and prosperity. Here is a metaphor. The life of the growing embryo or unborn baby depends on its connection through the umbilical cord to the mother. This cord carries its lifeblood. It is the lifeline for the development of the unborn baby. If it is cut prematurely and unwisely, the lifeblood will cease and the result will be death. Likewise, when our connection to the Covenant is cut off for whatever reason, it is as though our spiritual connection with Bahá'u'lláh ceases to exist. Thus the soul will have no protection and its progress will be impeded.

With this in mind we also need to be careful about any loose or unwise use of the word 'Covenant-breaker'. It has been noted at times that some Bahá'ís have a tendency to jump the gun and label another believer as a Covenant-breaker simply because this person has broken a law or failed to observe a rule of conduct. No one in the Bahá'í community locally or nationally has the authority to label anyone as a Covenant-breaker. Only the Head of the Faith, the Universal House of Justice, can make such a grave decision.

Materialistic Methodology and Spiritual Reality

Using materialistic methodology to verify or validate a spiritual reality or phenomenon is fraught with serious challenges. The current highly material approach to scientific research has also been applied to research studies on spiritual and religious issues, which may lead to questionable results. This is because spiritual phenomena cannot be measured, calculated and quantified in the same way as is done in a laboratory for biological or mechanical research studies. The Universal House of Justice writes:

> Although the reality of God's continuous relationship with His creation and His intervention in human life and history are the very essence of the teachings of the Founders of the revealed religions, dogmatic materialism today insists that even the nature of religion itself can be adequately understood only through the use of an academic methodology designed to ignore the truths that make religion what it is . . . [86]

Moreover:

> Problems will arise, rather, if an attempt is made to impose, on the Bahá'í community's own study of the Revelation, materialistic methodologies and attitudes antithetical to its very nature. The Faith is not the possession of any among us, but belongs to Bahá'u'lláh. Through the Covenant, which is a distinguishing feature of His Revelation, He has specified in unmistakable terms the means by which He wills to preserve the integrity of His message and to guide the implementation of His prescriptions for humankind. If one accepts the Bahá'í Teachings, one cannot, in good conscience, claim to be studying the Faith while ignoring the centrality of Bahá'u'lláh's Covenant to all aspects of the religion He has established.[87]

Further:

> The training of some scholars in fields such as religion and history seems to have restricted their vision and blinded them to the culturally determined basis of elements of the approach they have learned. It causes them to exclude from consideration factors which, from a Bahá'í point of view, are of fundamental importance. Truth in such fields cannot be found if the evidence of Revelation is systematically excluded and if discourse is limited by a basically deterministic view of the world.
>
> Some of the protagonists in the discussions on the Internet have implied that the only way to attain a true understanding of historical events and of the purport of the sacred and historical records of the Cause of God is through the rigid application of methods narrowly defined in a materialistic framework. They have even gone so far as to stigmatize whoever proposes a variation of these methods as wishing to obscure the truth rather than unveil it . . .
>
> The Universal House of Justice does not see itself obliged to

prescribe a new scientific methodology for Bahá'í academics who make study of the Faith, its teachings and history the subject of their professional activities. Rather has it concentrated on drawing the attention of these friends to the inadequacy of certain approaches from a Bahá'í point of view, urging them to apply to their work the concept which they accept as Bahá'ís: that the Manifestation of God is of a higher realm and has a perception far above that of any human being. He has the task of raising humankind to a new level of knowledge and behaviour. In this, His understanding transcends the traditions and concepts of the society in which He appears . . .

. . . Although, in conveying His Revelation, the Manifestation uses the language and culture of the country into which He is born, He is not confined to using terminology with the same connotations as those given to it by His predecessors or contemporaries; He delivers His message in a form which His audience, both immediate and in centuries to come, is capable of grasping. It is for Bahá'í scholars to elaborate, over a period of time, methodologies which will enable them to perform their work with this understanding. This is a challenging task, but not one which should be beyond the scope of Bahá'ís who are learned in the Teachings as well as competent in their scientific disciplines.[88]

Our knowledge of spiritual reality is very limited. In contrast with science, where scientific phenomena can be measured in the framework of material methodology, in the spiritual world we are highly dependent on religious scriptures and Writings for understanding intangible realities. The Baha'i Writings teach us that the human soul is an emanation of the spiritual worlds of God. Our minds are very limited in comprehending such intangible and non-material entities. In the Writings the soul has been referred to as 'a sign of God', a 'heavenly gem', 'a mystery . . . no mind, however acute, can ever hope to unravel'.[89] Such a 'mystery' is given to us by God, Whose essence is the Sublime Mystery. Also, we understand that the spiritual and physical worlds are not separate worlds or entities; they are part of one realm of existence. In one of His Tablets revealed in Baghdad, Bahá'u'lláh explains the limitations of human understanding of the essence of the soul as follows:

> Wert thou to ponder in thine heart, from now until the end that hath no end, and with all the concentrated intelligence and understanding

which the greatest minds have attained in the past or will attain in the future, this divinely ordained and subtle Reality, this Sign of the revelation of the All-Abiding, All-Glorious God, thou wilt fail to comprehend its mystery or to appraise its virtue.[90]

Although a daunting task, the study of the reality of the world around us in light of the Revelation of Bahá'u'lláh is one with which Bahá'í scholars are becoming increasingly familiar. As scientific knowledge evolves and the World Order of Bahá'u'lláh unfolds, new patterns of social relationships will be revealed, fulfilling Bahá'u'lláh's purpose 'to effect a transformation in the whole character of mankind that shall manifest itself both outwardly and inwardly, that shall affect both its inner life and external conditions.'[91]

8

The Covenant: The Individual, the Community and the Institutions

> A community is a comprehensive unit of civilization composed of individuals, families and institutions that are originators and encouragers of systems, agencies and organizations working together . . . it is a composition of diverse, interacting participants that are achieving unity in an unremitting quest for spiritual and social progress.
>
> *The Universal House of Justice* [1]

Unity is the hallmark of the Covenant in protecting the community from the assault of Covenant-breakers and their attempts to cause division and create doubt and discord among believers. When Bahá'ís are united and armed with the love of Bahá'u'lláh and firmness in the Covenant, nothing can erode their faith. 'In order to establish the unity of all humanity,' writes Brent Poirier,

> the Bahá'í community must protect its own internal unity. Just as Jesus said 'Ye are the salt of the earth: but if the salt have lost his savour, wherewith shall it be salted?' In like manner, how can the Bahá'í community unify humanity, if it is itself divided? Bahá'ís are enjoined repeatedly to associate with all peoples; but are emphatically warned to not associate with those few who seek division for selfish reasons, who violate Bahá'u'lláh's Covenant that is the primary instrument to maintain the unity of the Bahá'ís themselves.
>
> In the past every divine Revelation has faced the forces of opposition from without, and division from within, and these have sundered these faith communities. Bahá'u'lláh promises that these forces will not divide His Faith, but will only cause its light of concord and integrity

to burn more brightly. He established a written Covenant, appointing His eldest son 'Abdu'l-Bahá as His Successor, and directing all of the Bahá'ís to turn to Him.[2]

'Today no soul has any station or enjoys any title except the soul who is firm in the Covenant and steadfast in the Testament, who entirely forgets himself and is released from the world,' wrote 'Abdu'l-Bahá.[3] The individual as the single unit of the community plays an important role in preserving unity and steadfastness in the Covenant. This steadfastness is not limited to shunning Covenant-breakers and persevering against the attacks of internal and external enemies of the Faith. Rather, it has much wider implications for the life of believers. It requires obedience to all laws and commandments enshrined in the teachings of the Faith. From daily reading of the sacred Writings to avoidance of backbiting, from obedience to the laws and ordinances of this mighty Revelation and its institutions to chastity and rectitude of conduct, all are part of our faithfulness to the Covenant of Bahá'u'lláh. It is beyond the scope of this chapter to go into the details of each aspect of obedience to Bahá'í laws and administrative institutions and therefore, for the sake of brevity, this chapter will address some challenges which the Bahá'í community, individuals and especially the youth, face in a changing world where the disintegration of the old world order has created a climate of lawlessness, divisiveness and moral decline.

Before we discuss those issues let's reflect on the significance of deepening in the Covenant of our beloved Cause. Shoghi Effendi wrote to a National Spiritual Assembly:

> The education of the members of the community in the principles and essential verities underlying the Covenants of Bahá'u'lláh and 'Abdu'l-Bahá as well as the Administrative Order of the Faith – the twin pillars sustaining the spiritual life and the institutions of every organized Bahá'í community – must, at all costs, be vigorously pursued and systematically intensified.[4]

In this statement Shoghi Effendi makes it abundantly clear that the Covenant and the Administrative Order of the Cause are both vital in sustaining the spiritual life and the institutions of the Faith. Expounding further on the necessity of obtaining 'a far deeper understanding of

THE COVENANT: THE INDIVIDUAL, THE COMMUNITY AND THE INSTITUTIONS

the Covenants of both Bahá'u'lláh and the Master', he wrote:

> This is the rock foundation without which no sound super-structure can be built. Neither the administration, nor the general teaching work of the Cause . . . will progress, or be able to accomplish anything, unless the believers are truly firm, deep, spiritually convinced Bahá'ís. An intellectual grasp of the Teachings is purely superficial; with the first real test such believers are shaken from the bough!⁵

The Bahá'í Writings also examine and refine the quality of attitudes of the believers serving the institutions of the Faith at different levels. A message in 2010 from the Universal House of Justice to a Conference of the Continental Boards of Counsellors makes it clear:

> And those who are called upon from among the ranks of such enkindled souls to serve on the institutions of that mighty system understand well the Guardian's words that 'their function is not to dictate but to consult, and consult not only among themselves, but as much as possible with the friends whom they represent'. 'Never' would they be 'led to suppose that they are the central ornaments of the body of the Cause, intrinsically superior to others in capacity or merit and sole promoters of its teachings and principles.' 'With extreme humility,' they approach their tasks and 'endeavour, by their open-mindedness, their high sense of justice and duty, their candour, their modesty, their entire devotion to the welfare and interests of the friends, the Cause, and humanity to win, not only the confidence and the genuine support and respect of those whom they serve, but also their esteem and real affection.'
>
> . . . Composed of such individuals and such institutions, the community of the Greatest Name becomes that spiritually charged arena in which powers are multiplied in unified action. It is of this community that 'Abdu'l-Bahá writes: 'When any souls grow to be true believers, they will attain a spiritual relationship with one another, and show forth a tenderness which is not of this world. They will all of them, become elated from a draught of divine love, and that union of theirs, that connection, will also abide forever . . .'⁶

Although, as mentioned above, it is not possible to discuss specific Bahá'í laws and obedience to them in this chapter, it is nevertheless important to take note of the following warning (as well as assurance) from the Universal House of Justice:

> Obedience to the Laws of Bahá'u'lláh will necessarily impose hardships in individual cases. No one should expect, upon becoming a Bahá'í, that his faith will not be tested, and to our finite understanding of such matters these tests may occasionally seem unbearable. But we are aware of the assurance which Bahá'u'lláh Himself has given the believers that they will never be called upon to meet a test greater than their capacity to endure.[7]

Spiritual and Moral Requisites

We live in a world in which moral values are rapidly declining and the light of religious beliefs is becoming increasingly dim. Shoghi Effendi depicted the situation of the world in these words: 'A world spiritually destitute, morally bankrupt, politically disrupted, socially convulsed, economically paralyzed, writhing, bleeding and breaking up beneath the avenging rod of God.'[8] He explained that in such a world, '[h]uman character is debased, confidence is shaken, the nerves of discipline are relaxed, the voice of human conscience is stilled, the sense of decency and shame is obscured, conceptions of duty, of solidarity, of reciprocity and loyalty are distorted, and the very feeling of peacefulness, of joy and of hope is gradually extinguished.'[9]

Let's reflect on how the followers of Bahá'u'lláh are expected to live a Bahá'í life at such a difficult time. In *The Advent of Divine Justice*, the beloved Guardian described three spiritual prerequisites for the success of Bahá'í undertakings which he considered to 'stand out as preeminent and vital': rectitude of conduct, a chaste and holy life, and freedom from prejudice. Citing these prerequisites in their letter to the 2010 Counsellors' Conference, quoted above, the Universal House of Justice advised that in light of the condition of the world today, believers should reflect on the implications of the Guardian's observations for the Bahá'í community worldwide.[10]

With regard to rectitude of conduct the House of Justice stated that according to Shoghi Effendi, 'justice, equity, truthfulness, honesty, fair-mindedness, reliability, and trustworthiness' must 'distinguish every phase of the life of the Bahá'í community'.[11] Furthermore, the

THE COVENANT: THE INDIVIDUAL, THE COMMUNITY AND THE INSTITUTIONS

Guardian called for 'an abiding sense of undeviating justice' in a 'strangely disordered world'. . . . 'Profound is the confusion that threatens the foundations of society,' comments the House of Justice, 'and unwavering must be the resolve of all those involved in Bahá'í activity, lest the slightest trace of self-interest becloud their judgement.'[12] Subsequently, in the same letter, there is reference to the Guardian's

> 'forthright comments' concerning the importance of a chaste and holy life . . . The forces at work on the hearts and minds of the young, to whom the Guardian directed his appeal most fervently, are pernicious indeed. Exhortations to remain pure and chaste will only succeed to a limited degree in helping them to resist these forces. What needs to be appreciated in this respect is the extent to which young minds are affected by the choices parents make for their own lives, when, no matter how unintentionally, no matter how innocently, such choices condone the passions of the world – its admiration for power, its adoration of status, its love of luxuries, its attachment to frivolous pursuits, its glorification of violence, and its obsession with self-gratification. It must be realized that the isolation and despair from which so many suffer are products of an environment ruled by an all-pervasive materialism.[13]

The House of Justice then proceeds to the third prerequisite, freedom from prejudice, which the Guardian addressed

> stating patently that 'any division or cleavage ' in the ranks of the Faith 'is alien to its very purpose, principles and ideals'. He made clear that the friends should manifest 'complete freedom from prejudice in their dealings with peoples of a different race, class, creed, or colour'. He went on to discuss at length the specific question of racial prejudice, 'the corrosion of which', he indicated, had 'bitten into the fibre, and attacked the whole social structure of American society' and which, he asserted at the time, 'should be regarded as constituting the most vital and challenging issue confronting the Bahá'í community at the present stage of its evolution.'[14]

In this message of 2010, the Universal House of Justice focuses attention on the fact that the Guardian's analysis written 70 years ago is just as valid now as it was then and ask the believers to reflect on its implications. For instance, living one's life with purity of heart and chastity is a daily challenge, especially among the youth who live in a world engulfed by all types of moral decadence and frivolous behaviour. But believers who are destined to bring about a new world order and a transformation of society are called upon to set an example which will stand out as a contrast to the dark side of moral decline around them. The Guardian made it clear what such an example implies:

> Such a chaste and holy life, with its implications of modesty, purity, temperance, decency, and clean-mindedness, involves no less than the exercise of moderation in all that pertains to dress, language, amusements, and all artistic and literary avocations. It demands daily vigilance in the control of one's carnal desires and corrupt inclinations. It calls for the abandonment of a frivolous conduct, with its excessive attachment to trivial and often misdirected pleasures. It requires total abstinence from all alcoholic drinks, from opium, and from similar habit-forming drugs. It condemns the prostitution of art and of literature, the practices of nudism and of companionate marriage, infidelity in marital relationships, and all manner of promiscuity, of easy familiarity, and of sexual vices.[15]

In many parts of the world, especially in the West, there has been an obsession with sexuality. In fact, sexuality and violence are among the most common problems of society in that part of the world. 'The world today is submerged, amongst other things, in an over-exaggeration of the importance of physical love, and a dearth of spiritual values,' writes Shoghi Effendi.[16] He warned that

> the chosen ones of God . . . should not look at the depraved conditions of the society in which they live, nor at the evidences of moral degradation and frivolous conduct which the people around them display. They should not content themselves merely with relative distinction and excellence. Rather they should fix their gaze upon nobler heights . . .[17]

With regard to moral rectitude, the Master stated, 'In brief, let each one of you be as a lamp shining forth with the light of the virtues

THE COVENANT: THE INDIVIDUAL, THE COMMUNITY AND THE INSTITUTIONS

of the world of humanity. Be trustworthy, sincere, affectionate and replete with chastity. Be illumined, be spiritual, be divine, be glorious, be quickened of God, be a Bahá'í.'[18] He, moreover, elucidated the manner through which believers 'may stand out distinguished' through their conduct:

> Should any one of you enter a city, he should become a centre of attraction by reason of his sincerity, his faithfulness and love, his honesty and fidelity, his truthfulness and loving-kindness towards all the peoples of the world, so that the people of that city may cry out and say: 'This man is unquestionably a Bahá'í . . .' Not until ye attain this station can ye be said to have been faithful to the Covenant and Testament of God. For He hath, through irrefutable Texts, entered into a binding Covenant with us all, requiring us to act in accordance with His sacred instructions and counsels.[19]

And Bahá'u'lláh exalts the significance of righteous acts in these words:

> One righteous act is endowed with a potency that can so elevate the dust as to cause it to pass beyond the heaven of heavens. It can tear every bond asunder, and hath the power to restore the force that hath spent itself and vanished . . . Be pure, O people of God, be pure; be righteous, be righteous . . .[20]

Shoghi Effendi, referring to the American believers, writes of a 'double crusade, first to regenerate the inward life of their own community, and next to assail the long-standing evils that have entrenched themselves in the life of their nation'.[21] In such an environment the youth should become champions of self-discipline and examples of freedom from enslavement to the moral decadence of the Western world. 'Abdu'l-Bahá writes,

> The primary purpose, the basic objective, in laying down powerful laws and setting up great principles and institutions dealing with every aspect of civilization, is human happiness; and human happiness consists only in drawing closer to the Threshold of Almighty God, and in securing the peace and well-being of every individual member, high and low alike, of the human race; and the supreme agencies for

accomplishing these two objectives are the excellent qualities with which humanity has been endowed.[22]

The Relationship between Bahá'í Scholars and the Community

The Covenant of Bahá'u'lláh gives rise to a Bahá'í community which will increasingly become known for its fostering of creative development and for its encouragement of individual expression. The Covenant also provides guiding principles by which a Bahá'í scholar can exemplify that harmony of faith and reason which is a hallmark of the Bahá'í Dispensation.[23]

In the Bahá'í Writings, the believers have been encouraged to show respect toward those who strive to acquire knowledge. Shoghi Effendi stated that '(t)he Cause needs more Bahá'í scholars, people who not only are devoted to it . . . but also have a deep grasp of the Teachings and their significance, and who can correlate its beliefs with the current thoughts and problems of the people of the world.'[24]

Commenting on the relationship between the Bahá'í community at large and its scholars, the Universal House of Justice writes:

> In the field of Bahá'í scholarship we feel that it is most important not to stifle the development of Bahá'í scholars by an attitude of censorship or undue criticism. We believe that both the International Teaching Centre and the Boards of Counsellors can render valuable services in this area by encouraging budding scholars and by promoting within the Bahá'í community an atmosphere of tolerance for the views of others. At the same time the fundamental core of the believers' faith should be strengthened by an increasing awareness of the cardinal truth and vital importance of the Covenant, and an ever-growing love for Bahá'u'lláh.[25]

And,

> Those believers with the capacity and opportunity to do so have repeatedly been encouraged in their pursuit of academic studies by which they are not only equipped to render much needed services to the Faith, but

are also provided with the means to acquire a profound insight into the meaning and the implications of the Baháʾí Teachings.[26]

With the expansion of the Faith and the Baháʾí community, there will be increasing numbers of Baháʾís who will become experts in different fields, and likewise there will be experts who will embrace the Faith. Their input will bring knowledge, experience and skills to the community. Consequently, the institutional life of the Baháʾí community will also develop. This underlines the need for close collaboration between Baháʾí academics and the Baháʾí community as well as the institutions of the Faith.

While there have been comments implying that there exist two categories of believers designated 'administrators' and 'academics', the Universal House of Justice felt that the believers should recognize 'the unsoundness of such a concept'.[27] It furthermore underlined the fact that:

> In the nature of Baháʾí administration, there is no class of believers who serve as 'administrators'. Baháʾís from diverse fields of endeavour including academia can be elected or appointed to administrative service.[28]

Likewise, there are believers within the institutions of the Administrative Order who are referred to as "learned" in the Faith, but they, like academics, are part of the community and not above the believers at large. Also, 'misleading and invidious labels' which unfortunately may persist in the Baháʾí community such as 'traditionalists' and 'liberals' are viewed as a 'divisive habit of mind' which are a carry-over from non-Baháʾí society and a product of an immature concept of life.[29]

The Baháʾí institutions, whether elected or appointed, are responsible for the promotion of learning and the operation of the affairs of the Baháʾí community, assisted by individuals including those whose 'intellectual pursuits, qualities or character, and devotion to the Cause, particularly fit them to contribute their services'.[30] For example, members of the Continental Board of Counsellors who are appointed with specific tasks for a limited period of time will carry forward the functions of protection and propagation of the Cause to 'diffuse the Divine Fragrances, to edify the souls of men, to promote learning, to improve the character of all men and to be, at all times and under all conditions, sanctified and detached from earthly things'.[31] These individuals, like the Hands of the Cause, have no interpretative or authoritative function such as that exercised by the Centre of the Covenant and the Guardian. Their task is to encourage the friends in deepening their knowledge of the Cause and to execute the twin functions of protection and propagation.

Within the Bahá'í community, friends with diverse professional backgrounds endeavour to apply the Bahá'í principles for the good of mankind. The Universal House of Justice reminds us that

> all Bahá'ís, whatever their professions, are challenged to reflect on the implications of our common struggle to achieve Bahá'u'lláh's purpose for the human race, including the use of our intellectual resources to gain deeper understanding of that Revelation and to apply its principles. In pursuing this course that has been set for it so explicitly and emphatically by its Founder, the Bahá'í community acts through the institutions that He has provided.
>
> Scholarly endeavours are not an activity apart from this organic process, answering to standards and operating on authority outside it. The House of Justice believes that part of the difficulty that some Bahá'í academics are having with the question of prepublication review may arise from the fact that, in their scholarly work, such believers do not see themselves as full participants in this process, free to act with the spiritual autonomy they exercise in other aspects of their lives. What the Bahá'í community is engaged in bringing into visible expression is a new creation.[32]

And as we have seen earlier, it emphasizes that

> it is no doubt helpful to keep in mind that Bahá'ís who are trained in various academic disciplines do not constitute a discrete body within the community. While the Bahá'í institutions benefit on an ongoing basis from the advice of believers in many fields of specialization, there is obviously no group of academics who can claim to speak on behalf of Bahá'í scholars generally. Scholarly qualifications enable individuals to make greatly valued contributions to the work of the Cause, but do not set those possessing them apart from the general body of the believers.[33]

Although this statement lays stress on the lack of a privileged class standing apart from the rest of the Baháʼí community, this does not mean that valuable contributions in the arts and sciences or in the study of Baháʼí Writings are not appreciated. Nor should one underestimate the dedicated services which scores of Baháʼí academics and scholars have rendered to the Faith with the love of Baháʼuʼlláh in their hearts. Many of them labour selflessly – teaching, pioneering and serving on various institutions of the Faith – with humility and love, without drawing attention to their important contributions in their fields.

It is important for all Baháʼís, academics as well as others, to apply the teachings of Baháʼuʼlláh to their own lives as well as to the life of the community and society at large, as a document from the Baháʼí World Centre makes clear:

> [C]entral to the capacity of a Baháʼí community to lead a process of transformation is the ability of its members and institutions to apply the Revelation of Baháʼuʼlláh to various aspects of life and thereby establish consistent patterns of change. In fact, learning to apply the Teachings to achieve progress could be taken as the very definition of Baháʼí social and economic development.[34]

Thus, the relationship between Baháʼí academics and the community should be characterized by a seamless flow of reciprocal collaboration. What will ensure the strength of the bond is the fact that we all are servants of Baháʼuʼlláh working together to build a new world order. As the Universal House of Justice writes:

> The Baháʼí community is an association of individuals who have voluntarily come together, on recognizing Baháʼuʼlláh's claim to be the Manifestation of God for this age, to establish certain patterns of personal and social behaviour and to build the institutions that are to promote these patterns.[35]

Mutual respect and fellowship

In welcoming Baháʼí academics or scholars from different disciplines, their integration into the Baháʼí community needs to be characterized by an 'atmosphere of mutual respect and tolerance'.[36] On the other hand, Bahá'í scholars should also be participants in the work of the plans of the Cause and in community activities. They should guard against 'the temptation of intellectual pride'[37] so rampant in some circles of the professional community, especially in the West. The friends, whether scholars or not, should avoid the 'fomenting of discord' in the community.[38]

There is a need for a loving and encouraging attitude on the part of the community toward Bahá'í scholars, and likewise a nurturing and supportive attitude from professionals in the Faith who are willing to offer their knowledge and services to the institutions of the Cause.

Moderation

Shoghi Effendi stated that Bahá'u'lláh

> inculcates the principle of 'moderation in all things'; declares that whatsoever, be it 'liberty, civilization and the like', 'passeth beyond the limits of moderation' must 'exercise a pernicious influence upon men'; observes that western civilization has gravely perturbed and alarmed the peoples of the world; and predicts that the day is approaching when the 'flame' of a civilization 'carried to excess' will devour the cities'.[39]

And Bahá'u'lláh's own words read:

> The civilization, so often vaunted by the learned exponents of arts and sciences, will, if allowed to overleap the bounds of moderation, bring great evil upon men. Thus warneth you He Who is the All-Knowing. If carried to excess, civilization will prove as prolific a source of evil as it had been of goodness when kept within the restraints of moderation.[40]

Even in the practice of our Faith, Baha'u'llah counsels moderation. For example, we might ask ourselves about the benefits of reading the Writings for long periods of time. On this subject, Baha'u'llah exhorts us:

> Pride not yourselves on much reading of the verses or on a multitude of pious acts by night and day; for were a man to read a single verse with joy and radiance it would be better for him than to read with lassitude all the Holy Books of God, the Help in Peril, the Self-Subsisting. Read

ye the sacred verses in such measure that ye be not overcome by languor and despondency. Lay not upon your souls that which will weary them and weigh them down, but rather what will lighten and uplift them, so that they may soar on the wings of the Divine verses towards the Dawning-place of His manifest signs; this will draw you nearer to God, did ye but comprehend.[41]

Relating Bahá'í teachings to current issues

'If the Bahá'ís want to be really effective in teaching the Cause', writes Shoghi Effendi,

> they need to be much better informed and able to discuss intelligently, intellectually, the present condition of the world and its problems. We need Bahá'í scholars, not only people far, far more deeply aware of what our teachings really are, but also well-read and well-educated people, capable of correlating our teachings to the current thoughts of the leaders of society.
>
> We Bahá'ís should, in other words, arm our minds with knowledge in order to better demonstrate to, especially, the educated classes, the truths enshrined in our Faith.[42]

We live in a changing world in which, with the passage of time, the needs and requirements of people will also change. With the unprecedented expansion of communication technologies, the breakdown of traditional beliefs and the crumbling of the old world order, all Bahá'ís – whether scholars or not – need to recognize and reflect upon these changes in order to apply the healing message of Bahá'u'lláh:

> The remedy the world needeth in its present-day afflictions can never be the same as that which a subsequent age may require. Be anxiously concerned with the needs of the age ye live in, and center your deliberations on its exigencies and requirements.[43]

Bahá'í scholars and teachers can play an important role by participating in social discourse and by promoting the relevance and applicability of the teachings of the Faith to many contemporary social and humanitarian issues.

As to how to relate Bahá'í concepts and principles to social, economic and other current problems, there is no one particular approach to all circumstances. Moreover, the requirements of time and place and of the socio-cultural sensitivity of the people of a region may make discussion of the application of certain Bahá'í teachings unsuitable or irrelevant in a given situation. However, the Universal House of Justice has emphasized that 'an increasing number of believers will be able to analyse the problems of mankind in every field and to show how the Teachings solve them . . . '[44]

In one of his talks the late Peter Khan gave the following example of a possible approach:

1) What are the 'problems of mankind' which are of major concern to the people in this region?
2) How can these problems be analysed at a fundamental level (beyond the superficial level of partisan politics) to expose the deep and basic issues?
3) What Bahá'í teachings are relevant to these issues?
4) How can this analysis be used to devise means of presenting the Bahá'í Faith to people in such a manner that they see the relevance of the teachings to present-day needs, and the efficacy of the Faith as a solution to the problems besetting them?[45]

The purpose of this approach is not only to generate knowledge but also to nurture scholars from diverse backgrounds who will be able to analyse and respond to the pressing problems of global society by sharing fundamental principles enshrined in the Bahá'í Writings. In the same talk, Khan eloquently discussed various aspects of the application of Bahá'í principles, commenting on a particularly challenging aspect:

> One difficulty which must be faced is that so many contemporary issues are presented in terms of partisan politics, and are generally analysed on that basis. Bahá'ís addressing these issues are consequently in danger of becoming unwittingly embroiled in a potentially-divisive partisan political discussion, which could convey the erroneous impression that the Bahá'í teachings favour one partisan approach over another. The Guardian faced a similar difficulty in the analysis of world

events presented in his World Order letters; his resolution of the problem is described in the following passage taken from a letter written on his behalf:

> 'There is, however, one case in which one can criticize the present social and political order without being necessarily forced to side with or oppose any existing regime. And this is the method adopted by the Guardian in his Goal of a New World Order. His criticisms of the world conditions beside being very general in character are abstract; that is, instead of condemning existing institutional organizations it goes deeper and analyses the basic ideas and conceptions which have been responsible for their establishment . . .'[46]

The Challenge of Detachment in a Consumer Culture

In a world dominated by a materialistic philosophy of life and its offspring of atheism, consumerism and secularism, it is not easy to find an acceptable place for the virtue of detachment from a worldly lifestyle, including giving free rein to carnal desires. However, this virtue is valued in the Bahá'í community, as among the adherents of most religions. We also find some appreciation for detachment in the field of medicine, not as a virtue but as a practical means of enhancing public health and preventing disease.

In a world where the light of religion and divine education is darkened, understanding of the true meaning and spiritual significance of detachment is limited. For example, in the field of psychology and other behavioural sciences, to speak about the value of detachment is likely to be perceived as odd and old-fashioned.

In the ocean of the Revelation of Bahá'u'lláh, however, detachment and other virtues associated with it illumine the world of humanity. Frequent reference is made to detachment from and renunciation of the material world, as in these words:

> Blessed are they that have soared on the wings of detachment and attained the station which, as ordained by God, overshadoweth the entire creation, whom neither the vain imaginations of the learned, nor the multitude of the hosts of the earth have succeeded in deflecting from His Cause.[47]

In the Tablets of the Divine Plan 'Abdu'l-Bahá addresses the North American believers as 'heavenly armies' and characterizes them as those who are 'entirely freed from the human world, transformed into celestial spirits and have become divine angels'.[48] He challenges these 'heavenly armies' to 'uplift their magnanimity and be so illumined and detached' that should they be invited to accept 'the crown of the government of the whole world', they 'shall not condescend and shall refuse to accept it'.[49]

This kind of detachment is a spiritual virtue and is profoundly connected to the Covenant. Many great teachers or administrators of the Faith who became violators of the Covenant were unable to detach themselves from the world and their greedy desire for leadership which caused them to succumb to their egotism.

Detachment has many ramifications in the life of the Bahá'í community. One example is detachment from insisting on one's own views and imposing one's ideas on others during the process of consultation. Detachment can disappear when a person boasts about his or her great services as an officer of a Spiritual Assembly, or contributions to the Fund, and so on.

Sometimes lack of detachment and pure love for Bahá'u'lláh may deprive us from obeying a Bahá'í law such as the sacred law of Ḥuqúqu'lláh (the Right of God). Here the believer's detachment can be tested without any one noticing. This is a law to which obedience is strongly enjoined by Bahá'u'lláh, yet there is no sanction against a person who fails to pay his share of Ḥuqúqu'lláh. It is left entirely to the conscience of the individual. But there will be spiritual consequences. An essential feature of discharging this responsibility is that it must be done not only honestly but also 'with the utmost joy and radiance and in a spirit of perfect humility and lowliness'.[50] It should also be carried out in a 'spirit of willing submission and contentment'.[51] Without such requisites the payments will not be acceptable.[52]

There is a moving story about an event which took place in the early years of the Faith during the Ministry of the Báb which demonstrates absolute obedience and detachment. The Báb sent a message to Mullá Ḥusayn in Mashhad to go to Mazindaran while hoisting the Black Standard. Two hundred and two companions joined him for this long journey toward that region of northern Iran.

As soon as Mullá Ḥusayn had determined to pursue the way that led to

Mázindarán, he, immediately after he had offered his morning prayer, bade his companions discard all their possessions. 'Leave behind all your belongings,' he urged them, 'and content yourselves only with your steeds and swords, that all may witness your renunciation of all earthly things, and may realise that this little band of God's chosen companions has no desire to safeguard its own property, much less to covet the property of others.' Instantly they all obeyed and, unburdening their steeds, arose and joyously followed him. The father of Badí' was the first to throw aside his satchel, which contained a considerable amount of turquoise which he had brought with him from the mine that belonged to his father. One word from Mullá Husayn proved sufficient to induce him to fling by the road-side what was undoubtedly his most treasured possession, and to cling to the desire of his leader.[53]

In other circumstances, detachment may have nothing to do with material issues such as high position, business transactions or service to the Cause. For example, detachment from personal expectations of a spiritual nature can also become a test. For instance, the Báb gave the following enlightening explanation of the manner in which a believer should worship God:

> Worship thou God in such wise that if thy worship lead thee to the fire, no alteration in thine adoration would be produced, and so likewise if thy recompense should be paradise. Thus and thus alone should be the worship which befitteth the one True God. Shouldst thou worship Him because of fear, this would be unseemly in the sanctified Court of His presence, and could not be regarded as an act by thee dedicated to the Oneness of His Being. Or if thy gaze should be on paradise, and thou shouldst worship Him while cherishing such a hope, thou wouldst make God's creation a partner with Him, notwithstanding the fact that paradise is desired by men.
>
> Fire and paradise both bow down and prostrate themselves before God. That which is worthy of His Essence is to worship Him for His sake, without fear of fire, or hope of paradise.
>
> Although when true worship is offered, the worshipper is delivered from the fire, and entereth the paradise of God's good-pleasure, yet such should not be the motive of his act. However, God's favour and grace ever flow in accordance with the exigencies of His inscrutable wisdom.

> The most acceptable prayer is the one offered with the utmost spirituality and radiance; its prolongation hath not been and is not beloved by God. The more detached and the purer the prayer, the more acceptable is it in the presence of God.[54]

We conclude this section with these words of supplication from a prayer revealed by 'Abdu'l-Bahá:

> O God, my God! Fill up for me the cup of detachment from all things, and in the assembly of Thy splendours and bestowals, rejoice me with the wine of loving Thee. Free me from the assaults of passion and desire, break off from me the shackles of this nether world, draw me with rapture unto Thy supernal realm, and refresh me amongst the handmaids with the breathings of Thy holiness.[55]

The Insidious Influence of Materialism

As Bahá'ís, we often perceive obedience to the Covenant in the light of protection issues such as attacks from enemies or the pernicious influence of Covenant-breakers. However, obedience to the Covenant is a lifelong process. Among many other challenges is that of living a life with moral integrity, and resisting the corrosive and insidious influence of materialistic thoughts and lifestyle.

Believers in the Most Great Name are like an island surrounded by a sea of consumerism, self-indulgence and seductive media publicity that encourages self-gratification. As the 'devouring flame'[56] of materialism penetrates increasingly into the fabric of the society around us, protection from material corruption and preservation of the quality of Bahá'í life become a challenge to reckon with.[57] Excessive freedom, laxity in moral conduct, and indifference toward spiritual insights into the true purpose of life, as well as the breakdown of the institution of marriage, are but a few examples of a world in disarray.

'Abdu'l-Bahá writes that

> although material civilization is one of the means for the progress of the world of mankind, yet until it becomes combined with Divine civilization, the desired result, which is the felicity of mankind, will not be attained . . . Material civilization is like the body. No matter how

infinitely graceful, elegant and beautiful it may be, it is dead. Divine civilization is like the spirit, and the body gets its life from the spirit, otherwise it becomes a corpse. It has thus been made evident that the world of mankind is in need of the breaths of the Holy Spirit. Without the spirit the world of mankind is lifeless, and without this light the world of mankind is in utter darkness.[58]

And Shoghi Effendi elaborated on the spread of 'cancerous' materialism in human society: 'born originally in Europe, carried to excess in the North American continent, contaminating the Asiatic peoples and nations, spreading its ominous tentacles to the borders of Africa, and now invading its very heart . . .'[59] This underlines the seriousness of the challenge we face in contemporary society and calls to mind another statement of the Guardian in which he quotes Bahá'u'lláh:

> Small wonder that Bahá'u'lláh, the Divine Physician, should have declared: 'In this day the tastes of men have changed, and their power of perception hath altered. The contrary winds of the world, and its colors, have provoked a cold, and deprived men's nostrils of the sweet savours of Revelation.'[60]

More recently, the Universal House of Justice, in a message to the Bahá'ís of Iran describing principles that embody the oneness of humankind, wrote that

> religion without science soon degenerates into superstition and fanaticism, while science without religion becomes the tool of crude materialism; that true prosperity, the fruit of a dynamic coherence between the material and spiritual requirements of life, will recede further and further out of reach as long as consumerism continues to act as opium to the human soul . . .[61]

'Abdu'l-Bahá's promise to the Bahá'ís of the West that mental tests would be sent by the Almighty to purify and prepare them for 'their noble mission' further underscores our responsibility to overcome these problems.[62] Bahá'í youth, who are at the forefront of this changing world, need to study the Writings, in particular Shoghi Effendi's *The Advent of Divine Justice*, to gain a deeper understanding of their role and responsibility in the face of the unhealthy effects of a materialistic concept of life and habits of thinking.

The Guardian clearly emphasized the impact of materialism when he wrote:

> The gross materialism that engulfs the entire nation at the present hour; the attachment to worldly things that enshrouds the souls of men; the fears and anxieties that distract their minds; the pleasure and dissipations that fill their time, the prejudices and animosities that darken their outlook, the apathy and lethargy that paralyse their spiritual faculties – these are among the formidable obstacles that stand in the path of every would-be warrior in the service of Bahá'u'lláh, obstacles which he must battle against and surmount in his crusade for the redemption of his own countrymen.[63]

This statement draws our attention to the 'apathy and lethargy' that 'paralyse' the 'spiritual faculties' of individuals. This is a by-product of the 'gross materialism' which can seriously undermine if not cripple our motivation to be faithful and obedient to the Bahá'í laws and the Covenant of Bahá'u'lláh. One of the problems which confront young people in particular and even more so those in academic circles, is attraction to materialistic theories and assumptions promoting denial of the existence of God or misinterpretation of the origin of divinity and religion.

Materialism and notions of God and religion

During the past few decades there has been increasing literature and discourse, particularly in the academic community, that denies the existence of God and propagates theories that propound a biological basis for spiritual reality and religion.

Materialistic philosophy contends that matter is the core and primary basis of reality; that there is no such thing as spiritual or metaphysical reality. Whatever cannot be defined as a form of matter or a physical entity does not exist. A number of materialistic neuroscientists claim to have found a way to explain human consciousness, the soul and the mind. They believe that these are by-products or derivatives of neurobiological activities of the brain.

Many writers and researchers with that frame of mind argue that the human brain has evolved by natural selection. Based on this theory, they propose that religious beliefs must have also been developed through the same kind of processes. To them, religion and spirituality are products of molecular brain activity and have therefore evolved along with the brain through natural selection.[64]

These statements raise more questions than they can answer. First of all, scientific truth or reality is not absolute, but relative. Second, not every scientific finding or research study result is based on proven facts. Third, to insure the reliability of a research undertaking and the validity of its findings, the methodology used must be sound and relevant to the subject of the research. Methodologies used to explore issues such as the nature of religion, the essence or qualities of the soul, spirituality and the existence of God are mostly methodologies developed and used for the evaluation and measurement of physical conditions or entities. Although research can provide, for example, a scale to measure the effect of spiritual life on longevity, there is no scale to measure or quantify the nature and reality of the soul and spirituality. It is like measuring the length or width of love or compassion. Moreover, these researchers' approach in formulating the result is very reductionist.[65]

Such researchers assume that the existence of religion, revelation, and even the concept of God are the result of brain cell activity. This is particularly the case when they speak of the temporal lobe of the brain where religious thoughts or religious fervour is reportedly greater in patients with certain brain disorders such as temporal lobe epilepsy. However, they fail to respond to the fundamental question about who created the human brain in the first place.[66] Many researchers in these pursuits are atheists or are sceptical of the existence of divine reality. Their research theories are in line with a materialistic ideology of human nature. Many have been influenced by philosophers such as Kant, Marx, Engels and psychiatrists such as Freud who portrayed religion as an 'illusion' and attacked religious beliefs on those grounds. They are often in search of a material substitute for religion and God.

In recent years some youth in the Bahá'í community have become alienated from the Faith as a result of being influenced by this pervasive literature challenging the existence of God or misrepresenting the existence of God, giving it a biological explanation such as there being a God part or particle in the brain to explain the origin of the religious notion of God and religion itself. Many of these youth who are disillusioned about or question the existence of God feel too shy, embarrassed or simply uncomfortable to discuss the matter with their parents or friends, thinking that this would be perceived as a betrayal of the family and Bahá'í community in which they were brought up. Gradually they may drift away, initially showing no interest in attending Bahá'í gatherings and reading the Writings, and eventually leaving the Faith.

It is hard to know how many youth are so affected, but with the rise of indifference toward religious belief in society and increasing mistrust and scepticism toward God and religion, it is important for Bahá'ís to be aware of such a possibility. The remedy is to lovingly enquire about such thoughts and openly discuss these issues in order to assist young people to explore and understand Bahá'í teachings on the subject. Any strongly negative, punitive, or emotional reaction on the part of parents may prove counter-productive. Exposing youth to the Bahá'í Writings on the existence of God, reflecting together about the purpose of creation, and seeking assistance from other knowledgeable and trusted believers in such a way as not to antagonize and further alienate these young minds may be helpful.

The Bahá'í Writings are very clear that God's essence is unknowable and is far beyond the understanding of the human mind and intellect. Bahá'u'lláh tells us that 'The door of the knowledge of the Ancient Being hath ever been, and will continue for ever to be, closed in the face of men. No man's understanding shall ever gain access unto His holy court.'[67] He then explains that God, however, as a token of His mercy has sent the Day Stars of His divine guidance (the Prophets) and has made knowledge of them the same as knowledge of God.[68]

Those interested in the Bahá'í view of proofs of the existence of God may wish to read 'Abdu'l-Bahá's Tablet to Auguste Forel, *Some Answered Questions* and many other passages from the Writings as well as works published by Bahá'í scholars such as William Hatcher's logical proof of the existence of God. All Bahá'ís, especially youth and young intellectuals, are encouraged to study the Writings on these subjects in order to be deepened and prepared to share the wealth of these Writings with those seeking to understand questions about God and His existence. Such knowledge is also important for their own spiritual well-being, for should they fail to acquire it they can easily become influenced by the atheistic ideologies and scepticism which are growing in popularity and which may 'paralyse' their 'spiritual faculties' and weaken their firmness in the Covenant.

Bahá'í Youth and the Covenant

Throughout the history of the Faith, Bahá'í youth have demonstrated heroism in firmness in the Covenant. From Rúḥu'lláh Várqá, the 12-year-old martyr during the Heroic Age whose story is told in Chapter 4, to 17-year-old Mona Mahmudnizhad of Shiraz and other youth of the Formative Age of the Bahá'í Dispensation, there have been countless youth who arose like lions of steadfastness in the Covenant. The emergence of women, children and youth, who sacrificed and remained steadfast, especially since the Islamic Revolution in Iran, has been a remarkable characteristic of the firmness in the Covenant in the Bahá'í Faith. An understanding of the dynamic power of the Covenant on the part of the rising generation in the Bahá'í community is therefore very important.

A letter on behalf of Shoghi Effendi written to Bahá'í youth in Germany and Austria in 1949 states,

> He read with interest the report of the activities of the Youth, and was particularly pleased to see that Dr Grossmann had given a course on the Covenant. The Youth must ponder deeply over the significance and implications of the Covenants of Bahá'u'lláh and 'Abdu'l-Bahá, for these form the hub of the Bahá'í wheel, so to speak, the point of unity and strength for all the believers all over the world. Without these Covenants the Divine Protection of God over this new world Faith would not exist. Obedience to these Covenants is the stronghold of all the Bahá'ís, everywhere.
>
> The Youth must grasp this fundamental truth, for this will strengthen them in their service to the Cause, as nothing else can or will.
>
> Another thing he wants the young people to do is to set an example in obedience to the Administration, and to rise above the tendency, alas, so pronounced in some of the friends, to consider personalities instead of *principles*. This Cause is based on spiritual laws, and we must consider these, and obey them, and not lose time in thinking about the individual person's peculiarities, or opinions . . .

[In the hand of the Shoghi Effendi:] *May the Beloved bless, sustain and guide you, to enable you, to acquire a fuller understanding of the implications of God's Covenant in this day, and contribute effectively to its clarification and its comprehension by the believers.*[69]

And from another letter to the youth:

> The Guardian's message to you is that you should constantly strive to mirror forth in your private lives, and also in your social relationships, the beauty, purity and regenerative power of the Message of Bahá'u'lláh. The Bahá'í youth of today should be an example to the youth of the world, and should therefore live up to the highest standards of conduct. Nothing short of such a close, united and concrete adherence to the ideals and teachings of the Faith by every young Bahá'í man and woman can impress and attract to it the serious attention and consideration of the world outside.[70]

The Universal House of Justice identified six requisites for the development of spiritual growth, emphasizing that

> Bahá'u'lláh has stated quite clearly in His Writings the essential requisites for our spiritual growth, and these are stressed again and again by 'Abdu'l-Bahá in His Talks and Tablets. One can summarize them briefly in this way:
> 1. The recital each day of one of the Obligatory Prayers with purehearted devotion.
> 2. The regular reading of the Sacred Scriptures, specifically at least each morning and evening, with reverence, attention and thought.
> 3. Prayerful meditation on the teachings, so that we may understand them more deeply, fulfil them more faithfully, and convey them more accurately to others.
> 4. Striving every day to bring our behaviour more into accordance with the high standards that are set forth in the Teachings.
> 5. Teaching the Cause of God.
> 6. Selfless service in the work of the Cause and in the carrying on of our trade or profession.[71]

In a letter to the National Spiritual Assembly of Canada dated 24 July

THE COVENANT: THE INDIVIDUAL, THE COMMUNITY AND THE INSTITUTIONS

2013, the Universal House of Justice elaborated on the widening range and nature of activities of the Association for Bahá'í Studies to include and inspire large numbers of Bahá'í youth:

> The upcoming youth conferences, which will draw tens of thousands of young people, are representative of swelling numbers who, shaped by the institute process at the dawning of their maturity, will set their footsteps firmly in the path of learning and action that will extend throughout their academic studies and beyond. The House of Justice looks to rising generations of Bahá'ís to wholeheartedly address a wide range of intellectual challenges, overcome all pitfalls and obstacles, and render service for the betterment of the world. In the decades ahead, then, a host of believers will enter diverse social spaces and fields of human endeavour. To this arena, pregnant with possibilities, the Association for Bahá'í Studies can offer an important contribution.[72]

It is befitting to conclude this chapter with the following passage from a message from the Universal House of Justice to the Youth Congress in Paraguay in the year 2000:

> Be not dismayed if your endeavors are dismissed as utopian by the voices that would oppose any suggestion of fundamental change. Trust in the capacity of this generation to disentangle itself from the embroilments of a divided society. To discharge your responsibilities, you will have to show forth courage, the courage of those who cling to standards of rectitude, whose lives are characterized by purity of thought and action, and whose purpose is directed by love and indomitable faith. As you dedicate yourselves to healing the wounds with which your peoples have been afflicted, you will become invincible champions of justice.[73]

9
'Abdu'l-Bahá: Centre of the Covenant and Perfect Exemplar

In the Revelation of Bahá'u'lláh, 'Abdu'l-Bahá occupies a station which is unique and unprecedented in the history of religion. He is the 'Perfect Exemplar', 'the Mystery of God'. We are still striving to understanding the mystery of His presence in the Dispensation of Bahá'u'lláh.

Significance of the Station of 'Abdu'l-Bahá

In His sacred Books and Tablets Bahá'u'lláh praised and extolled 'Abdu'l-Bahá's rank and station. Shoghi Effendi, in *The Dispensation of Bahá'u'lláh*, enumerates the lofty titles and appellations that refer to 'Abdu'l-Bahá:

> He is, and should for all time be regarded, first and foremost, as the Centre and Pivot of Bahá'u'lláh's peerless and all-enfolding Covenant, His most exalted handiwork, the stainless Mirror of His light, the perfect Exemplar of His teachings, the unerring Interpreter of His Word, the embodiment of every Bahá'í ideal, the incarnation of every Bahá'í virtue, the Most Mighty Branch sprung from the Ancient Root, the Limb of the Law of God, the Being 'round Whom all names revolve,' the Mainspring of the Oneness of Humanity, the Ensign of the Most Great Peace, the Moon of the Central Orb of this most holy Dispensation – styles and titles that are implicit and find their truest, their highest and fairest expression in the magic name 'Abdu'l-Bahá. He is, above and beyond these appellations, the 'Mystery of God' . . .[1]

In the Súriy-i-Ghuṣn (Tablet of the Branch), moreover, Bahá'u'lláh writes of 'Abdu'l-Bahá, 'Render thanks unto God, O people, for His appearance; for verily He is the most great Favour unto You,'² while in another Tablet He states that He made 'Abdu'l-Bahá 'a shelter for all mankind', 'a shield unto all who are in heaven and on earth'.³ 'Abdu'l-Bahá's life is an example of simplicity and humility. Dr Yúnis Khán (Youness Afroukhteh), who served the Master for nine years as His secretary, recounts how some of the Persian Bahá'ís liked to compose poems about 'Abdu'l-Bahá. If someone was inspired to write a poem about His servitude, that was acceptable to the Master and the writer would be the recipient of His affectionate favours. But if anyone sang His praises or exalted His name, the Master would be displeased and would even ask that person to repent or beg for forgiveness:

> The only rank that the Master assumed exclusively for Himself was the position of Interpreter of the Book. And the reason for this was that if anyone, based on the divine utterances and Tablets revealed in praise of the one 'Who had branched from the Ancient Root' tried to glorify 'Abdu'l-Bahá, He would respond: 'I am the Interpreter of the Book and all these appellations mean 'Abdu'l-Bahá' [Servant of Bahá'u'lláh]. ⁴

During the ministry of 'Abdu'l-Bahá, some of the Bahá'ís were so excited by Him that they wanted to honour Him with a station equal to that of Bahá'u'lláh and the Báb or even superior to the station of the Báb. But the Master refused to accept this mistaken glorification and frequently warned the believers against such assumptions. He clearly stated, 'This is my firm, my unshakeable conviction, the essence of my unconcealed and explicit belief . . . My station is the station of servitude – a servitude which is complete, pure and real . . .'⁵ Those Bahá'ís who exaggerated His station by perceiving Him as equal to Bahá'u'lláh unfortunately contributed to confusion on this matter and unwittingly played into the hand of the enemies of the Faith, who took advantage of this confusion by maliciously alleging that 'Abdu'l-Bahá was claiming prophethood.⁶

The Guardian points out that the exalted titles conferred upon 'Abdu'l-Bahá by Bahá'u'lláh must never be construed as meaning that 'Abdu'l-Bahá was the recipient of a station 'identical with, or equivalent to, that of His Father, the Manifestation Himself.'⁷ In fact, 'Abdu'l-Bahá Himself commented on the Tablet of the Branch:

I affirm that the true meaning, the real significance, the innermost secret of these verses, of these very words, is my own servitude to the sacred Threshold of the Abhá Beauty, my complete self-effacement, my utter nothingness before Him. This is my resplendent crown, my most precious adorning. On this I pride myself in the kingdom of earth and heaven. Therein I glory among the company of the well-favoured! ... No one is permitted to give these verses any other interpretation.[8]

Furthermore, in rejecting the accusation of the Covenant-breakers who claimed that the Master was equating His station as the Centre of the Covenant with that of the Manifestation of God, the Guardian stated that this was their way 'to poison the minds' of the loyal followers of Bahá'u'lláh.[9] Shoghi Effendi points out that ' 'Abdu'l-Bahá is not a Manifestation of God, that He gets His light, His inspiration and sustenance direct from the Fountain-head of the Bahá'í Revelation; that He reflects even as a clear and perfect Mirror the rays of Bahá'u'lláh's glory...'[10]

In true servitude there is a gift of humility to surrender and submit to the will of one's Lord. 'A true servant abides in the depths of lowliness and humility, and not in the heights of glory,' writes Adib Taherzadeh, going on to elaborate on the relationship of 'Abdu'l-Bahá to Bahá'u'lláh: "'Abdu'l-Bahá occupies the lowest plane of servitude, a plane to which no other human being can ever descend. Bahá'u'lláh is the Manifestation of glory and is at the summit of majesty.'[11] He uses an analogy in which Bahá'u'lláh is likened to the peak of a mountain while 'Abdu'l-Bahá is the lowest valley. When it rains and the water pours from the top of the mountain to the deepest valley, the valley will contain a large amount of water, the source of sustenance. In this metaphor the rainwater pouring down into the valley below is the Word of God revealed by Bahá'u'lláh, and becomes the source of inspiration and enlightenment in the person of 'Abdu'l-Bahá.[12]

'Abdu'l-Bahá explains that there are three stations in the world of creation. The highest is the station of God, which is beyond our comprehension. The second is the station of the Manifestation of God, which is also inaccessible. The third is the station of man, and the most praiseworthy station for man is that of servitude. When a person dwells in this station, he grows closer to God and becomes the recipient of grace and bounty.[13]

'ABDU'L-BAHÁ: CENTRE OF THE COVENANT AND PERFECT EXEMPLAR

Personal Relationship between 'Abdu'l-Bahá and Bahá'u'lláh

While the Tablets of Bahá'u'lláh reveal all the glowing terms for and titles of 'Abdu'l-Bahá, the reverence and humility which the Master expressed toward the Blessed Beauty are beyond words. Although the intimate family relationship continued at home, the attitude of Bahá'u'lláh's faithful children toward their Father was far from ordinary, as Taherzadeh goes on to explain:

> the station of Bahá'u'lláh as the Manifestation of God completely overshadowed His position as a physical father. 'Abdu'l-Bahá, the Greatest Holy Leaf and the Purest Branch looked upon Bahá'u'lláh not merely as their father, but as their Lord, and because they had truly recognized His station, they acted at all times as most humble servants at His threshold. 'Abdu'l-Bahá always entered the presence of Bahá'u'lláh with such genuine humility and reverence that no one among His followers could express the spirit of lowliness and utter self-effacement as He did. The humility of 'Abdu'l-Bahá as He bowed before His Father, or prostrated Himself at His feet, demonstrated the unique relationship which existed between this Father and His faithful sons and daughter.[14]

In fact, whenever the Master went to visit Bahá'u'lláh at the Mansion of Mazra'ih or Bahjí, as soon as He saw the Mansion He dismounted from His steed and walked the rest of the road as a respect to His Lord Whose presence he wished to attain.[15]

This spirit of utter lowliness and humility was an inherent quality of the Master toward Bahá'u'lláh. 'Abdu'l-Bahá was a child in Baghdad when one day the Blessed Beauty intimated to him His own Station as a Manifestation of God. On hearing this, 'Abdu'l-Bahá instantly acknowledged the truth of Bahá'u'lláh's Mission and 'prostrated Himself at His feet and in humility and earnestness begged Bahá'u'lláh to grant Him the privilege of laying down His life in His path'.[16] Juliet Thompson, who met 'Abdu'l-Bahá and became one of His disciples, commented on that fateful moment of 'Abdu'l-Bahá's life in Baghdad: 'The sacrifice of life at least, was accepted and prolonged for fifty-six years in prison and exile.'[17]

While Bahá'u'lláh called Him the 'Master', a mark of honour

bestowed upon 'Abdu'l-Bahá alone among the entire family, the Master chose to be the servant, thus longing to be known as "Abdu'l-Bahá' (Servant of Bahá) as His most cherished title and honour. Bahá'u'lláh's response to 'Abdu'l-Bahá's absolute humility and self-effacement was an outpouring of loving admiration and affection. Such an expression of genuine love for the Master did not sit well with some members of the Holy Family, especially with 'Abdu'l-Bahá's half-brother Mírzá Muḥammad-'Alí, or with Mahd-i-'Ulyá, Muḥammad-'Alí's mother. One of the reasons that 'Abdu'l-Bahá chose to stay in 'Akká, instead of moving with Bahá'u'lláh to the Mansions of Mazra'ih and Bahjí, was to dampen their fierce jealousy. This was a voluntary and yet very painful decision on the part of the Master. It was difficult for Him to be separated from His Father and to be deprived from having the bounty of being in the presence of Bahá'u'lláh, Who was also longing to see His Most Great Branch.[18]

In 'Abdu'l-Bahá we find a perfect harmony between the spiritual powers and the physical and intellectual powers. A Biblical scholar once remarked about 'Abdu'l-Bahá that He is the 'Ambassador to Humanity'. Horace Holley, who first saw 'Abdu'l-Bahá in Thonon in 1911, described Him as 'majestic, strong, yet infinitely kind, He appeared like some just king that very moment descended from His throne to mingle with a devoted people'.[19]

Shoghi Effendi identified different dimensions of the person of 'Abdu'l-Bahá: one is the essentially human side of Him. Although the Master's station is radically different from that occupied by Bahá'u'lláh and the Bab, nevertheless He is the perfect Exemplar of the Bahá'í Faith and is endowed with 'superhuman knowledge'; He is regarded as the 'stainless mirror' reflecting the light of Bahá'u'lláh.[20]

'Abdu'l-Bahá's Life of Servitude

'Abdu'l-Bahá lived a very simple life. His secretary and chronicler during his journey to the West, Mírzá Maḥmúd-i-Zarqání, records that He was very generous when it came to spending for whatever would uphold the dignity of the Faith, and that He would assist the sick, the poor and those in distress. But as for Himself, He did not own a good winter coat. His companions had to beg Him over and over for permission to buy Him a new coat.[21]

He ate very simple meals and was detached from material wealth. While in the United States, some of the Bahá'ís made every effort to convince Him to accept some money, but He declined their offer, advising that they should distribute it among the poor. They brought presents for the members of His family and the Master responded, 'They are acceptable, but the best of all presents is the love of God . . .' which would be kept in the treasuries of the hearts. He told them that He would convey to His family the love of the Bahá'ís, which was the most precious of gifts.[22]

When World War I broke out, after having lived 55 years in exile and prison 'Abdu'l-Bahá's life was threatened by the Ottoman authorities and once again He became virtually a prisoner of that oppressive government. During the war 'Abdu'l-Bahá was kept busy attending to the needs of the people around Him, as Dr Esslemont recounts:

> He personally organized extensive agricultural operations near Tiberias, thus securing a great supply of wheat, by means of which famine was averted, not only for the Bahá'ís but for hundreds of the poor of all religions in Haifa and 'Akká, whose wants He liberally supplied. He took care of all, and mitigated their sufferings as far as possible. To hundreds of poor people He would give a small sum of money daily. In addition to money He gave bread. If there was no bread He would give dates or something else. He made frequent visits to 'Akká to comfort and help the believers and poor people there.[23]

Annamarie Honnold takes up the story:

> Food was stored in underground pits and elsewhere. This He distributed to inhabitants, regardless of religion or nationality. The food was systematically rationed. Having started His preparations as early as 1912, He averted tragedy in the dark days of 1917 and 1918.
>
> At war's end the British were quick to recognize His painstaking accomplishments. He was to be knighted on 27 April 1920, at the residence of the British Governor in Haifa at a ceremony held especially for Him. British and religious dignitaries came to honour Him on this auspicious occasion. His unselfish acts had won Him the love and respect of high and low alike. 'Abdu'l-Bahá consented to accept the knighthood – but he was not impressed with worldly honour or

ceremony. Even a formality must be simplified. An elegant car was sent to bring Him to the Governor's residence, but the chauffeur did not find the Master at His home. People scurried in every direction to find Him. Suddenly He appeared '. . . alone, walking His kingly walk, with that simplicity of greatness which always enfolded Him.

Isfandíyár, His long-time faithful servant, stood near at hand. Many were the times when he had accompanied the Master on His labours of love. Now, suddenly, with this elegant car ready to convey his Master to the Governor, he felt sad and unneeded. Intuitively, 'Abdu'l-Bahá must have sensed this – He gave him a sign. Isfandíyár dashed off – the horse was harnessed, the carriage brought to the lower gate and the Master was driven to a side entrance of the garden of the Governor. Isfandíyár was joyous – he was needed even yet. Quietly, without pomp, 'Abbás Effendi arrived at the right time at the right place and did honour to those who would honour Him when He was made Sir 'Abdu'l-Bahá 'Abbás, K.B.E. – a title which He almost never used.[24]

In His service to humanity the Master sacrificed His comfort and rest for others and would even give away His own food or clothes. While in prison in 'Akká He would nurse with His own hands the sick and dying prisoners.[25] Life was extremely difficult in the beginning. The room given to 'Abdu'l-Bahá to stay in was formerly a morgue on the ground floor. Besides the severe heat during the day, the humidity of the air adversely affected the Master's health for the rest of His life. The life the prisoners lived, with its filthy conditions, severe restrictions and lack of proper food and hygiene, took its toll. Soon the majority of the prisoners were afflicted with terrible infectious diseases. Only 'Abdu'l-Bahá and one other believer were unaffected for a period of time, during which they would attend to the needs of the sick, nursing them day and night.[26] Despite all this misery and other suffering, the Master kept His composure and was serene and happy.

One of the prison attendants asked Him, 'How is it you laugh and sing when prisoners ironed [referring to the chains carried by the prisoners] in this way usually cry out, weep and lament?' 'Abdu'l-Bahá replied, 'I rejoice because you are doing Me a great kindness; you are making Me very happy.' Then He told them that for a long time He wished to know the feelings of prisoners behind the iron bars, to experience what they have been subjected to. This imprisonment for the Cause of God gave Him that opportunity.[27]

The enormous and often daily services 'Abdu'l-Bahá rendered were not only for the Bahá'í community, but also for the ordinary people of 'Akká and Haifa. One of His daughters described His life after Bahá'u'lláh moved to Bahjí as follows:

> The life of the Master in 'Akka was full of work for others' good. He would rise very early, take tea, then go forth to His self-imposed labours of love. Often He would return very late in the evening, having had no rest and no food... The Arabs called Him the 'Lord of Generosity'... It would be impossible to write even a small part of the many compassionate acts of love and charity wrought by the Master; all His life was spent in ministering service to every unhappy creature who came to Him.[28]

Lua Getsinger, an early American Bahá'í who made several pilgrimages to visit 'Abdu'l-Bahá in the prison city of 'Akká and who lived with the family teaching English to His daughters for some months, recounted her personal observation of the Master's devotion to helping poor and sick people. One day the Master asked her to go and attend a person who was very ill and poor, as He was very busy that day. He told her, 'take him food and care for him as I have been doing'. She was told where this man was to be found and gladly agreed; she was proud that 'Abdu'l-Bahá had entrusted her with a task of His own.

> Lua went, but she returned quickly. 'Master,' she exclaimed, 'surely you cannot realize to what a terrible place you sent me! I almost fainted from the awful smells, the dirty rooms, the low condition of that man and his house. I ran away before I should catch some terrible disease.' 'Abdu'l-Bahá looked at her sadly and like a firm father. 'If you want to serve God,' He said, 'you must serve your fellow man, for in him do you see the image and likeness of God.'[29]

The Master told Lua to go back to that man's house and follow His instructions to bathe and feed him and to clean his house, thus teaching her how to serve her fellow human beings as He did.[30]

We conclude this chapter with the following passage for consideration and inspiration. These are the last words spoken by 'Abdu'l-Bahá to his followers prior to His departure from North America in December 1912:

> It is my hope that you may become successful in this high calling so that like brilliant lamps you may cast light upon the world of humanity and quicken and stir the body of existence like unto a spirit of life. This is eternal glory. This is everlasting felicity. This is immortal life. This is heavenly attainment. This is being created in the image and likeness of God. And unto this I call you, praying to God to strengthen and bless you.[31]

10

'Be Thou Assured'

> Be moreover assured beyond all shadow of doubt that no matter how strenuously the enemies of God's Faith may exert themselves to extinguish its fire, they will but cause its flame to burn the more fiercely, its light to shine the more brightly, and its heat to grow the more intense.
>
> *Shoghi Effendi*[1]

With the Revelation of Bahá'u'lláh comes an outpouring of loving encouragement and assurance for those facing trials and tribulations in the path of their Lord. This chapter contains a number of excerpts from the Writings on this theme, some of which appear in a small compilation entitled *Be Thou Assured*.[2]

> I say unto thee the truth, that I am with you in spirit and in heart, that I rejoice by your joy and am happy by your happiness; and hear with the ear of spirit your calling and scent with the spiritual nostrils the fragrances of your garden.
>
> *'Abdu'l-Bahá*[3]

> The source of courage and power is the promotion of the Word of God, and steadfastness in His Love.
>
> *Bahá'u'lláh*[4]

> Such is My plight, wert thou to ponder it in thine heart. Let not, however, thy soul grieve over that which God hath rained down upon Us. Merge thy will in His pleasure, for We have, at no time, desired anything whatsoever except His Will, and have welcomed each one of His irrevocable decrees. Let thine heart be patient, and be thou not dismayed. Follow not in the way of them that are sorely agitated.
>
> *Bahá'u'lláh*[5]

You shall in truth become the lighted torches of the globe. Fear not, neither be dismayed, for your light shall penetrate the densest darkness. This is the Promise of God, which I give unto you. Rise! and serve the Power of God! *'Abdu'l-Bahá* [6]

Walk, therefore, with a sure step and engage with the utmost assurance and confidence in the promulgation of the divine fragrances, the glorification of the Word of God and firmness in the Covenant. Rest ye assured that if a soul ariseth in the utmost perseverance and raiseth the Call of the Kingdom and resolutely promulgateth the Covenant, be he an insignificant ant he shall be enabled to drive away the formidable elephant from the arena, and if he be a feeble moth he shall cut to pieces the plumage of the rapacious vulture. Endeavour, therefore, that ye may scatter and disperse the army of doubt and of error with the power of the holy utterances. . . *'Abdu'l-Bahá* [7]

There is no refuge in the world today except the Cause of Bahá'u'lláh. The believers must rest assured that, having the Faith, they have everything. They must place their lives in the Hand of God, and, confident of His mercy and protection, go on teaching the Cause and serving it, no matter what happens . . . *Shoghi Effendi* [8]

The harder you strive to attain your goal, the greater will be the confirmations of Bahá'u'lláh, and the more certain you can feel to attain success. Be cheerful, therefore, and exert yourself with full faith and confidence. For Bahá'u'lláh has promised His Divine assistance to everyone who arises with a pure and detached heart to spread His Holy Word, even though he may be bereft of every human knowledge and capacity, and notwithstanding the forces of darkness and of opposition which may be arrayed against him. The goal is clear, the path safe and certain, and the assurances of Bahá'u'lláh as to the eventual success of our efforts quite emphatic. Let us keep firm, and whole-heartedly carry on the great work which He has entrusted into our hands.

Shoghi Effendi [9]

The friends must realize the Power of the Holy Spirit which is manifest and quickening them at this time through the appearance of Bahá'u'lláh. There is no force of heaven or earth which can affect them

'BE THOU ASSURED'

if they place themselves wholly under the influence of the Holy Spirit and under its guidance . . .   *Shoghi Effendi* [10]

Dear friends, as the world passes through its darkest hour before the dawn, the Cause of God, shining ever more brightly, presses forward to that glorious break of day when the Divine Standard will be unfurled and the Nightingale of Paradise warble its melody.
The Universal House of Justice [11]

At all times do I speak of you and call you to mind. I pray unto the Lord, and with tears I implore Him to rain down all these blessings upon you, and gladden your hearts, and make blissful your souls, and grant you exceeding joy and heavenly delights . . .
'Abdu'l-Bahá [12]

Ye live, all of you, within the heart of 'Abdu'l-Bahá, and with every breath do I turn my face toward the Threshold of Oneness and call down blessings upon you, each and all.   *'Abdu'l-Bahá* [13]

These are fate-laden days. The storms of test and trials continue, but however dark the clouds may be, they cannot dim the light appearing on the horizon.   *The Universal House of Justice* [14]

Not a moment passes that you are not in our thoughts. At every turn we remember you and take pride in retelling the accounts of your fortitude and fidelity. Our constant prayers are with you, and in the Holy Shrines we beseech the Blessed Beauty to protect and sustain you.
The Universal House of Justice [15]

To conclude this chapter, the following is from a prayer revealed by the beloved Master:

Thou seest me, O my God, bowed down in lowliness, humbling myself before Thy commandments, submitting to Thy sovereignty, trembling at the might of Thy dominion, fleeing from Thy wrath, entreating Thy grace, relying upon Thy forgiveness, shaking with awe at Thy fury. I implore Thee with a throbbing heart, with streaming tears and a yearning soul, and in complete detachment from all things, to make Thy lovers as rays of light across Thy realms, and to aid Thy chosen servants to exalt Thy Word, that their faces may turn beauteous and bright with splendour, that their hearts may be filled with mysteries, and that every soul may lay down its burden of sin. Guard them then from the aggressor, from him who hath become a shameless and blasphemous doer of wrong…

Heroes are they, O my Lord, lead them to the field of battle. Guides are they, make them to speak out with arguments and proofs. Ministering servants are they, cause them to pass round the cup that brimmeth with the wine of certitude. O my God, make them to be songsters that carol in fair gardens, make them lions that couch in the thickets, whales that plunge in the vasty deep.[16]

Bibliography

'Abdu'l-Bahá. *Memorials of the Faithful*. Trans. M. Gail. Wilmette, IL: Bahá'í Publishing Trust, 1971.

— *Paris Talks: Addresses given by 'Abdu'l-Bahá in 1911* (1912). London: Bahá'í Publishing Trust, 12th ed. 1995.

— *The Promulgation of Universal Peace: Talks Delivered by 'Abdu'l-Baha During His Visit to the United States and Canada in 1912* (1922, 1925). Comp. H. MacNutt. Wilmette, IL: Bahá'í Publishing Trust, 2nd ed. 1982.

— *The Secret of Divine Civilization*. Trans. M. Gail. Wilmette, IL: Bahá'í Publishing Trust, 1957.

— *Selections from the Writings of 'Abdu'l-Bahá*. Comp. Research Department of the Universal House of Justice. Haifa: Bahá'í World Centre, 1978.

— *Some Answered Questions* (1908). Comp. L. Clifford Barney. Wilmette, IL: Bahá'í Publishing Trust, 3rd ed. 1981.

— *Tablets of Abdul-Baha Abbas*. 3 vols. Chicago: Bahá'í Publishing Society, 1909–1916.

— *Tablets of the Divine Plan*. Wilmette, IL: Bahá'í Publishing Trust, 1975.

— 'Tablet to Dr. Auguste Henri Forel', in *The Bahá'í World 1968–1973*, vol. XV, pp. 37–43.

— *The Will and Testament of 'Abdu'l-Bahá*. Wilmette, IL: Bahá'í Publishing Trust, 1944.

Mírzá Abu'l-Faḍl-i-Gulpáygání. *Letters and Essays, 1886–1913*. Trans. Juan R.I. Cole. Los Angeles: Kalimát Press, 1985.

— *Miracles and Metaphors*. Trans. Juan Ricardo Cole. Introduction by Amin Banani. Los Angeles: Kalimát Press, 1981

Afroukhteh, Dr Youness. *Memories of Nine Years in 'Akká*. Trans. Riaz Masrour. Oxford: George Ronald, 2003.

The Báb. *Selections from the Writings of the Báb.* Haifa: Bahá'í World Centre, 1976.

Bahá'í Canada. Periodical. Thornhill, Ontario: National Spiritual Assembly of the Bahá'ís of Canada.

Bahá'í International Community. *The Bahá'í Question: Cultural Cleansing in Iran.* New York: Bahá'í International Community, 2005.

— *The Bahá'í Question: Iran's Secret Blueprint for the Destruction of a Religious Community.* New York: Bahá'í International Community, 1993.

— *Inciting Hatred: Iran's Media Campaign to Demonize Bahá'ís.* Special Report. New York: Bahá'í International Community, 2011.

— *Inciting Hatred: The Baha'is of Semnan, A Case Study in Religious Hatred.* Special Report. New York: Bahá'í International Community, 2012. Available at: www.bic.org/inciting-hatred.

Bahá'í Prayers: A Selection of Prayers Revealed by Bahá'u'lláh, The Báb, and 'Abdu'l-Bahá. Wilmette, IL: Bahá'í Publishing Trust, rev. ed. 1991

The Bahá'í World: An International Record. Vol. V (1932–1934), Wilmette, IL: Bahá'í Publishing Trust; vol. 8 (1938–1940), Wilmette, IL: Bahá'í Publishing Trust; vol. XII (1950–1954), Wilmette, IL: Bahá'í Publishing Trust; vol. XIII (1954–1963), Haifa, The Universal House of Justice; vol. XIV (1963–1968), Haifa: The Universal House of Justice, 1970; vol. XV (1968–1973), Haifa: Bahá'í World Centre, 1976; vol. XVIII (1979–1983), Haifa: Bahá'í World Centre, 1986.

Bahá'í World Faith: Selected Writings of Bahá'u'lláh and 'Abdu'l-Bahá. Wilmette, IL: Bahá'í Publishing Trust, rev. ed. 1956.

Bahíyyih Khánum; The Greatest Holy Leaf. Haifa: Bahá'í World Centre, 1982.

Bahá'u'lláh. *Epistle to the Son of the Wolf.* Trans. Shoghi Effendi. Wilmette, IL: Bahá'í Publishing Trust, rev. ed. 1976.

— *Gleanings from the Writings of Bahá'u'lláh.* Trans. Shoghi Effendi. Wilmette, IL: Bahá'í Publishing Trust, 2nd ed. 1976.

— *The Hidden Words of Bahá'u'lláh.* Trans. Shoghi Effendi. Wilmette, IL: Bahá'í Publishing Trust, 1970; New Delhi: Bahá'í Publishing Trust, 1987.

— *The Kitáb-i-Aqdas: The Most Holy Book.* Haifa: Bahá'í World Centre, 1992.

— *Kitáb-i-Íqán: The Book of Certitude.* Trans. Shoghi Effendi. Wilmette, IL: Bahá'í Publishing Trust, 2nd ed. 1950, 1981.

— *Prayers and Meditations by Bahá'u'lláh.* Trans. Shoghi Effendi. Wilmette, IL: Bahá'í Publishing Trust, 1938, 1987.

— *The Seven Valleys and the Four Valleys.* Trans. M. Gail with A-K. Khan. Wilmette, IL: Bahá'í Publishing Trust, rev. ed. 1975.

BIBLIOGRAPHY

— *The Summons of the Lord of Hosts: Tablets of Bahá'u'lláh.* Haifa: Bahá'í World Centre, 2002.

— *Tablets of Bahá'u'lláh Revealed after the Kitáb-i-Aqdas.* Comp. Research Department of the Universal House of Justice. Haifa: Bahá'í World Centre, 1978.

Balyuzi, H. M. *'Abdu'l-Bahá.* Oxford: George Ronald, 1971.

— *Bahá'u'lláh: The King of Glory.* Oxford: George Ronald, 1980.

Beauregard, M.; O'Leary, D. *The Spiritual Brain: A Neuroscientist's Case for the Existence of the Soul.* New York: Harper, 2007.

Be Thou Assured: A Compilation from the Bahá'í Writings prepared by the Continental Board of Counsellors in the Americas. National Spiritual Assembly of the Bahá'ís of Canada, White Mountain Publications, 1996.

Berger, David M. 'Recovery and Regression in Concentration Camp Survivors: A Psychodynamic Re-evaluation', in *Canadian Journal of Psychiatry*, vol. 30 (1985), pp. 54–9.

Blomfield, Lady. *The Chosen Highway.* London: Bahá'í Publishing Trust, 1940. RP Oxford: George Ronald, 2007.

Common Ground: website available at: http://www.commongroundgroup.net/2013/05/20/why-do-bahai-babies-go-to-prison-in-iran/.

The Compilation of Compilations. Prepared by the Universal House of Justice 1963–1990. 2 vols. Sydney: Bahá'í Publications Australia, 1991.

Crisis and Victory. Comp. Research Department of the Universal House of Justice. London: Bahá'í Publishing Trust, 1988.

Developing Distinctive Bahá'í Communities. Evanston, IL: National Spiritual Assembly of the Bahá'ís of the United States, 1998.

The Divine Art of Living: Selections from Writings of Bahá'u'lláh and 'Abdu'l-Bahá. Comp. M. H. Paine. Wilmette, IL: Bahá'í Publishing Trust, 4th rev. ed. 1979.

Esslemont, J. E. *Bahá'u'lláh and the New Era.* Wilmette IL: Bahá'í Publishing Trust, 1980.

Faizí, Abu'l-Qásim. *Milly: A Tribute to Amelia E. Collins.* Oxford: George Ronald, 1977.

Faizi, Gloria. *Stories about 'Abdu'l-Bahá.* New Delhi: Bahá'í Publishing Trust, 1993.

Ferraby, John. *All Things Made New.* London: Bahá'í Publishing Trust, 1975.

Freud, Sigmund. *Civilization and its Discontents.* Trans. James Strachey. New York: W.W. Norton, 1961.

Ghadirian, A-M. 'Intergenerational Responses to the Persecution of the Bahá'ís of Iran', in *International Handbook of Multigenerational Legacies of Trauma*. Ed. Yael Danieli. New York: Plenum Press, 1998.

— *Materialism: Moral and Social Consequences*. Oxford: George Ronald, 2010.

— 'Psychological and Spiritual Dimensions of Persecution and Suffering', in *The Journal of Bahá'í Studies*, vol. 6, no. 3 (1994), pp. 1–26.

Hakim-Samandari, Christine. 'A Victory over Violence: A Personal Testimony', in *World Order*, vol. 20, no. 1 (Fall 1985).

Harper, Barron. *Lights of Fortitude*. Oxford: George Ronald, RP 2007.

Hatcher, William. 'A Scientific Proof of the Existence of God', in *Journal of Bahá'í Studies*, vol. 5 (1994), no. 4.

Honnold, Annamarie. *Vignettes from the Life of 'Abdu'l-Bahá*. Oxford: George Ronald, rev. ed. 1991.

Human Rights Activists News Agency (HRANA). 'Two infants along with their mothers in grave danger in Semnan Prison, Iran', 7 December 2012.

Ḥuqúqu'lláh: The Right of God. Comp. Research Department of the Universal House of Justice. London: Bahá'í Publishing Trust, 1986.

The Institution of the Counsellors. Comp. Research Department of the Universal House of Justice. Haifa: Bahá'í World Centre, 2001.

Khan, Janet A.; Khan, Peter J. *Advancement of Women: A Bahá'í Perspective*. Wilmette, IL: Bahá'í Publishing Trust, 1998.

Khan, Peter. 'Relating the Faith to Current Issues', undated talk, unpublished.

— 'Some Aspects of Bahá'í Scholarship', in *Journal of Bahá'í Studies*, vol. 9 (1999), no. 4.

Lample, Paul. *Creating a New Mind*. Riviera Beach, FL: Palabra Publications, 1999.

— *Revelation and Social Reality*. West Palm Beach, FL: Palabra Publications, 2009.

Lights of Guidance: A Bahá'í Reference File. Comp. H. Hornby. New Delhi: Bahá'í Publishing Trust, 5th ed. 1997.

Nabíl-i-A'ẓam (Muḥammad-i-Zarandí). *The Dawn-Breakers: Nabíl's Narrative of the Early Days of the Bahá'í Revelation*. Trans. Shoghi Effendi. Wilmette, IL: Bahá'í Publishing Trust, 1932.

Nakhjavani, Bahiyyih. *Asking Questions: A Challenge to Fundamentalism*. Oxford: George Ronald, 1990.

Poirier, Brent. Blog, available at: bahai-covenant.blogspot.com/2010/12/covenant-protects-from-schism.html.

BIBLIOGRAPHY

— *Twin Covenants of the Bahá'í Faith*. Online article, 1998. Available at http://bahai-library.com/poirier_twin_covenants.

The Power of the Covenant. 3 parts. National Spiritual Assembly of the Baha'is of Canada. Thornhill, ON: Bahá-í Canada Publications, 1976–7.

Psychology and Knowledge of Self. Compilation prepared at the Bahá'í World Centre, 1994.

Rights and Responsibilities: The Complementary Roles of the Individual and Institutions. Thornhill, ON: Bahá'í Canada Publications, 1997.

Ruhe-Schoen, Janet. *A Love Which Does Not Wait*. Riviera Beach, FL: Palabra Publications, 1998.

The Ruhi Foundation. *Reflections on the Life of the Spirit*. Riviera Beach, FL: Palabra Publications, 1987.

Rutter, Michael. 'Resilience in the Face of Adversity', in *British Journal of Psychiatry*, No. 147 (1985), pp. 598–611.

Scholarship. Comp. Research Department of the Universal House of Justice. Mona Vale, NSW: Bahá'í Publications Australia, 1995.

Sears, William; Quigley, Robert. *The Flame*. George Ronald: Oxford, 1972.

Shoghi Effendi. *The Advent of Divine Justice* (1939). Wilmette, IL: Bahá'í Publishing Trust, 1984.

— *Bahá'í Administration: Selected Messages 1922-1932*. Wilmette IL: Bahá'í Publishing Trust, 1980.

— *Dawn of a New Day: Messages to India 1923-1957*. New Delhi: Bahá'í Publishing Trust, n.d.

— *Citadel of Faith: Messages to America, 1947–1957*. Wilmette, IL: Bahá'í Publishing Trust, 1965.

— *God Passes By* (1944). Wilmette, IL: Bahá'í Publishing Trust, rev. ed. 1974.

— *The Light of Divine Guidance: The Messages from the Guardian of the Bahá'í Faith to the Bahá'ís of Germany and Austria*. 2 vols. Hofheim-Langenhain: Bahá'í-Verlag, 1982, 1985.

— *Messages to America 1932-1946*. Wilmette, IL: Bahá'i Publishing Trust, 1947. Published online by the Project Gutenberg.

— *Messages to the Bahá'í World 1950–1957*. Wilmette, IL: Bahá'í Publishing Trust, 2nd ed. 1971.

— *Messages to Canada*. Thornhill, ON: National Spiritual Assembly of the Bahá'ís of Canada, 1965.

— *Messages of Shoghi Effendi to the Indian Subcontinent 1923-1957*. Comp. Iran Furutan Muhajír. New Delhi: Bahá'í Publishing Trust, rev. ed. 1995.

— *Principles of Bahá'í Administration*. London: Bahá'í Publishing Trust, 1950.

— *The Promised Day Is Come* (1941). Wilmette, IL: Bahá'í Publishing Trust, rev. ed. 1980.

— *Unfolding Destiny: The Messages from the Guardian of the Bahá'í Faith to the Bahá'í Community of the British Isles*. London: Bahá'í Publishing Trust, 1981.

— *The World Order of Bahá'u'lláh: Selected Letters by Shoghi Effendi* (1938). Wilmette, IL: Bahá'í Publishing Trust, 2nd rev. ed. 1974.

Star of the West: The Bahai Magazine. Periodical, 25 vols. 1910–1935. Vols. 1–14 RP Oxford: George Ronald, 1978. Complete CD-ROM version: Talisman Educational Software/Special Ideas, 2001.

Taherzadeh, Adib. *The Child of the Covenant: A Study Guide to the Will and Testament of 'Abdu'l-Bahá*. Oxford: George Ronald, 2000.

— *The Covenant of Bahá'u'lláh*. Oxford: George Ronald, 1992.

— *The Revelation of Bahá'u'lláh*. 4 vols. Oxford: George Ronald, 1974–1987.

Thompson, Juliet. *'Abdu'l-Bahá: The Center of the Covenant*. Wilmette, IL: Bahá'í Publishing Committee, 1948.

— *Abdul-Bahá's First Days in America: From the Diary of Juliet Thompson*. East Aurora, NY: The Roycrofters, n.d. (1924?). RP Lansing, MI: H-Bahai, 2004.

Tillich, Paul. *Dynamics of Faith*, New York: Harper & Row, 1957.

The Universal House of Justice. *The Constitution of the Universal House of Justice*. Haifa: Bahá'í World Centre, 1972.

— *Individual Rights and Freedoms in the World Order of Bahá'u'lláh: A Statement by the Universal House of Justice*. Letter to the Followers of Bahá'u'lláh in the United States of America, 29 December 1988. Wilmette, IL: Baha'í Publishing Trust, 1989.

— *Issues Related to the Study of the Baha'i Faith*. Wilmette IL: Baha'i Publishing Trust, 1999.

— *Messages from the Universal House of Justice 1963–1986: The Third Epoch of the Formative Age*. Comp. Geoffry W. Marks. Wilmette, IL: Bahá'í Publishing Trust, 1996.

— Message to the Bahá'ís of the World, Riḍván 153, 1996.

— Message to Believers Gathered for Terrace Events, 24 May 2001.

— Message to the Conference of the Continental Boards of Counsellors, 28 December 2010.

— Message to the Iranian Believers Throughout the World, Bahá 154 B.E. Wilmette, IL: Persian/American Affairs Office, Bahá'í National Center, August 1997. Translation from Persian.

— Second Message to World Congress, 26 November 1992.

— *To Champion the Cause of Justice: Messages from the Universal House of Justice to the Youth Congresses in the Americas, 1998-2002*, West Palm Beach, FL: Palabra Publications, 2002.

— *Wellspring of Guidance: Messages from the Universal House of Justice 1963-1968*. Wilmette, IL: Bahá'í Publishing Trust, 1976.

Vahman, Fereydun. *160 Years of Persecution*. Sweden: Baran Publishers, 2010.

Ward, Allan. *239 Days: 'Abdu'l-Bahá's Journey in America*. Wilmette, IL: Bahá'í Publishing Trust, 1979.

White, Roger (comp.). *A Compendium of Volumes of the Bahá'í World: An International Record, I-XII*. Oxford: George Ronald, 1981.

Whitehead, O. Z. *Some Early Bahá'ís of the West*. Oxford: George Ronald, 1977.

Wilson, Edward O. *On Human Nature*. Cambridge, MA: Harvard University Press, 1978.

Zarqání, Mírzá Maḥmúd. *Maḥmúd's Diary: The Diary of Mírzá Maḥmúd-i-Zar'qání Chronicling 'Abdu'l-Bahá's Journey to America*. Trans. M. Sobhani with S. Macias. Oxford: George Ronald, 1998.

References

Introduction
1. Bahá'u'lláh, quoted by Shoghi Effendi, 'The Dispensation of Bahá'u'lláh', in *The World Order of Bahá'u'lláh*, p. 109.
2. 'Abdu'l-Bahá, quoted by Shoghi Effendi, *Bahá'í Administration*, p. 123.
3. 'Abdu'l-Bahá, *Tablets of the Divine Plan*, p. 49.
4. 'Abdu'l-Bahá, Tablet to the Paris Assembly, 23 July 1919, in *Star of the West*, vol 10, no. 12, p. 226.
5. Letter on behalf of Shoghi Effendi to the Bahá'í community of Stuttgart, 30 May 1949, in *The Light of Divine Guidance*, vol. 2, p. 86.
6. Taherzadeh, *The Child of the Covenant*, p. 35.
7. 'Abdu'l-Bahá, quoted by Shoghi Effendi, 14 November 1923, in *Baha'i Administration*, p. 50.
8. Letter on behalf of Shoghi Effendi to the National Youth Committee of the Bahá'ís of Germany and Austria, 20 October 1949, in *The Light of Divine Guidance*, vol. 2, p. 89.
9. Baha'u'llah, Súriy-i-Haykal, para. 63, in Bahá'u'lláh, *Summons of the Lord of Hosts*, p. 34.
10. 'Abdu'l-Bahá, quoted by Shoghi Effendi, 'The Dispensation of Bahá'u'lláh', in *The World Order of Bahá'u'lláh*, p. 136.
11. Bahá'u'lláh, Hidden Words, Arabic no. 55.
12. Qur'án 29:2, quoted by Taherzadeh, *The Child of the Covenant*, p. 36.
13. Bahá'u'lláh, Tablet of Aḥmad, in *Bahá'í Prayers*, p. 208.
14. Taherzadeh, *The Child of the Covenant*, p. 35.
15. ibid. p. 36.
16. 'Abdu'l-Bahá, *Selections from the Writings of 'Abdu'l-Bahá*, no. 43. p. 87.
17. Letter from the Universal House of Justice to the National Spiritual Assembly of the United States, 7 September 1965, in *Lights of Guidance*, no. 1144.
18. Letter on behalf of Shoghi Effendi to an individual, 22 October 1949, in *Unfolding Destiny*, p. 456.
19. Letter on behalf of Shoghi Effendi to an individual, 18 December 1945, in *The Compilation of Compilations*, vol. II, no. 1308.

STEADFASTNESS IN THE COVENANT

1 **The Covenant of Bahá'u'lláh: Its Significance and a Brief History**
1. The Universal House of Justice, *The Institution of the Counsellors*, p. 26.
2. Bahá'u'lláh, *Kitáb-i-Aqdas*, para. 1, p. 19.
3. 'Abdu'l-Bahá, in *Star of the West*, vol. 4, no. 14, p. 237; also in *The Compilation of Compilations*, vol. I, no. 224.
4. 'Abdu'l-Bahá, *Tablets of Abdul-Baha Abbas*, p. 442.
5. 'Abdu'l-Bahá, in *Bahá'í World Faith*, pp. 357–8.
6. Bahá'u'lláh, *Gleanings*, CXXXIII, pp. 289–90.
7. Shoghi Effendi, *God Passes By*, p. 237.
8. ibid.
9. Bahá'u'lláh, *Tablets of Bahá'u'lláh Revealed After the Kitáb-i-Aqdas*, p. 221.
10. The Universal House of Justice, *The Constitution of the Universal House of Justice*, pp. 3–4.
11. Bahá'u'lláh, quoted by Shoghi Effendi, *The Advent of Divine Justice*, p. 77.
12. Shoghi Effendi, 'The Dispensation of Bahá'u'lláh', in *The World Order of Bahá'u'lláh*, p. 123.
13. The Báb, quoted by Bahá'u'lláh in *Epistle to the Son of the Wolf*, pp. 154–5.
14. ibid. p. 152.
15. The Báb, *Selections from the Writings of the Báb*, p. 104.
16. The Báb, quoted by Bahá'u'lláh in *Epistle to the Son of the Wolf*, p. 151.
17. Nabíl-i-A'ẓam, *The Dawn-Breakers*, p. 94.
18. Bahá'u'lláh, quoted by Shoghi Effendi, 'The Dispensation of Bahá'u'lláh', in *The World Order of Bahá'u'lláh*, p. 116.
19. Shoghi Effendi, *The Promised Day is Come*, p. 118.
20. Bahá'u'lláh, *Gleanings*, III, pp. 5–6.
21. Bahá'u'lláh, quoted by Shoghi Effendi, 'The Dispensation of Bahá'u'lláh' in *The World Order of Bahá'u'lláh*, p. 108.
22. Shoghi Effendi, ibid. p. 145.
23. Shoghi Effendi, *Messages to the Bahá'í World 1950–1957*, pp. 155–6 (emphasis added).
24. The Universal House of Justice, *The Compilation of Compilations*, vol. I, p. 111.
25. ibid.
26. Taherzadeh, *The Covenant of Bahá'u'lláh*, p. 99.
27. Letter from the *Universal House of Justice to an individual*, 23 March 1975, in *The Power of the Covenant, Part Two*, p. 10.
28. 'Abdu'l-Bahá, *The Promulgation of Universal Peace*, pp. 455–6.
29. 'Abdu'l-Bahá, quoted by Shoghi Effendi, 'The Dispensation of Bahá'u'lláh', in, p. 136.
30. Shoghi Effendi, 'This Hour, Crowded With Destiny', letter dated 18 August 1949, *Citadel of Faith*, p. 76.
31. Poirier, *Twin Covenants of the Bahá'í Faith*.
32. Shoghi Effendi, *Messages to Canada*, pp. 61–2.

REFERENCES

33 Letter on behalf of Shoghi Effendi to Anna Grossman, 15 April 1949, in *The Light of Divine Guidance*, vol. 2, p. 84.
34 'Abdu'l-Bahá, *Will and Testament*, para. 17.
35 Shoghi Effendi, *God Passes By*, p. 238.
36 ibid. p. 239.
37 ibid. p. 240.
38 Shoghi Effendi, 'The Dispensation of Bahá'u'lláh', in *The World Order of Bahá'u'lláh*, p. 144.
39 Shoghi Effendi, *God Passes By*, p. 328.
40 Letter on behalf of Shoghi Effendi to an individual, 25 March 1930, quoted by the Universal House of Justice, letter to an individual, 7 December 1969, in *Messages from the Universal House of Justice 1963-1986*, no. 75, p. 161.
41 Shoghi Effendi, *Messages to the Bahá'í World 1950-1957*, p. 84.
42 Shoghi Effendi, *God Passes By*, p. 214.
43 'Abdu'l-Bahá, *Will and Testament*, para. 36.
44 ibid. para. 13.
45 ibid. para. 24.
46 ibid. para. 16.
47 Shoghi Effendi, *God Passes By*, p. 324.
48 Shoghi Effendi, 'The Dispensation of Bahá'u'lláh', in *The World Order of Bahá'u'lláh*, p. 148.
49 'Abdu'l-Bahá, *Will and Testament*, para. 16.
50 Shoghi Effendi, 'The Dispensation of Bahá'u'lláh', in *The World Order of Bahá'u'lláh*, p. 150.
51 ibid. p. 148.
52 Letter from the Universal House of Justice to an individual, 7 December 1969, in *Messages from the Universal House of Justice 1963-1986*, no. 75, p. 156.
53 Letter from the Universal House of Justice to the National Spiritual Assembly of the Netherlands, 9 March 1965, ibid. no. 23, p. 53.
54 'Abdu'l-Bahá, *Will and Testament*, para. 17.
55 'Abdu'l-Bahá, quoted in a letter from the Universal House of Justice to an individual, 27 May 1966, in *Messages from the Universal House of Justice 1963-1986*, no. 35, p. 85.
56 Letter from the Universal House of Justice to the National Spiritual Assembly of the Netherlands, 9 March 1965, ibid. no. 23, p. 53.
57 ibid. p. 56.
58 Shoghi Effendi, 'The Dispensation of Bahá'u'lláh', in *The World Order of Bahá'u'lláh*, p. 153.
59 Shoghi Effendi, 'The World Order of Bahá'u'lláh', ibid. p. 23.
60 Letter from the Universal House of Justice to the National Spiritual Assembly of the Netherlands, 9 March 1965, in *Messages from the Universal House of Justice 1963-1986*, no. 23, p. 57.

STEADFASTNESS IN THE COVENANT

61 Letter from the Universal House of Justice to an individual, 27 May 1966, ibid. no. 35, p. 88.
62 'Abdu'l-Bahá, *Selections from the Writings of 'Abdu'l-Bahá*, no. 185, pp. 210-11.
63 ibid. no. 183, pp. 208–9.
64 Taherzadeh, *The Child of the Covenant*, p. 38.
65 'Abdu'l-Bahá, in *Star of the West*, Vol. VIII, no. 16, p. 219.
66 'Abdu'l-Bahá, ibid. no. 17, p. 222.
67 'Abdu'l-Bahá, *Tablets of the Divine Plan*, p. 51.
68 'Abdu'l-Bahá, quoted by Shoghi Effendi, *God Passes By*, p. 238.
69 ibid. p. 239.
70 ibid.
71 ibid.
72 Shoghi Effendi, *God Passes By*, p. 239.

2 Responses to the Covenant

1 'Abdu'l-Bahá, *Selections from the Writings of 'Abdu'l-Bahá*, no. 192, p. 228.
2 Bahá'u'lláh, *Prayers and Meditations*, LXI, p. 97.
3 Letter on behalf of Shoghi Effendi to an individual, 18 December 1945, in *The Compilation of Compilations*, vol. II, no. 1308.
4 The Báb, quoted by Shoghi Effendi, *The Advent of Divine Justice*, p. 39.
5 Taherzadeh, *The Covenant of Bahá'u'lláh*, p. 181.
6 ibid.
7 Taherzadeh, *The Revelation of Bahá'u'lláh*, vol. 1, p. 28.
8 Taherzadeh, *The Covenant of Bahá'u'lláh*, p. 181.
9 ibid. p. 182.
10 'Abdu'l-Bahá, *Memorials of the Faithful*, pp. 97–101.
11 ibid. p. 98.
12 Taherzadeh, *The Revelation of Bahá'u'lláh*, vol. 1, p. 27.
13 'Abdu'l-Bahá, *Memorials of the Faithful*, p. 100.
14 Bahá'u'lláh, *Gleanings*, XLV, pp. 99-100.
15 Bahá'u'lláh, *Prayers and Meditations*, VIII, pp. 10–11.
16 ibid. p. 11.
17 Shoghi Effendi, *God Passes By*, pp. 309–10.
18 ibid. pp. 292–3.
19 'Abdu'l-Bahá, in *Star of the West*, Vol. 13, no. 1, pp. 21-2.
20 White, *A Compendium of Volumes of the Bahá'í World*, p. 33.
21 Letter from the Universal House of Justice to the Iranian believers resident in other countries throughout the world, 10 February 1980, in *Crisis and Victory*, no. 69, p. 35.
22 Letter from the Universal House of Justice to the Bahá'ís of the World, 26 January 1982, ibid. no. 70, pp. 35–6.
23 Letter on behalf of Shoghi Effendi to an individual, 4 April 1930, ibid. no. 62, p. 33.

REFERENCES

24 'Abdu'l-Bahá, *Selections from the Writings of 'Abdu'l-Bahá*, no. 196, p. 238.
25 Letter on behalf of Shoghi Effendi to the Local Spiritual Assembly of Panama, 26 January 1950, in *The Compilation of Compilations*, vol. I, no. 323.
26 Bahá'u'lláh, *Gleanings*, XVII, pp. 42–3.
27 Bahá'u'lláh, *Bahá'í Prayers*, p. 211.
28 Letter from the Universal House of Justice to the Bahá'ís of the World, 2 January 1986, *Messages from the Universal House of Justice 1963–1986*, no. 447, p. 706.
29 The Universal House of Justice, in *Crisis and Victory*, p. 36.
30 Shoghi Effendi, *Bahá'í Administration*, , p. 164.
31 Shoghi Effendi, 'The Unfoldment of World Civilization', in *The World Order of Bahá'u'lláh*, pp. 195–6.
32 Bahá'u'lláh, Hidden Words, Persian no. 40.
33 Thompson, 'Abdu'l-Bahá, *The Center of the Covenant*, p. 9.
34 ibid.
35 ibid. p. 7.
36 Bahá'u'lláh, *Kitáb-i-Íqán*, p. 198.
37 ibid. pp. 198–9.
38 ibid. p. 199.
39 ibid. p. 200.
40 Taherzadeh, *The Revelation of Bahá'u'lláh.*, vol. 1, p. 109.
41 ibid. p. 110.
42 ibid, pp. 112–13.
43 Shoghi Effendi, *Bahá'í Administration*, pp. 60–61.
44 'Abdu'l-Bahá, quoted by Shoghi Effendi, 'The World Order of Bahá'u'lláh', in *The World Order of Bahá'u'lláh*, p. 17.
45 Shoghi Effendi, *The Advent of Divine Justice*, p. 15.
46 Bahá'u'lláh, quoted by the Universal House of Justice, in *The Bahá'í World*, vol. XVIII, pp. 10–11.

3 Opposition and the Capacity to Respond

1 Shoghi Effendi, 12 August 1941, in *Messages to America*, pp. 51-2.
2 Letter from the Universal House of Justice to all National Spiritual Assemblies, 26 November 1974, in *Messages from the Universal House of Justice 1963–1986*, no. 152, p. 285.
3 Shoghi Effendi, 'The World Order of Bahá'u'lláh: Further Considerations', in *The World Order of Bahá'u'lláh*, p. 17.
4 Shoghi Effendi, *The Advent of Divine Justice*, pp. 41–2.
5 Shoghi Effendi, 12 August 1941, in *Messages to America*, pp. 51–2.
6 ibid.
7 Bahá'u'lláh, *Gleanings*, XXIX, p. 72.
8 ibid.
9 ibid. CLXIII, p. 341.

10 Letter from the Universal House of Justice to all National Spiritual Assemblies, 26 November 1974, in *Messages from the Universal House of Justice 1963–1986*, no. 152, p. 285.
11 ibid. p. 284.
12 Message from the Universal House of Justice to the International Teaching Conference, Hong Kong, November 1976, ibid. no. 181, p. 346.
13 Letter from the Universal House of Justice to all National Spiritual Assemblies, 26 November 1974, ibid. no. 152, p. 285.
14 Shoghi Effendi, *God Passes By*, p. 410.
15 ibid. p. 412.
16 'Abdu'l-Bahá, in *The Power of the Covenant*, Part 3, p. 58.
17 Bahá'u'lláh, in *Bahá'í Prayers*, p. 210.
18 Shoghi Effendi, 12 August 1941, in *Messages to America*, p. 51.
19 ibid.
20 'Abdu'l-Bahá, in *Crisis and Victory*, p. 24.
21 Bahá'u'lláh, quoted by Shoghi Effendi, *The Advent of Divine Justice*, p. 82.
22 'Abdu'l-Bahá, in *The Power of the Covenant*, Part 3, p. 60.
23 ibid.
24 Shoghi Effendi, *The Advent of Divine Justice*, p. 35.
25 Bahá'u'lláh, *Gleanings*, XXIX, p. 72.
26 *The Power of the Covenant*, Part 3, pp. 53–5.
27 Letter from Shoghi Effendi to an individual, 30 August 1939, ibid. p. 62.
28 'Abdu'l-Bahá, *Selections from the Writings of 'Abdu'l-Bahá*, no. 12, p. 27.
29 ibid. no. 207, pp. 260–61.
30 Letter from the Universal House of Justice to an individual, 4 January 1979, in *The Compilation of Compilations*, vol. I, no. 230.
31 Shoghi Effendi, 12 August 1941, in *Messages to America*, p. 51.
32 ibid.
33 Letter from the Universal House of Justice to an individual, 23 March 1975, in *The Compilation of Compilations*, vol. I, p. 112.
34 ibid., in *The Power of the Covenant*, Part 2, p. 7.
35 'Abdu'l-Bahá, *Selections from the Writings of 'Abdu'l-Bahá*, no. 185, p. 210.
36 Letter on behalf of Shoghi Effendi, 29 July 1946, in *Lights of Guidance*, no. 602, p. 183.
37 ibid.
38 Letter on behalf of Shoghi Effendi, 30 November 1944, in *Lights of Guidance*, no. 604, p. 184; see also Shoghi Effendi, *Principles of Bahá'í Administration*, pp. 22–3.
39 Taherzadeh, *The Covenant of Bahá'u'lláh*, p. 337.
40 'Abdu'l-Bahá, *Will and Testament*, para. 48.
41 'Abdu'l-Bahá, in *Bahá'í World Faith*, pp. 357–8.
42 Letter from the Universal House of Justice to an individual, 23 March 1975, in *Developing Distinctive Baha'i Communities*, no page.

REFERENCES

43 'Abdu'l-Bahá, *Selections from the Writings of 'Abdu'l-Bahá*, no. 187, pp. 215–16.
44 'Abdu'l-Bahá, *Tablets of the Divine Plan*, p. 51.
45 Bahá'u'lláh, Hidden Words, Persian no. 57.
46 'Abdu'l-Bahá, in *Bahá'í World Faith*, p. 431.
47 ibid. p. 438.
48 ibid. p. 430.
49 Letter on behalf of Shoghi Effendi to an individual, 28 November 1944, in *Principles of Bahá'í Administration*, p. 22.
50 Letter on behalf of Shoghi Effendi to an individual, 19 March 1945, in *Developing Distinctive Bahá'í Communities*, no page.
51 Letter from the Universal House of Justice to the National Spiritual Assembly of Hong Kong, 30 March 1976, in *The Compilation of Compilations*, vol. I, no. 293.
52 Letter from the Universal House of Justice to the National Spiritual Assembly of Panama, 2 October 1975, in *Devoloping Distinctive Bahá'I Communities*, no page.
53 Letter on behalf of the Universal House of Justice to an individual, 9 April 2008, available at: http://www.bcca.org/bia/Responding%20to%20Criticism%20and%20Opposition%20on%20the%20%20%20%20%20%20Internet.pdf.
54 Letter on behalf of Shoghi Effendi to an individual, 28 November 1944, in *Principles of Bahá'í Administration*, p. 22.
55 Letter from the Universal House of Justice to a National Spiritual Assembly, 29 October 1974, in *Lights of Guidance*, no. 611, p. 186.
56 Letter on behalf of Shoghi Effendi to an individual, 15 April 1949, in *The Light of Divine Guidance*, vol. 2, p. 84; see also *The Compilation of Compilations*, vol. I, no. 353.
57 Letter from the Universal House of Justice to all National Spiritual Assemblies, 7 April 1999, in *Bahá'í Canada*, June 1999, regarding the compilation *Issues Related to the Study of the Baha'i Faith*.
58 ibid.
59 ibid.
60 ibid.
61 ibid.
62 Bahá'í International Community, *Inciting Hatred: The Baha'is of Semnan*, pp. 10–11.
63 ibid. p. 21.
64 ibid.
65 Bahá'u'lláh, quoted by Shoghi Effendi, *The Promised Day is Come*, p. 80.
66 Bahá'u'lláh, *Kitáb-i-Íqán*, para. 175, p. 164.
67 *The Power of the Covenant*, Part 3, p. 14.
68 ibid. p. 12.

69 Bahá'u'lláh, quoted by Shoghi Effendi, *The Promised Day is Come*, p. 83.
70 Shoghi Effendi, 'The World Order of Bahá'u'lláh: Further Considerations', in *The World Order of Bahá'u'lláh*, p. 18.
71 Shoghi Effendi, 'The Unfoldment of World Civilization', ibid. p. 180.
72 ibid. pp. 180–81.
73 'Abdu'l-Bahá, *The Will and Testament of 'Abdu'l-Bahá*, para. 3.
74 Bahá'u'lláh, *Gleanings*, CX, p. 215.
75 The Universal House of Justice, Second Message to World Congress, 26 November 1992, p. 4.
76 Shoghi Effendi, *The Advent of Divine Justice*, p. 82.
77 Letter from the Universal House of Justice to the International Teaching Centre, 10 October 1976, in *The Institution of the Counsellors*, p. 16; see also *The Compilation of Compilations*, vol. I, no. 355.

4 Persecution, Resilience and Heroism

1 Letter on behalf of Shoghi Effendi to an individual, 4 April 1930, in *Crisis and Victory*, no. 62, p. 33.
2 Letter on behalf of Shoghi Effendi to an individual, 5 November 1931, in *The Compilation of Compilations*, vol. II, no. 1274.
3 Rutter, 'Resilience in the Face of Adversity', p. 598.
4 Tillich, *Dynamics of Faith*, p. 2.
5 Ghadirian, 'Psychological and Spiritual Dimensions of Persecution and Suffering', p. 20. Original version published in *Bahá'í Studies Notebook*, vol. 3, no. 1/2 (1983), p. 60.
6 See Ghadirian, 'Psychological and Spiritual Dimensions of Persecution and Suffering'.
7 See Berger, 'Recovery and Regression in Concentration Camp Survivors'.
8 Ghadirian, 'Intergenerational Responses to the Persecution of the Bahá'ís of Iran', p. 524.
9 'Abdu'l-Bahá, *The Promulgation of Universal Peace*, p. 451.
10 Letter on behalf of Shoghi Effendi to an individual 22 November 1936, in *The Compilation of Compilations*, vol. II, no. 1282.
11 Shoghi Effendi, 23 December 1922, in *Bahá'í Administration*, p. 27.
12 Bahá'í International Community, *The Bahá'í Question: Cultural Cleansing in Iran*, p. 6.
13 Hakim-Samandari, 'A Victory over Violence', p. 9.
14 Ghadirian, 'Psychological and Spiritual Dimensions of Persecution and Suffering', pp. 14–17.
15 Letter from the Universal House of Justice to all National Spiritual Assemblies, 10 May 1984, in *Messages from the Universal House of Justice 1963-1986*, no. 395, p. 626.
16 Bahá'í International Community, *The Bahá'í Question: Iran's Secret Blueprint for the Destruction of a Religious Community*.
17 ibid. pp. 24–6.

REFERENCES

18 Bahá'u'lláh, *Prayers and Meditations*, XCIV, pp. 158-9.
19 Bahá'u'lláh, *The Seven Valleys*, pp. 8-9.
20 Taherzadeh, *The Revelation of Bahá'u'lláh*, vol. 4, pp. 302-3.
21 ibid. vol. 2, p. 94.
22 Khan and Khan, *Advancement of Women*, p. 218.
23 ibid. p. 213.
24 Shoghi Effendi, cable dated 30 October 1933, in *Messages to America*, p. 3.
25 *The Bahá'í World*, vol. V, p. 409; see also Harper, *Lights of Fortitude*, p. 109.
26 Ghadirian, 'Intergenerational Responses to the Persecution of the Bahá'ís of Iran'.
27 ibid. pp. 528-9.
28 Bahá'í International Community, *Inciting Hatred: Iran's Media Campaign to Demonize Bahá'ís*, p. 26.
29 Bahá'í International Community, *The Bahá'í Question: Cultural Cleansing in Iran*, p. 15.
30 Bahá'í International Community, *Inciting Hatred: Iran's Media Campaign to Demonize Bahá'ís*, p. 32.
31 Bahá'í International Community, *Inciting Hatred: The Baha'is of Semnan*, p. 12.
32 *Iran Press News*, 24 July 2012.
33 Human Rights Activists News Agency (HRANA), 'Two infants along with their mothers in grave danger in Semnan Prison, Iran', 7 December 2012; see also http://news.gooya.com/politics/archives/2013,4,158328.php.
34 ibid.
35 See http://www.commongroundgroup.net/2013/05/20/why-do-bahai-babies-go-to-prison-in-iran/.
36 ibid.
37 Bahá'u'lláh, in *Bahá'í Prayers*, p. 211.
38 Bahá'í International Community, *The Bahá'í Question: Cultural Cleansing in Iran*, p. 25.
39 ibid. p. 26.
40 ibid.
41 ibid. p. 24.
42 ibid. p. 28.
43 ibid.
44 ibid. pp. 25, 29.
45 Bahá'u'lláh, *The Seven Valleys*, p. 9.
46 Bahá'u'lláh, *Hidden Words*, Arabic no. 50.
47 Vahman, *160 Years of Persecution*, pp. 455-6.
48 Letter from the Universal House of Justice to the Baha'i students deprived of access to higher education in Iran, 9 September 2007, pp. 1-2.
49 ibid. p. 2.
50 Personal communication from Shakib Nasrullah, 27 November 2011.
51 Taherzadeh, *The Revelation of Bahá'u'lláh*, vol. 4, p. 63.

STEADFASTNESS IN THE COVENANT

52 ibid. pp. 58-9.
53 ibid. p. 64.
54 'Abdu'l-Bahá, 'Supplication', in *The Bahá'í World*, vol. XVIII, p. 290.
55 The Universal House of Justice, 'Message to the Iranian Believers Throughout the World, Bahá 154 B.E.' Translation from Persian, p. 1.
56 ibid. p. 2.
57 ibid. p. 3.
58 ibid.
59 ibid. pp. 4-5.
60 Bahá'u'lláh, *Gleanings*, CLI, p. 321.
61 Available at: http://www.akhbar-rooz.com/ article.jsp? essayId=16659.
62 The Universal House of Justice, 'Message To Believers Gathered for Terrace Events', 24 May 2001, p. 3.
63 Letter from the Universal House of Justice to the Bahá'ís of the World, 3 November 1980, in *Messages from the Universal House of Justice 1963–1986*, no. 267, p. 466.
64 Bahá'u'lláh, quoted by Shoghi Effendi, 'The Dispensation of Bahá'u'lláh', in *The World Order of Bahá'u'lláh*, p. 108.
65 Bahá'u'lláh, *Tablets of Bahá'u'lláh Revealed After the Kitáb-i-Aqdas*, pp. 246-7.
66 Bahá'u'lláh, in *Crisis and Victory*, pp. 22-3.

5 Steadfastness in the Covenant

1 'Abdu'l-Bahá, *Tablets of the Divine Plan*, p. 51.
2 ibid. pp. 51-2.
3 Bahá'u'lláh, *Gleanings*, CLIII, pp. 325-6.
4 'Abdu'l-Bahá, *Selections from the Writings of 'Abdu'l-Bahá*, no. 185, pp. 210-11.
5 ibid.
6 ibid.
7 Taherzadeh, *The Revelation of Bahá'u'lláh*, vol. 2, pp. 438-9.
8 ibid. p. 440.
9 ibid.
10 ibid. p. 442.
11 ibid. pp. 441-3.
12 Israfil is believed in Islam to be the angel appointed to sound the trumpet on the Day of Resurrection to raise the dead at the bidding of the Lord.
13 'Abdu'l-Bahá, *Selections from the Writings of 'Abdu'l-Bahá*, no. 8, p. 23.
14 *Bahíyyih Khánum: The Greatest Holy Leaf*, no. 40, p. 148.
15 ibid. no. 41, p. 148.
16 ibid. no. 48, p. 163.
17 ibid. pp.163-4.
18 ibid. no. 6, pp. 33-4.
19 ibid. pp. 35-6.

REFERENCES

20 ibid. no. 6, p. 10.
21 ibid. no. 49, p. 165–6.
22 ibid. p. 167.
23 Bahá'u'lláh, *Gleanings*, XVII, pp. 42–3.
24 Balyuzi, *Bahá'u'lláh: The King of Glory*, p. 96–7, based on Nabil-i-A'ẓam, *The Dawn-Breakers*.
25 Nabil-i-A'ẓam, *The Dawn-Breakers*, pp. 633–4.
26 Balyuzi, *Bahá'u'lláh: The King of Glory*, p. 97.
27 Thompson, ''Abdu'l-Bahá's First Days in America', pp. 34–5.
28 Ruhe-Schoen, *A Love Which Does Not Wait*, p. 4.
29 ibid. p. 11.
30 ibid. p. 16.
31 ibid.
32 ibid. p. 18.
33 Khan and Khan, *Advancement of Women*, p. 178.
34 Ruhe-Schoen, *A Love Which Does Not Wait*, p. 19.
35 ibid.
36 Metelmann, *Lua Getsinger, Herald of the Covenant*, , pp. 55–56.
37 Sears and Quigley, *The Flame*, p. 102.
38 ibid.
39 Ruhe-Schoen, *A Love Which Does Not Wait*, p. 30.
40 Sears and Quigley, *The Flame*, p. 130.
41 ibid. p. 134.
42 ibid. pp. 121–2.
43 Harper, *Lights of Fortitude*, pp. 139-40.
44 ibid., based on Faizi, *Milly*, p. 19.
45 *The Bahá'í World*, vol. XIII, pp. 834-41.
46 *The Bahá'í World*, vol. XIV, p. 313.
47 ibid. p. 314.
48 ibid. pp. 314–15.
49 ibid. p. 315.
50 Letter from the Universal House of Justice to all National Spiritual Assemblies, 27 October 1987, compilation distributed to Counsellors and Auxiliary Board members, 2004.

6 Scholarship and the Covenant

1 Bahá'u'lláh, quoted by Shoghi Effendi, 'The Dispensation of Bahá'u'lláh', in *The World Order of Bahá'u'lláh*, p. 109.
2 Bahá'u'lláh, Lawḥ-i-Dinyá, in *Tablets of Bahá'u'lláh Revealed after the Kitáb-i-Aqdas*, p. 96.
3 Lample, *Creating a New Mind*, p. 4.
4 The Universal House of Justice, Riḍván Message 2010, para. 29.
5 Shoghi Effendi, 'The Unfoldment of World Civilization' in *The World Order of Bahá'u'lláh*, p. 163.

6 Bahá'u'lláh, quoted by Shoghi Effendi, 'The Dispensation of Bahá'u'lláh', in *The World Order of Bahá'u'lláh*, p. 107.
7 Bahá'u'lláh, Súriy-i-Haykal, in *The Summons of the Lord of Hosts*, para. 66, p. 35.
8 'Abdu'l-Bahá, *Some Answered Questions*, no. 83, pp. 297–9.
9 ibid.
10 Khan, 'Some aspects of Bahá'í Scholarship', p. 46.
11 'Abdu'l-Bahá, in *Scholarship*, no. 60, pp. 29–30.
12 'Abdu'l-Bahá, *The Secret of Divine Civilization*, p. 34.
13 ibid. p. 35.
14 Bahá'u'lláh, *Kitáb-i-Aqdas*, para. 173, p. 82.
15 'Abdu'l-Bahá, *Selections from the Writings of 'Abdu'l-Bahá*, no. 72, p. 110.
16 ibid.
17 ibid.
18 Notes to the *Kitáb-i-Aqdas*, p. 250.
19 The Universal House of Justice, in *Scholarship*, no. 39, p. 18.
20 Bahá'u'lláh, Lawḥ-i-Burhán, in *Tablets of Bahá'u'lláh Revealed after the Kitáb-i-Aqdas*, p. 208.
21 Bahá'u'lláh, *Kitáb-i-Íqán*, para. 154, pp. 145–6.
22 'Abdu'l-Bahá, *The Secret of Divine Civilization*, p. 21.
23 ibid. p. 22.
24 Bahá'u'lláh, *Gleanings*, CLIV, p. 329.
25 'Abdu'l-Bahá, *The Secret of Divine Civilization*, p. 109.
26 Bahá'u'lláh, *Gleanings*, CLIV, p. 330.
27 The Universal House of Justice, in *Scholarship*, no. 64, p. 31.
28 Bahá'u'lláh, *Gleanings*, CXV, pp. 245–6.
29 Taherzadeh, *The Child of the Covenant*, p. 33.
30 Nakhjavani, *Asking Questions*, p. 41.
31 ibid. p. 42.
32 Letter from the Universal House of Justice to an individual, 27 May 1966, in *Messages from the Universal House of Justice 1963-1986*, no. 35, p. 87.
33 Bahá'u'lláh, *Kitáb-i-Íqán*, para. 237, p. 214.
34 ibid. para. 175, p. 164.
35 ibid. para 15, p. 15.
36 Bahá'u'lláh, quoted by Shoghi Effendi, *The Promised Day is Come*, p. 83.
37 Nakhjavani, *Asking Questions*, p. 26.
38 ibid. p. 28.
39 The Universal House of Justice, in *Issues Related to the Study of the Bahá'í Faith*, p. 20.
40 Letter on behalf of Shoghi Effendi to the Spiritual Assembly of Istanbul, quoted in *Messages from the Universal House of Justice 1963-1986*, no. 111, pp. 216-17.
41 The Universal House of Justice, *Issues Related to the Study of the Bahá'í Faith*, p. 36.

REFERENCES

42 Bahá'u'lláh, quoted in *Messages from the Universal House of Justice 1963-1986*, no. 206, p. 376.
43 Taherzadeh, *The Revelation of Bahá'u'lláh*, vol. 1, p. 325.
44 ibid.
45 ibid.
46 'Abdu'l-Bahá, *Memorials of the Faithful*, p. 200.
47 'Abdu'l-Bahá, *The Secret of Divine Civilization* pp. 33-4.
48 'Abdu'l-Bahá, in *Scholarship*, no. 60, p. 30.
49 'Abdu'l-Bahá, *The Secret of Divine Civilization*, p. 33.
50 ibid. p. 34.
51 Bahá'u'lláh, Lawḥ-i-Maqṣúd, in *Tablets of Bahá'u'lláh Revealed after the Kitáb-i-Aqdas*, p. 171.
52 'Abdu'l-Bahá, *The Secret of Divine Civilization*, pp. 23-4.
53 Letter from the Universal House of Justice to an individual, 23 March 1983, in *Scholarship*, no. 64, p. 32.
54 The Universal House of Justice, in *Scholarship*, no. 64, p. 31.
55 Research Department at the World Centre, 3 January 1979, in *Messages from the Universal House of Justice 1963-1986*, no. 217, pp. 390-91.
56 Taherzadeh, *The Covenant of Bahá'u'lláh*, p. 263.
57 Bahá'u'lláh, *Kitáb-i-Aqdas*, para. 41, p.34.
58 Bahá'u'lláh, *Epistle to the Son of the Wolf*, p. 83.
59 Bahá'u'lláh, *Gleanings*, V, p. 8.
60 The Universal House of Justice, in *Scholarship*, no. 61.
61 Letter from the Universal House of Justice, 10 June 1966, *Messages from the Universal House of Justice 1963-1986*, pp. 93-4.
62 Letter on behalf of Shoghi Effendi to the National Spiritual Assembly of India and Burma, 5 September 1936, in *Dawn of a New Day*, p. 61.
63 'Abdu'l-Bahá, *The Secret of Divine Civilization*, p. 34.
64 Bahá'u'lláh, *Epistle to the Son of the Wolf*, pp. 74-5.
65 'Abdu'l-Bahá, *The Secret of Divine Civilization*, p. 21.
66 Bahá'u'lláh, Lawḥ-i-Ḥikmat, in *Tablets of Bahá'u'lláh Revealed after the Kitáb-i-Aqdas*, p. 151.
67 Bahá'u'lláh, Tablet to an individual, in *The Compilation of Compilations*, vol. II, no. 2212.
68 Taherzadeh, *The Revelation of Bahá'u'lláh*, vol. 2, p. 44.
69 Amin Banani, Introduction to Mírzá Abu'l-Faḍl Gulpáygání, *Miracles and Metaphors*, p. ix.
70 ibid. p. xviii.
71 ibid. p. ix.
72 ibid. p. ix.
73 'Abdu'l-Bahá, in *Scholarship*, no. 30, pp.14-15.
74 Amin Banani, Introduction to Mírzá Abu'l-Faḍl Gulpáygání, *Miracles and Metaphors* p. xix.
75 Quoted in Taherzadeh, *The Revelation of Bahá'u'lláh*, vol. 2, p. 45.

76 ibid.
77 Mírzá Abu'l-Faḍl Gulpáygání, *Letters and Essays*, p. xv.
78 Harper, *Lights of Fortitude*, p. 372.
79 ibid. p. 378.
80 ibid.
81 ibid. p. 370.
82 ibid. p. 379; see also the memorial article in *The Bahá'í World*, vol. XVIII, pp. 635–51.

7 Tests of the Covenant among Scholars and Teachers of the Faith

1 Baha'u'llah, *Gleanings*, CXV, pp. 245–6.
2 Taherzadeh, *The Child of the Covenant*, p. 189.
3 Balyuzi, *'Abdu'l-Bahá*, p. 220.
4 Shoghi Effendi, *Citadel of Faith*, p. 34.
5 Shoghi Effendi, *The Advent of Divine Justice*, pp. 41–2.
6 'Abdu'l-Bahá, quoted in Balyuzi, *'Abdu'l-Bahá*, pp. 220–21.
7 The Universal House of Justice, in *Scholarship*, p. 31.
8 'Abdu'l-Bahá, *Selections from the Writings of 'Abdu'l-Bahá*, no. 155, p. 182.
9 'Abdu'l-Bahá, in *Psychology and Knowledge of Self*, no. 20.
10 Bahá'u'lláh, Kalimát-i-Firdawsíyyih, in *Tablets of Bahá'u'lláh Revealed after the Kitáb-i-Aqdas*, p. 70.
11 'Abdu'l-Bahá, *Will and Testament*, para. 21.
12 Letter on behalf of Shoghi Effendi to an individual, 8 January 1949, in *Unfolding Destiny*, p. 454.
13 Letter on behalf of Shoghi Effendi to an individual, 10 December 1947, in *The Compilation of Compilations*, vol. II, no. 1318.
14 Freud, *Civilization and its Discontents*, pp. 25, 28.
15 'Abdu'l-Bahá, *Paris Talks*, no. 34, p. 108.
16 The Universal House of Justice, *Individual Rights and Freedoms*, p.11.
17 Letter on behalf of Shoghi Effendi to an individual, 18 February 1954, in *Lights of Guidance*, no. 391.
18 The Ruhi Foundation, *Reflections on the Life of the Spirit*, p. 27.
19 Bahá'u'lláh, *Hidden Words*, Arabic no. 59.
20 Bahá'u'lláh, *Kitáb-i-Íqán*, para. 77, p. 70.
21 ibid. para. 48, p. 46.
22 Bahá'u'lláh, *Hidden Words*, Arabic no. 59.
23 'Abdu'l-Bahá, *The Secret of Divine Civilization*, p. 116.
24 ibid.
25 ibid. pp. 96–7.
26 See Taherzadeh, *The Revelation of Bahá'u'lláh*, vol. 2, p. 217.
27 ibid. pp. 264-7, 272-3.
28 'Abdu'l-Bahá, *Tablets of Abdul-Baha Abbas*, p. 460; also in *Bahá'í World Faith*, p. 384.

REFERENCES

29 Bahá'u'lláh, Lawḥ-i-Ḥikmat, in *Tablets of Bahá'u'lláh Revealed after the Kitáb-i-Aqdas*, p. 143.
30 Bahá'u'lláh, Lawḥ-i-Siyyid-i-Mihdíy-i-Dahají, ibid. pp. 198–9.
31 Bahá'u'lláh, Lawḥ-i-Ḥikmat, ibid. p. 143.
32 Bahá'u'lláh, Lawḥ-i-Siyyid-i-Mihdíy-i-Dahají, ibid. p. 199.
33 Taherzadeh, *The Revelation of Bahá'u'lláh*, vol. 2, p. 274.
34 Bahá'u'lláh, Lawḥ-i-Siyyid-i-Mihdíy-i-Dahají, in *Tablets of Bahá'u'lláh Revealed after the Kitáb-i-Aqdas*, p. 200.
35 ibid. p. 196.
36 Taherzadeh, *The Revelation of Bahá'u'lláh*, vol. 2, p. 273.
37 Bahá'u'lláh, quoted in a letter from the Universal House of Justice to all National Spiritual Assemblies, in *Messages from the Universal House of Justice 1963–1986*, no. 206, p. 376.
38 Letter on behalf of Shoghi Effendi to an individual, 8 January 1949, in *Unfolding Destiny*, p. 454.
39 ibid. p. 453.
40 Letter on behalf of Shoghi Effendi to an individual, 14 December 1941, in *The Compilation of Compilations*, vol. II, no. 1295.
41 Bahá'u'lláh, *Hidden Words*, Persian no. 6.
42 Bahá'u'lláh, *Gleanings*, CV, p. 211.
43 'Abdu'l-Bahá, *Tablets of Abdul-Baha Abbas*, p. 136.
44 Bahá'u'lláh, Aṣl-i-Kullu'l-Khayr (Words of Wisdom), in *Tablets of Bahá'u'lláh, Revealed after the Kitáb-i-Aqdas*, p. 156.
45 Bahá'u'lláh, *Gleanings*, CXXV, p. 265.
46 'Abdu'l-Bahá, *Selections from the Writings of 'Abdu'l-Bahá*, no. 15, p. 30.
47 Taherzadeh, *The Covenant of Bahá'u'lláh*, p. 167.
48 Bahá'u'lláh, Kalimát-i-Firdawsíyyih, in *Tablets of Bahá'u'lláh Revealed after the Kitáb-i-Aqdas*, p. 64.
49 Bahá'u'lláh, *Gleanings*, LXXXII, p. 159.
50 ibid. V, pp. 7–8.
51 Letter from the International Teaching Centre, 9 August 1984, in *Bahá'í Canada*, vol. 9, no. 5 (July 1987), quoting Bahá'u'lláh, *Prayers and Meditations*, no. CLXXXIV.
52 Letter from the Universal House of Justice to an individual, 19 October 1993, in *Issues Related to the Study of the Bahá'í Faith*, p. 14.
53 ibid. pp. 14–15.
54 ibid. p. 15.
55 ibid.
56 ibid. p. 16.
57 ibid. p. 17.
58 The Universal House of Justice, *Individual Rights and Freedoms in the World Order of Bahá'u'lláh*, p. 12.
59 'Abdu'l-Bahá, quoted in a letter from the Universal House of Justice, 8 February 1998, in *Issues Related to the Study of the Bahá'í Faith*, p. 41.

60 ibid. p. 43.
61 ibid.
62 Bahá'u'lláh, *Gleanings*, CLIX. p. 336.
63 'Abdu'l-Bahá, Tablet to the Hague, *Selections from the Writings of 'Abdu'l-Bahá*, no. 227, p. 303.
64 ibid. p. 305.
65 Letter from the Universal House of Justice to an individual, 27 May 1966, in *Messages from the Universal House of Justice 1963–1986*, no. 35, p. 88.
66 The Universal House of Justice, in *Issues Related to the Study of the Bahá'í Faith*, p. 31.
67 ibid.
68 'Abdu'l-Bahá, *Will and Testament*, para. 17.
69 Letter from the Universal House of Justice to an individual, 12 June 1984, in *Messages from the Universal House of Justice 1963–1986*, no. 397, p. 629.
70 Letter on behalf of Shoghi Effendi to an individual, 8 December 1935, ibid.
71 'Abdu'l-Bahá, *Some Answered Questions*, no. 3, p. 8.
72 ibid. p. 9.
73 'Abdu'l-Bahá, *The Promulgation of Universal Peace*, p. 363.
74 ibid. p. 12.
75 Abdu'l-Baha, *Selections from the Writings of 'Abdu'l-Bahá*, no. 23, pp. 52–3.
76 Letter on behalf of Shoghi Effendi to an individual, 8 December 1935, quoted in *Messages from the Universal House of Justice 1963–1986*, no. 397, p. 629.
77 ibid. p. 630.
78 'Abdu'l-Bahá, *Selections from the Writings of 'Abdu'l-Bahá*, no. 97, p. 126.
79 'Abdu'l-Bahá, *The Promulgation of Universal Peace*, p. 455.
80 Bahá'u'lláh, *Kitáb-i-Íqán*, para. 233, p. 211.
81 ibid. p. 46.
82 Bahá'u'lláh, Súriy-i-Mulúk, in *The Summons of the Lord of Hosts*, para. 114, p. 234.
83 Bahá'u'lláh, *The Kitáb-i-Aqdas*, para. 1, p. 19.
84 ibid.
85 'Abdu'l-Bahá, in *The Compilation of Compilations*, vol. I, no. 251.
86 The Universal House of Justice, in *Issues Related to the Study of the Bahá'í Faith*, p. 3.
87 ibid. p. 33.
88 ibid. pp. 37–9.
89 Bahá'u'lláh, *Gleanings*, LXXXII, pp. 158–9.
90 ibid. LXXXIII, p. 165.
91 Bahá'u'lláh, Kitáb-i-Íqán, para. 270, p. 240.

REFERENCES

8 The Covenant: The Individual, the Community and the Institutions

1. The Universal House of Justice, Message to the Baháʼís of the World, Riḍván 153, 1996.
2. Poirier, bahai-covenant.blogspot.com/2010/12/covenant-protects-from-schism.html.
3. ʻAbduʼl-Baha, Tablet quoted in *Star of the West*, vol.VIII, no. 16, p. 218.
4. Letter from Shoghi Effendi to the National Spiritual Assembly of Germany, 28 June 1950, in *The Light of Divine Guidance*, vol. 1, p. 162.
5. Letter on behalf of Shoghi Effendi to Dr Hermann Grossmann, 11 April 1949, ibid. vol. 2, pp. 83-4.
6. The Universal House of Justice, Message to the Conference of the Continental Boards of Counsellors, 28 December 2010.
7. Letter from the Universal House of Justice to the National Spiritual Assembly of the United States, 7 September 1965, in *Developing Distinctive Baháʼí Communities*, section 15.32.
8. Shoghi Effendi, *The Promised Day Is Come*, p. 16.
9. Shoghi Effendi, ʻThe Unfoldment of World Civilizationʼ, in *The World Order of Baháʼuʼlláh*, p. 187.
10. The Universal House of Justice, Message to the Conference of the Continental Boards of Counsellors, 28 December 2010.
11. ibid.
12. ibid.
13. ibid.
14. ibid.
15. Shoghi Effendi, *The Advent of Divine Justice*, p. 30.
16. Letter on behalf of Shoghi Effendi to an individual, 28 September 1941, quoted in a letter from the Universal House of Justice to all National Spiritual Assemblies, 6 February 1973, in *Messages from the Universal House of Justice, 1963-1986*, no. 126, p. 233.
17. Letter from Shoghi Effendi to the Spiritual Assembly of Teheran, 20 October 1924, in *The Compilation of Compilations*, vol. I, no. 122.
18. ʻAbduʼl-Bahá, *The Promulgation of Universal Peace*, p. 453.
19. ʻAbduʼl-Bahá, *Selections from the Writings of ʻAbduʼl-Bahá*, no. 35, p. 71.
20. Baháʼuʼlláh, *Gleanings*, CXXXI, p. 287.
21. Shoghi Effendi, *The Advent of Divine Justice*, p. 41.
22. ʻAbduʼl-Bahá, *The Secret of Divine Civilization*, p. 60.
23. Letter from the International Teaching Centre, 9 August 1984, on Baháʼí Scholarship, in *Baháʼí Canada*, vol. 9, no. 5 (July 1987).
24. Letter from Shoghi Effendi to an individual, 21 October 1943, in *Scholarship*, no. 13, p. 5.
25. Memorandum from the Universal House of Justice to the International Teaching Centre, 10 February 1981, ibid. no. 77, p. 28.
26. Letter from the Universal House of Justice to an individual, 19 October 1993, ibid. no. 50, p. 17.

27 Letter from the Universal House of Justice, 3 June 1997, in *Issues Related to the Study of the Bahá'í Faith*, no. 8.
28 ibid.
29 Letter from the Universal House of Justice, 19 May 1995, ibid. no. 5.
30 Letter from the Universal House of Justice, 14 March 1996, ibid. no. 6.
31 ibid., referring to the Will and Testament of 'Abdu'l-Bahá, para. 21.
32 Letter from the Universal House of Justice, 5 October 1993, ibid. no.2.
33 Letter from the Universal House of Justice, 20 July 1997, ibid. no. 9.
34 Document prepared at the Bahá'í World Centre, in Lample, *Revelation and Social Reality*, p. 128.
35 Letter from the Universal House of Justice, 2 July 1996, in *Issues Related to the Study of the Bahá'í Faith*, no. 7.
36 The Universal House of Justice, in *Scholarship*, no.14, p. 6.
37 ibid. no. 64, p. 31.
38 ibid. no. 63, p. 31.
39 Shoghi Effendi, quoted in *Rights and Responsibilities: The Complementary Roles of the Individual and Institutions*, p. 8.
40 Bahá'u'lláh, *Gleanings*, CLXIV, pp. 342-3.
41 Bahá'u'lláh, *The Kitáb-i-Aqdas*, para. 149, pp. 73-74.
42 Letter on behalf of Shoghi Effendi to an individual, 5 July 1949, in *Scholarship*, no. 34, p. 16.
43 Bahá'u'lláh, *Gleanings*, CVI, p. 213.
44 Letter from the Universal House of Justice to an individual, 19 January 1983, in *The Compilation of Compilations*, vol. II, no. 1636.
45 Peter J. Khan, 'Relating the Faith to Current Issues', undated talk, unpublished.
46 ibid, quoting a letter on behalf of Shoghi Effendi to an individual, 2 March 1934, in *Lights of Guidance*, p. 451.
47 Bahá'u'lláh, *Gleanings*, XIV, p. 34.
48 'Abdu'l-Bahá, *Tablets of the Divine Plan*, p. 49.
49 ibid. pp. 50-51.
50 Bahá'u'lláh, in *Ḥuqúqu'lláh*, no. 2.
51 ibid. no. 51.
52 ibid. no. 27.
53 Nabíl-i-A'ẓam, *The Dawn-Breakers*, p. 329.
54 The Báb, *Selections from the Writings of the Báb*, pp. 77-8.
55 'Abdu'l-Bahá, in *Bahá'í Prayers*, p. 58.
56 Shoghi Effendi, 28 July 1954, in *Citadel of Faith*, p. 125.
57 See Ghadirian, *Materialism: Moral and Social Consequences*, p. 93.
58 'Abdu'l-Bahá, *Selections from the Writings of 'Abdu'l-Bahá*, no. 227, p. 302.
59 Shoghi Effendi, 28 July 1954, in *Citadel of Faith*, p.125.
60 Shoghi Effendi, *The Promised Day is Come*, p. 114.
61 The Universal House of Justice, Message to the Bahá'ís of Iran, 2 March 2013.

REFERENCES

62 Shoghi Effendi, *Bahá'í Administration*, p. 50.
63 Shoghi Effendi, 19 July 1956, in *Citadel of Faith*, p. 149.
64 See Wilson, *On Human Nature*, Ch. 1.
65 See Ghadirian, *Materialism: Moral and Social Consequences*, pp. 128-32.
66 See Beauregard and O'Leary, *The Spiritual Brain: A Neuroscientist's Case for the Existence of the Soul*.
67 Bahá'u'lláh, *Gleanings*, XXI, p. 49.
68 ibid.
69 Letter on behalf of Shoghi Effendi to the National Youth Committee of the Bahá'ís of Germany and Austria, 20 October 1949, in *The Light of Divine Guidance*, vol. 2, p. 89.
70 Letter on behalf of Shoghi Effendi 17 March 1937, in *The Light of Divine Guidance*, vol. 1, pp. 87-8.
71 Letter from the Universal House of Justice to the National Spiritual Assembly of the Bahá'ís of Norway, 1 September 1983, in Messages from the Universal House of Justice, 1963-1986, no. 375, p. 589.
72 Letter from the Universal House of Justice to the National Spiritual Assembly of Canada, 24 July 2013 (unpublished).
73 The Universal House of Justice, Message to the Youth Congress in Paraguay, 8 January 2000, in *To Champion the Cause of Justice*, pp. 6-7.

9 'Abdu'l-Bahá: Centre of the Covenant and Perfect Exemplar

1 Shoghi Effendi, 'The Dispensation of Bahá'u'lláh' in *The World Order of Bahá'u'lláh*, p. 134.
2 ibid. p. 135.
3 Bahá'u'lláh, quoted by Shoghi Effendi, *God Passes By*, p. 243.
4 Afroukhteh, *Memories of Nine Years in 'Akká*, p. 245.
5 Shoghi Effendi, 'The Dispensation of Bahá'u'lláh', in *The World Order of Bahá'u'lláh*, p. 133.
6 Ferraby, *All Things Made New*, p. 225; see also Afroukhteh, *Memories of Nine Years in 'Akká*.
7 Shoghi Effendi, 'The Dispensation of Bahá'u'lláh', in *The World Order of Bahá'u'lláh*, p. 136.
8 ibid. p. 138.
9 ibid.
10 ibid. p. 139.
11 Taherzadeh, *The Covenant of Bahá'u'lláh*, pp. 102-3.
12 ibid.
13 ibid.
14 ibid. p. 135.
15 ibid.
16 ibid. p. 102.
17 Thompson, *'Abdu'l-Bahá*, p. 9.
18 Taherzadeh, *The Covenant of Bahá'u'lláh*, p. 136.

STEADFASTNESS IN THE COVENANT

19 Balyuzi, *'Abdu'l-Bahá*, p. 6.
20 Shoghi Effendi, *God Passes By*, p. 242.
21 Balyuzi, *'Abdu'l-Bahá*, p. 374.
22 Ward, *239 Days: 'Abdu'l-Bahá's Journey in America*, p. 190.
23 Esslemont, *Bahá'u'lláh and the New Era*, p. 63.
24 Honnold, *Vignettes from the Life of 'Abdu'l-Bahá*, pp. 16–17.
25 Thompson, *'Abdul-Bahá*, p. 10.
26 Taherzadeh, *The Child of the Covenant*, p. 88.
27 Thompson, *'Abdul-Bahá*, p. 10.
28 Blomfield, *The Chosen Highway*, pp. 100–101, 103.
29 Faizi, *Stories About 'Abdu'l-Bahá*, p. 3.
30 ibid.
31 Abdu'l-Baha, *The Promulgation of Universal Peace*, p. 470.

10 'Be Thou Assured'

1 Letter from Shoghi Effendi to the National Spiritual Assembly of Persia, August 1927, in *Crisis and Victory*, no. 84, p. 45.
2 *Be Thou Assured: A Compilation from the Bahá'í Writings prepared by the Continental Board of Counsellors in the Americas*. National Spiritual Assembly of the Bahá'ís of Canada, White Mountain Publications, 1996.
3 'Abdu'l-Bahá, *Tablets of Abdul-Baha Abbas*, vol. 1, pp. 8–9.
4 Bahá'u'lláh, Aṣl-i-Kullu'l-<u>Kh</u>ayr, in *Tablets of Bahá'u'lláh Revealed after the Kitáb-i-Aqdas*, p. 156.
5 Bahá'u'lláh, *Gleanings*, LXII, p. 120.
6 'Abdu'l-Bahá, *Paris Talks*, no. 52, p. 177.
7 'Abdu'l-Bahá, *Selections from the Writings of 'Abdu'l-Bahá*, no. 184, pp. 209–10.
8 Letter on behalf of Shoghi Effendi to an individual, 8 May 1942, in *Messages of Shoghi Effendi to the Indian Subcontinent 1923–1957*, p. 217.
9 Letter on behalf of Shoghi, Effendi to an individual, 3 February 1937, in *Unfolding Destiny*, p. 436.
10 Letter on behalf of Shoghi Effendi to an individual, 11 August 1957, in *The Compilation of Compilations*, vol. II, no. 1721.
11 The Universal House of Justice, Message to the Bahá'ís of the World, Riḍván 1986, in *Messages from the Universal House of Justice 1963–1986*, no. 456, p. 726.
12 'Abdu'l-Bahá, *Selections from the Writings of 'Abdu'l-Bahá*, no. 17, p. 37.
13 ibid. no. 62, p. 193.
14 Letter from the Universal House of Justice to the followers of the Bahá'u'lláh in the Cradle of the Faith, 25 December 2007 (unpublished).
15 Letter from the Universal House of Justice to the believers in the Cradle of the Faith, 28 July 2008 (unpublished).
16 'Abdu'l-Bahá, *Selections from the Writings of 'Abdu'l-Bahá*, no. 190, pp. 224–5.

Index

'Abdu'l-Bahá (Master) 184-92
   and Bahá'u'lláh 184-8
   'Ambassador to Humanity' 188
   appellations and titles 184-5, 187-8, 190
   ascension of 26, 54, 98
   Centre of the Covenant 2-4, 9, 11, 117, 134, 160
   Covenant of xiv, 9-10, 160, 181
   Master xvi, 21
   Most Mighty Branch (Ghuṣn-i-A'zam) 3, 11
   Mystery of God 29, 184
   in North America 102, 133-4
   Perfect Exemplar 184-92
   servitude of 134, 185-92
   statements on Covenant xiii, xiv, 2, 9, 19, 20, 56, 93-4, 134, 154, 160, 194
       see also Covenant-breaking
   suffering of 14, 24-9, 35, 54
   and Tablet of the Branch, 134, 184-5
   and Universal House of Justice 14-15
   Will and Testament of 10-15, 19, 106
   Writings of 150
'Abdu'l-Ḥamid (Sultan) 14
'Abdu'l-Váhhab, Mírzá 101-2
Abhá Beauty 10, 11, 13, 15, 100, 151, 186
Abhá Kingdom, Realm 7, 19, 28, 97
abrogation 16, 117
abstinence 164
Abu'l-Faḍl Gulgáygání (Father of Excellence) 103, 123, 128-31
Abu'l-Qásim, Ḥájí Mírzá 132
academic
   community 116-17, 120, 123-5, 135, 178

methodology 156-7
studies 83, 116-17, 120, 123-4, 126, 135, 146-8, 166-73, 183
Ádhirbáyján 27
Administrative Order 5-6, 13-14, 46, 64, 134, 160-61, 167, 181
administrators 54, 82, 167, 174
Adrianople 5, 23, 96, 134, 141
advancement 31, 47, 116, 124, 132, 148
Advent of Divine Justice, The 64-5, 162, 177
adversity 33, 43, 46, 49, 51, 53, 64, 66, 68-70, 84-6, 99
affiliation, political 62
affiliation, religious 68, 83
affliction 25, 28-9, 31, 99, 11, 113, 171
Afnán (s) 3, 12, 13, 14, 131
Afnán, Mullá Ḥájí Mírzá Taqí 14
Africa 14, 38, 177
Afroukhteh, Dr Youess (Yúnis Khán) 185
agitation 18, 31, 46, 50, 94
aggression 40, 46, 49, 50, 100
Aghsán 3, 13
agriculture 189
'Akká 22, 24, 27, 130, 141, 188-91
alcohol 164
alienation 179-8
'Alí-Muḥammad, Mírzá (Varqá) 87-8
ambition 55, 63, 144
America(s) x, 9, 26-8, 35, 38, 75-6, 102, 125, 137, 163, 177
   Baháʼí community in 103, 130, 133-4, 165, 174, 192
   see also United States
American University (Beirut) 131
amnesia 68

225

Ámul 27
analogy 137, 144-5, 186, *see also* metaphor
angel(s) xiv, 20, 37, 95, 174
animosity 28, 178
antagonism 30, 46, 51, 149
anti-Baháʾí propaganda, rhetoric 62, 77, 79
apathy 178
apostle(s) 15
Apostle of Baháʾuʾlláh 24, 87
Apostolic (Heroic) Age 13, 43, 87, 181
appeal 29, 34, 42, 163
application of Baháʾí teachings and principles x, 6, 16, 114, 116, 135, 157, 168-9, 171-2
Áqá Ján, Mírzá 22-4, 140
arising 12, 26, 38, 46-7, 53, 56, 63, 100, 116, 141, 156, 194
Ark of Salvation 19
armaments 33
Army of Light 65
arrest 44, 63, 78-9, 82, 85-8, 96, 101
arrogance 43-4, 114, 125-7, 135
arson 63, 79
Asia, Asians 23-4, 177
assassination 96, 103
assault(s) 19, 42, 45, 49, 51, 70, 73, 159
of selfish desire 117, 133, 176
Association for Baháʾí Studies x, 147, 183
atheism, atheistic 64, 173, 179, 180
atoms of dust 145
atrocities 33, 48, 54, 74, 81
attack(s) xiii, 10, 20, 26, 28, 32-4, 40-41, 44-6, 51-5, 61-5, 73-4, 78, 94-5, 116-17, 124, 129, 153, 160, 163, 176, 179
attitude(s) 4, 46-9, 55, 56, 67-70, 90, 99, 107, 112, 118, 123-32, 142, 144, 145, 156, 161, 166, 170, 187
attributes 70, 112-15, 123-8, 145, 152
Australia 7
authenticity 16, 88, 149
authoritative interpretation of Sacred Text 6, 15-18, 61-2, 117-19, 149-51, 168
authority, authorities 3-4, 6, 16, 42, 54, 61-2, 117-18, 70, 72, 85, 96, 120, 144, 151-2, 155, 189
civil 6-7, 62
Auxiliary Board 51, 57, 65

Azal (Mírzá Yahyá) 24
Azízuʾlláh (Varqá) 87
Báb, the 4-5, 11, 22, 26, 27, 104, 118, 132, 174-5, 185
ascension of 54
Declaration of 3
Dispensation of 4, 6, 10, 122
Herald 4, 33
Qáʾim 121
sacrifice, suffering of 29, 84
Bábís 62, 95, 101, 118, 134
Badíʿ, father of 175
Baghdad 22, 27, 35, 141, 157, 187
Baháʾí(s) xiii, xvi, 3, 10, 19, 21, 30, 38-9, 41-2, 56-7, 145, 160-61, 167, 176, 185
academics and scholars x, 103, 110-17, 119-32, 135, 137-8, 143, 146-58 *passim*, 166-72, 180
attitude to opposition 49-53, 70, 109
cycle 6-7
community xvi, 7, 18-19, 40, 51-3, 110, 114-15, 159-74
demonization of 78-9
Dispensation 3, 6, 110, 119
Faith ix, 3, 6, 38, 40-46, 63
in Iran ix, xiv, 31, 33-4, 44, 62-3, 70-74, 76-91, 103, 141, 177, 181
institutions 46, 51-2, 114-15, 161, 167-8
life x, 1, 162-5
people of Bahá 11, 30, 65
state 6-7
teachers 88, 140-44, 171-2
in the West xiv, 26, 31, 46, 64, 103, 133-4, 165, 174, 177
Writings ix-x, xiv, 14-18, 47, 58-61, 69-70, 74, 92, 110, 115-17, 137-8, 180, 193-6
youth ix-x, xiv, 34, 82-7, 126, 165, 177-83
Baháʾí Institute of Higher Education (BIHE), 82, 86
Baháʾí International Community 77, 82
Baháʾí Proofs, The 129
Bahjí 187, 188, 191
Baháʾuʾlláh 3-4
and ʿAbduʾl-Bahá 184-8
arrest and imprisonment of 101-2

INDEX

ascension of 3, 54, 87, 150
blood of 25-6
Covenant of 1-4, 7-12, 64, 117, 129, 159 *see also* Covenant
Dispensation of 4-7, 13, 110, 119, 154
King of Glory 33
Revelation of ix-x, xvi, 2, 4-5, 17, 22, 48, 101, 110-12, 126, 156-8, 193
suffering of 20-21, 24-6, 29, 32, 47, 52, 54, 81, 84
Will and Testament of (Kitáb-i-'Ahdí) 3, 10-11
World Order of xiii, 11, 14, 16, 33 40, 43, 91, 158, 169, 173
Bahíyyih Khánum (Greatest Holy Leaf) 29, 97-101, 187
Balyuzi, Hasan 131-2
Banani, Amin 130
Bárfurúsh 76
bastinado 27
Bayán 4-5, 22
Be Thou Assured x, 193
benevolence 49, 126
betrayal 21, 54, 180
bewilderment 90
Bible 129
Bihjatu's-Sudur (Delight of the Hearts) 97
bird(s) 12, 26, 28, 89, 108, 115, 148
Birds of Heaven 154
Blessed Beauty, Perfection *see* Bahá'u'lláh
Blessed Tree 19
blessing 8, 17, 22-3, 43, 49, 53, 94, 98, 145, 152, 195
in disguise xiv, 30, 33-4, 40, 50, 65, 70, 77
blood relationship 57
bloodshed 5, 13, 30, 74-5, 77, 83, 85, 92, 103
Book of Certitude 35, 95, 115
brain 135, 138, 178-9
Britain, British government 131-2, 189
bullets 27, 72
burial of dead 44, 73, 90
Burning Bush 35
Bustan (Orchard) 125

Cairo 105, 129
calamity xiii, 25, 31, 33-4, 47, 77, 89, 98-9, 113
Canada x, 7, 75, 107-8, 182

cancer(ous) 57-8, 60
materialism 177
capacity ix, 5, 22, 48, 69, 89, 112, 113, 124, 126, 161, 166, 169, 183, 194
to endure xvi, 162
to love 69, 128
to respond to challenge 47
caprice of children 50
Cause of God 2, 10, 12-13, 19, 30, 38, 44, 56, 61, 63, 70, 74, 93, 116-17, 151, 156, 182, 195
cell(s), human 19, 138, 179
cell, prison 72, 86-7, 102
censorship 166
Central Figures ix, 26, 46, 51, 54, 62
Centre of the Covenant *see* 'Abdu'l-Bahá
certitude xv, 34-5, 44, 49, 63, 68, 90, 99, 127, 196
character, human x, 39, 67, 99, 113, 122-6, 129-30, 131, 137, 153, 158, 162, 167-8, 174
Charters 11
chaste and holy life 162-4
children 34, 49-50, 62, 72-3, 76, 80-81, 82, 87-8, 90, 100, 128, 187
China 38
Christ (Jesus) 7, 35, 87, 159
Christianity, Christian clergy 6, 64, 120
City of Certitude 35-6, 44
City of the Covenant (New York) 134
civil authorities 6-7, 62-3
civilization xiii, 4, 11, 47, 51, 53, 110-11, 113, 128, 152, 159, 165, 170, 176-7
divine 7, 176-7
dying 41
spiritual 153
civil rights 34, 60-61
clean-mindedness 164
clergy, divines 5, 15, 20, 31, 34, 42-4, 62-4, 74, 77, 117-20, 125, 149
Collins, Amelia (Milly) 106-7
Columbus, second 133
companionate marriage 164
Company on high 97
compassion 24, 77, 138, 179, 191
competition x, 125, 142
competitive superiority x, 135
concentration camp 34, 69
conscience 41, 73, 118, 138, 148, 156, 162, 174

227

constancy 8, 34, 49, 90, 94, 98, 136, 143, 182, 195
Constantine, Emperor 6
Constantinople (Istanbul) 141
Consul General (Persia) 96
consultation xv-xvi, 51, 151, 161, 174
consumerism 142, 173, 176-7
contempt 72, 92
contentment 67, 68, 174
contest(s), critical, dire 41-2, 44-5, 65
Continental Board of Counsellors x, 61, 161-2, 166-7
corruption 41, 50, 62, 136, 142, 164, 176
courage 44, 53, 67, 68, 70, 74, 81, 85, 87-8, 90, 97, 101, 127, 183, 193
Covenant ix-x, xiii-xiv, 1-4, 7-19, 20, 38, 64, 156, 159-62
   and detachment 174
   firmness, steadfastness in xiv, 1-3, 18-19, 44, 49-50, 51, 56-7, 81, 83-7, 93-109, 111, 112, 134, 154, 159-62, 181, 194
   of 'Abdu'l-Bahá xiv, 9-10, 134, 160, 181
   of Bahá'u'lláh 1-4, 7-12, 117, 129, 159
   Greater 8
   Lesser 8, 9
   metaphors for 18-19
   obedience to 176, 181
   opposition to 40, 60-61
   power of xiii, xvi, 1-2, 7, 18-19, 44, 56, 93, 155, 181
   and scholarship 112-20, 133, 135-7, 154, 156, 166
   and unity 159-62
   and youth 181
Covenant-breaker,-breaking 18, 20, 23, 24, 28-9, 54-61, 94-5, 98, 103, 133, 140-42, 144, 154, 186
   civil rights of 60-61
   contagious spiritual disease 55, 59
   shun, admonition to 56-9, 160
covetousness 175
cradle of the Administrative Order (North America) 134
Cradle of the Faith (Iran) 7, 30-31, 62, 89, 90, 103
Creative Word 34, 47, 69, 110
Crimson Book 3, 10
crisis and victory ix, 7, 32-3, 48, 92, 100, 109
crusade, 6, 9, 29, 165, 178

dark forces x, 40, 139, 143
Dawn-Breakers 134
debasement 50, 162
decadent theories 126
decadence, moral 164-5
decency 126, 162, 164
dead, burial of 44, 73, 90
death 29, 34, 35, 70-72, 74-5, 77, 85, 88, 97, 102, 122, 155
   belief about 67, 84, 108
deeds 2, 39, 90, 127
   not words 121
deepening xiv, 2, 9-10, 17, 49, 52, 56, 103, 109, 117, 129-30, 150, 160, 168, 180
   spiritual vaccination 59
defence
   of Bahá'ís 90-91, 100-01
   of the Covenant 20, 29, 95, 98, 117
   of the Faith ix-x, 40, 42, 46, 48, 115-17, 123, 129-32, 147
defence mechanism 46-7, 50, 66-8
dehumanization 71, 79
demoralization 73, 78, 83
denial 67-8, 77
   of education 82-3, 85
   of existence of God 46, 178
   of faith 75, 84, 144
dependence
   on self 68
   on God 126
depression 66, 81
deprivation 2, 29, 44, 55, 57, 73, 75, 81, 90, 93-4, 118, 140, 174, 177, 188
   of education 82-3
   of human contact 72
   of means of living 34, 70, 78
desecration of graves 44, 73, 79
despair, desperation xvi, 31, 67, 78, 86, 126, 163
detachment xv, 93-5, 128-9, 140-42, 173-6, 195
determination 20, 41, 53, 58, 67, 70, 75, 79, 85, 98, 100, 103, 107
deterministic view 156
Dhábih 117, 133
dialectic process 7, 32-3, 48, 89
digital age 18
disability, physical 107-8

INDEX

disciple(s) 36-7, 95, 187
discontent xvi, 68
discord 12, 49, 65, 159, 170
discouragement 31, 135
discrimination 34, 62, 73, 82-3
disillusionment 68, 91, 180
dismissal from employment 70
Dispensation of Bahá'u'lláh 4-7, 13, 110, 119, 154
Dispensation of Bahá'u'lláh, The 184
dispute(s) 17, 144, 150
dissension 39, 142
distinction, distinguish x, xv, 1, 3, 5-6, 11, 14, 17-18, 52, 54, 69, 114, 117, 119, 120-21, 124, 125, 134, 137, 142, 150, 152, 156, 162, 164-5
distortions of truth 73, 124
disunity 21, 149
divine(s) *see* clergy
divine assistance xvi, 30, 50, 52, 90, 194
divine guidance 15, 30, 93, 151, 180
divine philosophy 114, 128
division, divisive 15, 19, 51, 54, 61, 103, 118, 135, 149-51, 159-60, 163, 167, 172
dogmatic materialism 156
doubt 38, 45-6, 51, 52, 56, 61-2, 93, 98, 124, 132, 159, 193, 194
Dreyfus, Hippolyte 103-4
drugs, habit-forming 164
dust of complacency 89
dynamic coherence 177
dynamic forces, power 6, 19, 116, 181
dynamic process 1, 3

ecclesiastics 118 *see also* clergy
economy, economic(s) 34, 78, 90, 146, 162, 169, 172
education 67, 113-14, 137, 153, 160, 171
  denial of 34, 70, 78, 82-6
  divine, spiritual xiv, 69, 152, 154, 173
  material 152
  three kinds of 152
educator(s) 19, 86, 90, 124, 144, 152
ego xv-xvi, 21-3, 44, 117, 133, 135-7, 140, 142-3, 154-5
egocentricity, egotism x, xv, 55, 127, 134-7, 140-44, 155, 174
Egypt 96, 105, 128-9, 133
Elysée Palace Hotel (Paris) 103

emancipation 6, 38, 149
emergence of Bahá'í Faith ix, xiii-xiv, 6-7, 32, 43, 117
emotion(s) xvi, 34, 42, 46, 50, 66, 71-2, 80-81, 104, 105, 127, 180
empowerment xv, 47, 68, 69, 84, 126
encouragement xiii, 31, 48, 75, 86, 99, 100, 102, 103, 115, 123, 129, 148, 154, 159, 168, 193
  of individual expression 166
  of scholarship 114, 120, 148, 166, 180
endurance xiii, xvi, 18, 25, 28, 34, 44, 49, 68-9, 80, 90, 91-2, 94, 110, 144, 162
enemies xiii, 3, 24, 32-3, 41-52, 59, 65, 69, 81, 90, 92, 96, 100-01, 107, 160, 176, 185, 193
ego 117 *see also* ego, egotism
  external 10, 26, 62-4
  internal 10, 26, 61-2
Engels 179
envy 43, 100, 116, 143
Epistle to the Son of the Wolf 10, 127
Esslemont, Dr 189
Europe, European 38, 131, 148, 177
evil 136, 137, 139, 165, 170
Evin prison 86-7
evolution 33, 111, 163
  of Bahá'í Faith 6-7, 33, 109
  of Bahá'í scholarship xvi, 111
excellence 114, 123, 164, 166
executions 27, 44, 63, 70, 72, 76-8, 85, 102
  mock 71
exile 23, 34, 35-6, 99, 187, 189
existence of God, denial of 46, 178
expansion of consciousness 153
experts 114-15, 151, 167

fair-minded 52, 91, 92, 128, 162
faith 17, 18, 38, 49, 66-9, 87, 89, 99, 120, 123, 127, 129, 138-40, 146, 166, 183, 194
  and reason 166
  recantation of 44, 70, 71, 75, 78, 84-5, 88
  tests of xvi, 20-21, 24, 37, 57-8, 95, 159, 162
faithfulness ix, 1, 8, 12, 24, 34, 36, 51, 83, 87, 93, 98, 111, 124, 134, 160, 165, 178, 182

false accusations 34, 62, 70, 71, 78, 85
falsehood 3, 98, 137, 150
false promises 82-3
famine 189
fanaticism 20, 41, 46, 50, 73, 124, 177
Father of Excellence 129
Farā'id 129
fear 40, 42, 65, 67-9, 71, 73-4, 78, 107, 127, 175, 178, 194
fear of God 63, 75, 122, 127-8, 142, 175
fidelity 98, 134, 165, 195
fight or flight 49, 68
firebombing 63
fire xv, 35, 37, 58, 70, 89, 92, 100, 104-5, 125, 144, 175, 193
fire of the tongue 144
firmness in the Covenant ix-x, xiv, 1-2, 18, 44, 49, 85, 87-8, 93-4, 97-8, 103, 115-16, 133, 154-5, 159, 181, 194
first condition 93
first duty 1, 154-5
flexibility (of Bahá'í teachings) 4
forbearance 39, 46-7, 50, 68, 81, 126
foresight 43, 122
forgiveness xvi, 21, 55, 77, 99, 185
 by God 32, 55, 59, 101, 195
Formative Age, Period xiii, 13, 43, 181
freedom 90, 142, 154, 162-3, 165, 176 *see also* liberty
 and responsibility 148-9
France 71, 103
Freud 136, 179
frivolous pursuits 163

Gardener, The 91
Geneva, Lake of 27
Getsinger, Edward 103
Getsinger, Lua 85, 103-6, 191
Ghuṣn-i-Akbar 11
Ghuṣn-i-A'ẓam 3, 11
Giachery, Ugo 132
Glenwood Springs 27
God, existence of 46, 128, 178-80
God particle 179-80
God Passes By 19, 45
gold xv, 35, 118, 155
gold buttons 27
Golden Age 7, 43
graves, desecration of 44, 73, 79
Greatest Holy Leaf 29, 97-101, 187

Greatest Name 9, 24, 161 *see also* Most Great Name
Great Terror 21
Greece 153
greed 174
grief 57, 72, 77, 100, 141, 193
 of Central Figures 25-6, 28, 54, 98
Grossmann, Dr 181
Guardian *see* Shoghi Effendi
Gulf Islands 108
Gulpáygání, Abu'l-Faḍl 103, 123, 128-31

habits of mind, thinking 167, 178
Hakím, Dr Manúchihr 70-71
Hand(s) of the Cause 12-13, 76, 107, 129, 131-2, 136, 168
Hand of Divine Power 43, 51
happiness 106-7, 113, 116, 123, 126, 136, 139, 148, 165, 190, 193
hatred 12, 21, 28, 29, 31-2, 46-8, 59, 73, 77
 creating in children 73
 inciting 20, 34, 42, 50, 62-3, 77-9, 149
 transformation into love 69-70, 77
Ḥaydar-'Alí, Ḥájí Mírzá 95-7
heart(s) xiii, 2, 12, 18-19, 29, 47, 57-8, 69, 81, 89, 99, 128, 136, 138-40, 141, 143, 144, 148, 154, 193, 195-6
 faithful 124
 loving 50, 53, 93
 purity of 55, 130, 142, 147, 154, 164, 182, 189, 194
heart of the ocean 91
Hearst, Phoebe 133
Herald of the Covenant 103-4
Heroic (Apostolic) Age 13, 43, 87, 181
heroism ix, 13, 29, 38, 52, 66-7, 74, 78, 81, 82-8, 95, 97, 107-8, 127, 134, 181, 196
hidden mysteries 154
Hidden Words 108
higher nature 136
Hippocrates 153
Holley, Horace 188
Holy Land 97, 100, 104-5, 133, 153
Holy Spirit 15, 53, 112, 152, 177, 194-5
Honnold, Annamarie 189-90
Hotel du Parc, Thonon 27
Hudson River 27

INDEX

human nature 136, 179
Human Rights Activists News Agency (HRANA) 80
humiliation 27, 70, 81, 82
humility xv, 4, 17, 24, 95, 113, 115, 121, 123, 125-30, 135, 137, 140, 142-6, 161, 169, 174, 185-8
Ḥuqúqu'lláh 174
Ḥusayn, Mullá 174-5
Huxtable, Catherine and Clifford 107-8

idle fancy 32, 63, 101, 121
infidelity 164
ignorance 12, 21, 63, 73, 77, 92, 100, 118, 122, 130-31, 140
illusion 95, 114, 179
immorality 62, 74
immortality 35, 102, 153, 192
India 38, 105
individualism, culture of 125, 137
infallibility 112, 118, 149
  conferred 14-15
infants in prison 73, 79-81
injustice 31, 34, 80-81, 85, 137
institutions, Bahá'í 46, 51-2, 114-15, 161, 167-8
intellect(ual) 2, 10, 47, 64, 110, 114, 126, 137-40, 146, 161, 167-8, 171, 180, 188
  challenges 183
  honesty and humility 126
  pride 117, 125, 137, 170
  ridicule xiv
International Teaching Centre 146, 166
Internet 18, 60, 61, 149, 156
interpretation of Sacred Text 6, 15-18, 61-2, 117-19, 149-51, 168
'interpretive authority' 61-2
Interpreter 9, 184-6
Iraq 22, 36, 101
Iran, Iranians 7, 23, 30, 33-4, 43, 75, 81, 86, 90-91, 121, 129, 131, 174 *see also* Persia
Iranian authorities, government 7, 62-3, 70-71, 74, 75, 76-9, 82-3, 85
Iranian Bahá'ís ix, xiv, 31, 33-4, 44, 62-3, 70-74, 76-91, 103, 141, 177, 181
Iranian Taboo 91
iron, example of 70
Iron Age (of Faith) 13

Isfahan 76, 95, 104
Isfandíyár 190
'Ishqábád Temple 14
Islam xv, 52, 73, 96, 120, 121, 123, 128, 214
Islamic Republic of Iran 62, 70, 71, 76, 78 *see also* Iranian authorities
Islamic Revolution 7, 31, 34, 44, 82, 87, 181
Israel 62, 85
Israfil 97, 214
Istanbul (Constantinople) 141, 151

Jamál-i-Burújirdí 140
jealousy 63, 188
Jesus Christ 7, 35, 87, 159
Jewish doctors, prophets 153
junior youth 87
justice 3, 8, 34, 75, 137, 161, 162-3

Kant 179
Kazimayn, Iraq 101
K͟hádim'u'lláh 22
Khan, Janet, 75
Khan, Peter 75, 172-3
Khartoum 96
K͟hayru'lláh, Ibrahim 103, 133
Khedive (of Egypt) 27
Kitáb-i-'Ahdí 3, 8, 10
Kitáb-i-Aqdas 1-2, 6, 8, 11, 125, 154
Kitáb-i-Íqán 35, 95, 115
Knight(s) of Bahá'u'lláh 107-8
knights of the Lord 38
knowledge x, xv, 5, 22, 50, 52, 59, 109, 110-15, 120-23, 125, 130-40, 146-7, 151-8, 166-72, 180, 188, 194
  access to 111
  acquiring x, 112, 113, 115, 122, 138, 151-4, 166
  and the Covenant 1, 10, 112-20, 133, 135-7, 154-6, 166
  source of all 114, 154
  theological 44, 118, 119
Kurdistan 27

leadership, desire for x, 54-5, 63, 94, 118, 133, 140, 144, 174
Legion of Honour 71
leprosy 55, 59
lethargy 178

learned, the x, 113-15, 146, 157, 167,
    170, 173
  attributes and attitudes 123-8
  dictatorial views of 120, 151
  in Bahá 113, 136
  spiritually 122
'liberals' 167
liberty 24, 75, 149, 170 *see also* freedom
life-blood 19, 47, 155
lifeboat 19
line of succession 13
living martyrs 34, 85
London 27, 131
longevity, effect of spiritual life on 179
Lord of Hosts 20
love 20, 29, 35, 47, 50, 53, 64, 68, 81, 84,
    115, 126-7, 137-8, 145, 165, 179, 183
  between 'Abdu'l-Bahá and Bahá'u'lláh
    27, 35, 188
  of 'Abdu'l-Bahá for Greatest Holy Leaf
    99-100
  and Bahá'í scholars 115, 123, 169
  of believers for Bahá'í Cause,
    Bahá'u'lláh 29, 44, 47, 76, 81, 84-5,
    92, 101, 108, 123, 159, 166, 174
  divine 12, 161
  for God 25-6, 35, 74, 88, 93, 105,
    142, 189
  and faithfulness to Covenant ix, 1, 2
  of leadership 63, 118
  physical 164
  a protective force 53
  of self 139, 142, 144
  and steadfastness 3, 81, 193
  transformation of hate into 69-70, 77
lower nature 136
lowliness xv, 4, 124, 144-5, 174, 186,
    187, 195

magnanimity 47, 66-7, 71, 126, 144, 174
Mahd-i-'Ulyá 188
Maḥmúd-i-Zarqání, Mírzá 188
Mahmudnizhad, Mona 85, 181
Manifestation (Divine, of God) xiv, 1, 3,
    4, 8, 11, 20, 23, 36, 42, 44, 47, 55,
    69, 100, 110, 112, 115, 118-19, 140,
    145, 155, 157, 169, 185-7
manipulation 71, 73, 155
marriage 73, 77, 90, 164, 176
Mars (planet) 131

martyr(s) 13, 29, 30, 33, 34, 44, 62, 67,
    72, 75-7, 83-5, 87-9, 101-2, 127, 181
martyrdom 74-5, 82, 85, 104, 134
  of the Báb 27, 29, 95
Marx 179
Mashhad 174
materialism xiv, 35, 48, 64, 123-5, 127,
    135-6, 139-40, 151, 153, 163, 176-9
materialistic methodology 155-7
Maxwell, May 85
Mazindaran 174-5
Mazra'ih 187, 188
media, the 52, 62, 66, 78, 91, 176
medicine 57, 70-71, 135, 173
Memorials of the Faithful 121
Messianic Spirit 35
metaphor 18-19, 94, 129-30, 145, 155,
    186 *see also* analogy
Metelmann, Velda 104
Mihdíy-i-Dahají, Siyyid 140-42
mind, human 9, 19, 21, 22, 45, 50, 71,
    86, 110, 113, 124, 135, 138-40, 142,
    146, 152-4, 157-8, 163, 167, 171,
    178, 180, 186
mindset 123, 139, 167
Miracles and Metaphors 129-30
Mír 'Imád 23
Míshkín-Qalam 23-4
misrepresentation 42-3, 52, 63, 179
mob(s) 27, 44, 62, 63, 73
mock execution 71
moderation 141, 148, 164, 170
modesty 124-5, 131, 161, 164
Momen, Moojan 132
moon, the 131
moral behaviour, character, conduct 113,
    123, 162-5, 176
moral decadence, decline 160, 162, 164-5
moral integrity 50, 176
morality 52, 62, 66, 74, 116, 153
moral requisites 162-5
Most Great House (in Baghdad) 141
Most Great Name xvi, 54, 176 *see also*
    Greatest Name
Most Great Peace 4, 184
Mother Book 4, 6, 22
Mu'ayyad, Ḥabíb 130
Muhammad (Prophet) 36-7
Muhammad-'Alí, Mírzá 11, 23, 98, 133,
    188

232

INDEX

Muḥammad Sh̲áh 121
Muḥammad-'Alí, Mírzá (G̲h̲uṣn-i-Akbar) 11
murder 71, 80, 97
Muṣ̲h̲íru'l-Mulk, Governor of S̲h̲íráz 37
Muslims 31, 43, 73, 80, 90, 103, 129 *see also* Islam
mysteries xvi, 7, 17, 18, 20, 22, 30, 32, 35, 41, 53, 94, 117, 126, 131, 138, 140, 147, 154, 157-8, 196
Mystery of God ('Abdu'l-Bahá) 29, 184
mystic, mysticism 23, 35, 69, 138, 153

Nabíl-i-Akbar 128
Nabíl-i- A'ẓam 101
Nak̲h̲javani, Bahiyyih, 117, 119
narcissism 137, 139
National Spiritual Assembly 14, 52, 57, 160
  of the British Isles 132
  of Canada x, 182-3
  of the United States and Canada 75
natural selection 179
nature (world of) 89, 149
neurobiology 138, 178
New York 27, 104, 133-4
New York Times 82
Niagara 27
Nimrod 125
Nine Year Plan 108
non-violence 69, 100

obedience x, 1-2, 3, 35, 57-8, 93, 127, 131, 137, 148, 154-5, 160-2, 174, 176, 181
obligation(s) 3, 43, 61, 93, 98
obscurity, emergence from ix, xiv, 6-7, 32, 38, 117
ocean (metaphor) 5, 7, 18, 53, 90, 94, 112, 115, 125, 126, 130, 134, 173
ocean, midmost heart of 91
Ocean, Most Mighty 113
oneness of humankind 1, 19, 54, 100, 177, 184
open-mindedness 116, 161
opium 164
  of the human soul 177
opposites 32, 123, 137, 144-5
opposition x, xiv, 7, 20, 32-3, 40-65, 159-60, 194
  motives for 20, 42, 46, 48, 54, 56, 118

  response to 33, 39, 40-65, 67, 85, 109, 183
  will increase 38, 40-41, 43, 45-6, 48, 61, 65, 91
oppression ix, 28, 30-02, 34, 36, 48-50, 68-9, 78-9, 137
organic life, process 32, 111, 168
Orient 103
Ottoman 189

Pacific Ocean 108
paganism 64
paradise 4, 25, 175
paradox 20, 32, 91
Paraguay 183
Paris 27, 71, 103-4
partners
  with 'Abdu'l-Bahá 25
  with God 31, 175
passion(s) 55, 94, 123, 135, 163, 176
  for leadership x, 118
  for power 21, 42, 54, 133, 140, 142, 144, 155
patience xv, xvi, 24-5, 31. 46, 49-50, 72, 74, 109, 120, 145, 193
peace, peaceful 4, 29, 33, 46, 67, 69, 84, 101, 123, 139, 162, 165, 184
pearl 18, 125
people of Bahá 11, 30, 65 *see also* Bahá'ís
persecution ix, xiv, 20, 28, 30-34, 37, 44, 46, 48-50, 53, 62, 66-74, 76-81, 84, 86, 89-91, 95-7, 100, 103-5
perseverance 29, 32, 67, 69, 81, 82, 101, 160, 194
Persia, Persian(s) 3, 23-4, 36, 57, 75-6, 87, 91, 95-6, 103, 104, 134, 140, 185 *see also* Iran
Persian literature 125, 128
petition to the S̲h̲áh 75, 103-4
philosophy 64, 67, 114, 128, 146, 153, 173, 178, 179
pivot of oneness of mankind 1, 19
plague 59
pleasure principle 136
politics 33, 62, 77, 104, 131, 148, 162, 172-3
partisan 172
Poirier, Brent 159
poison 24, 26, 55, 59, 60, 113, 137, 144, 186

Port Said 105
power *see also* empowerment
  of the Covenant xiii, xvi, 1-2, 7,
    18-19, 44, 56, 93, 155, 181
  of community 161
  divine 31, 33, 42, 43, 48, 153
  of ego 140
  of faith 38, 66-8, 74
  of God 51, 65, 116, 194
  of governments 33, 49, 64, 104
  of the heart 138
  of the Holy Spirit 112, 194
  human 153
  of humility 145
  ideal 149
  of intellect, reason, understanding 17,
    38, 69, 112, 122, 137-8, 140, 146,
    150, 188
  of love 53, 74
  material 148
  of opposition 38, 40
  of orthodoxy 41-2, 64, 118
  of perception 177
  passion for 21, 42, 54, 133, 140, 142,
    144, 155
  of publication of high thoughts 116
  of Revelation of Bahá'u'lláh 22, 32, 44,
    69, 89, 109, 110-12, 182, 194
  of one righteous act 165
  source of 193
  spiritual 33, 188
  of truth 65
  of unity 53, 135
  of utterance 141, 145, 194
prayer xvi, 43, 50, 58, 90, 104, 108, 130,
    143, 153, 175-6, 182
  of 'Abdu'l-Bahá 26, 88, 176, 195-6
  of Bahá'u'lláh 21, 25, 146
  prolongation not beloved by God 176
prejudice 21, 43, 46, 50, 62-3, 69, 71, 79,
    162-3, 178
prepublication review 116
present-day requirements 116
pride x, 22, 23, 30, 63, 114, 115, 127,
    135, 141-5, 154, 170, 186, 195
  intellectual 117, 124-5, 135-7, 170
priest(s) *see* clergy, religious authorities
priestcraft 117
priesthood 117-20
Prime Minister (Persia) 103-4

prison 23-5, 27, 34, 35, 44, 47, 59, 63,
    69-73, 79-82, 86-7, 88, 90, 91, 96,
    101-2, 105, 129, 187, 189-91
  infants in 73, 79-81
  of self 35, 136, 139
professionals 71, 84, 117, 147, 157, 168,
    170
progressive unfoldment 45
progressive movements, perspectives 46,
    147
progressive revelation 110-11
promiscuity 164
Promised One 21, 43, 88, 89
proof xv, 129, 180, 196
prophecy 96, 129
protection
  of believers xiii-xiv, 19, 26, 28-9, 38,
    53, 59, 74, 93, 96, 103, 113, 127,
    142-3, 155, 159, 176, 194, 195
  of the Faith ix, xiii-xiv, 2, 8-10, 15, 19,
    20, 56, 61, 64-5, 91, 93, 96, 103,
    117, 151, 167-8, 176, 181
psychology 47-9, 81, 127, 138, 173
psychological
  dangers xiv
  intimidation 44, 71-3, 81
  reactions 49, 66-8
  tribulations 34, 70, 85
publication of high thoughts 116
Purest Branch 187
purity xiv, xv, 17, 24, 33, 58, 119, 122,
    129-30, 137-9, 141, 142, 150, 154,
    163-5, 176, 177, 182, 183, 185, 194

Qá'im 121
Quddús 76
Qur'án xv, 22, 87, 121, 129

race, racial 53, 163
  new 69
radiance xv, 12, 23, 29, 37, 49, 58, 93,
    98, 100, 170, 174, 176
Rafsanjan 63
rank(s) 4, 76, 92, 123-4, 151, 161, 163,
    184-5 *see also* station
rank on rank 53, 89
Ransom-Kehler, Keith 75-6, 85
Regina, Saskatchewan 108
reason, rational 150
reciprocity 19, 162, 169

INDEX

recognition
  of Bahá'í Faith ix, 6-7, 41, 52, 77
  of Manifestation of God xiv, 1-3, 8,
    21, 44, 112, 113, 115, 118-19,
    121, 125, 13, 140, 143, 145,
    154-5, 169, 187
rectitude 160, 162, 164, 183
reductionist view 127, 179
refinement 124, 141
refuting attack and criticism 52, 59, 116
relating Bahá'í teachings to current issues
  147, 171-2
religion(s) 3, 8, 10, 12, 15-16, 19, 20, 31,
  33, 42, 45, 51-2, 67, 93, 117, 153,
  156, 189
  mistrust of 46, 64, 173, 178-80
  purpose of 64, 151, 153
  and science 124, 154, 177
religious authorities 8, 63, 65, 77, 117-20,
  189
religious education 152 *see also* education
renunciation 26, 36, 135, 173, 175
repeating like a parrot 88
repression of Bahá'í Faith 6-7, 34, 38, 44,
  70, 71
research 2, 16, 66, 76, 116, 132, 143,
  155-6, 178-9
resilience 32, 49, 50, 66-9, 78, 85, 87,
  100
respect 28, 125, 147-8, 166, 169-70, 187,
  18
reverence 122, 182, 187
reward 75, 84, 85, 125, 139, 175
ridicule xiv, 34, 42, 46, 73
righteousness xiv, 2, 126, 165
Rúhu'lláh 84, 87-8
Ruhe Schoen, Janet 104
Rúz-bih 36-7

Sabz-i-Maydán 76
sacred law 174
sacred Lote-Tree 13
sacred places 73
sacrifice 26, 28, 29, 35, 70, 76, 86-7,
  89-90, 102, 107, 118, 121-2, 181,
  187, 190
  of self 29, 136, 139, 141
Sa'di 125
sages 152
saints, saintly 99, 108, 143

sanction 118, 149, 174
scapegoat 77, 103
scarlet fever 107
scepticism 179-80
scholars, scholarship x, 103, 110-17,
  119-32, 135, 137-8, 143, 146-58
  passim, 166-72, 180
school(s) xv, 34, 73, 79, 82, 130
schoolchildren 62-3, 73, 82
science 67-8, 71, 110, 112, 114-15, 138,
  140, 146, 147, 152-4, 155, 157-8,
  169-70, 173, 177, 178-9
  and religion 124, 154, 177
scientific methodology 157
scientific training 115, 146-7, 157
scripture, text, sacred Writings 6, 10,
  15-16, 19, 73, 110, 112, 119, 141-2,
  157, 160, 171, 182, 184
search for ourselves 137
secularism 173
security 37, 47, 81, 105, 117, 165
  of the state 96
sedition 39, 48, 92, 149
seeds of dissension 142
seeker 18, 96, 132
self 22, 55, 68, 94, 101, 113, 123, 126,
  135-7, 143-4
  insistent xvi
  prison of 35, 139
  two meanings of 136
self-advancement 132, 142
self-centredness 126, 135-6, 142, 144
self-deception xvi
self-discipline 120, 165
self-effacement 123, 124, 186-8
self-esteem 69
self-evaluation xvi, 135
self-glorification 121, 123-4, 125, 135,
  137
self-gratification 163, 176
self-indulgence 176
self-interest 163
selfishness x, 21, 23, 43, 55-6, 117, 125,
  133, 136-7, 141-4, 154, 159
selflessness 129-30, 169, 182
self-love 139, 142-3
self-sacrifice 29, 102, 136, 139, 141
Semnan 63, 79-80
sensory deprivation 72
service xv-xvi, 20, 21-3, 64, 75-6, 90,

96-7, 101, 105, 107-8, 114, 121, 128-9, 132, 133, 137, 161, 166-7, 169-70, 174-5, 178, 182, 194
  to humanity 71, 75, 123, 135-6, 139, 190-91
  path of 31, 98
  public 77
  of youth 181, 183
servitude 34-5, 89, 121, 128-9, 134, 144-5, 185-6, 188
seven stages 6-7
Seven Valleys, The 74
sexes, equality of 74. 79
sexuality 164
Shah 23, 75, 101, 103-4, 121
Shaykh Salmán 36-7
shame 84, 162, 196
shield 19, 91, 128, 185
Shiraz 37, 85, 101, 121, 131, 181
shock 52, 67, 72, 86
Shoghi Effendi (Guardian of the Cause)
  analysis of world events 163-4, 172-3
  authoritative interpreter 15-16, 17, 62, 119, 149-50, 168
  expounder of the Word of God 13-14
  foresight and vision 43
  infallibility 14-15
  passing of 16, 45, 151
  successor to 'Abdu'l-Bahá 10, 13, 62
  suffering of 54, 107
  Ten Year Plan of 6, 9
  study writings of 177
  see quotations throughout
sincerity xiv, xv, 22, 52, 55, 58, 96, 119, 130, 135, 139, 141-2, 165
six requisites for spiritual growth 182
Síyáh-Chál 27, 101-2
society 16, 41, 46, 79, 101, 114-15, 116, 123, 126, 135, 157, 167, 169, 180, 183
  contemporary 148-9, 177
  current issues of x, 114-15, 171-2
  Islamic 52, 74
  materialistic 125, 135, 176-7
  progress of xiii, 5, 111, 113, 147, 152, 159, 176
  Western 64, 66, 123, 137, 163-4
Socrates 153
solitary confinement 72, 86
Some Answered Questions 180

sorrow 20, 24-5, 27-8, 31 45, 54, 66-7, 72, 99, 105, 148
soul xiii, xiv, xvi, 12, 18, 21, 35, 40, 53, 55, 67, 69, 94-5, 97-8, 105, 117, 126, 135-6, 139, 141, 143-5, 148, 151-5, 157, 160-61, 167, 171, 177-9, 193-6
  of Bahá'u'lláh 25
spirit xv, 19, 29, 53, 63, 64, 87, 102, 108, 116, 126, 136, 138-9, 141, 174, 177, 187, 192
  of the Covenant xiii, 155
  freedom of 153
  immortality of 153
  of the age 151
  of obedience 131
Spiritual Assembly xv, 108, 174
  of Istanbul 151
  of Los Angeles 94
  of Regina 108
  of Toronto 107
  see also National Spiritual Assembly
spiritual
  attributes, virtues 49, 53, 64, 70, 112-13, 126, 137, 162-5, 173
  autonomy 168
  belief, conviction 67-9, 161
  civilization 153
  consequences 174
  dangers xiv
  descendants 134
  development, progress 66, 85, 143, 151, 153, 159, 182
  disease 55, 59
  education 69, 152
  faculties 178, 181
  health, well-being 55, 59, 155, 180
  insight 35, 36, 47, 67, 122, 176
  issues 46, 155
  laws 137, 181
  life 9, 66, 137, 160, 179
  power 33, 188
  principles, verities of Faith 10, 116
  reality 140, 155, 157, 178-9
  realization 35
  requirements xv, 162-3, 177
  response 68
  springtime 89
  transformation 123
  unity 111
  vaccination 59

world 157
spirituality 53, 61, 68, 70, 95, 127, 138, 143, 153, 161, 175-6, 179
spiritually charged arena 161
spiritually corrosive 149
spiritually learned 122-3, 127
starvation 70, 97
statesmanship 128
station 186
  of 'Abdu'l-Bahá 184-6, 188
  of Bahá'u'lláh 2, 4-5, 22, 145, 152, 187
  of (true) believers 2, 5, 160, 165, 173
  of defender of Faith 116
  eminent 113
  of individual 123, 145, 160
  of love 74
  of martyrdom 76
  most sublime 155
  of sacrifice 141
  of scholarship 124
steadfastness ix, xiii, 1-3, 8, 12, 21, 30, 32-4, 40, 47, 49-50, 73, 81-2, 85, 87-90, 93-102, 107, 11, 113, 160, 181, 193
  obligation of 3, 93
St Helena 108
stigma 62, 73, 156
stress 50, 66-8, 72
submission to the Will of God 35, 58, 63, 142, 186, 195
success 78, 133, 162, 192, 194
succession, successor 3-4, 8, 10-11, 13-14, 23, 26, 54, 62, 98, 119, 149, 160
Sudan 96
suffering ix, xiii, xiv, 13, 30-32, 42, 45, 48, 51, 54, 66-8, 72, 74-7, 84-6, 92, 96-7, 99, 105, 163, 189
  of Central Figures 20-29, 32, 51-2, 84, 99, 105, 107, 118, 141, 190
  of innocents 79-81
  of youth 81, 86, 88
Sulaymán Khán 44, 84
sun 19, 21, 49, 106, 115, 126, 134
Sun of Reality 153, 155
Sun of Truth 89, 94
superiority, sense of x, 120-21, 25, 135, 141, 143-4, 151, 161
superstition 177
Supreme Concourse 56, 93, 152

Súriy-i-Ghuṣn 184
Súriy-i-'Ibád 142
survival, survivors 34, 69, 72, 75, 107

Tablet(s) 21, 24, 25, 36-7, 39, 87, 141-2, 187
  of Aḥmad 22, 32, 47, 81, 98
  to America 26, 28, 32
  to Auguste Forel 180
  of the Branch 134, 184-5
  of Carmel 11
  of the Divine Plan 11, 19, 174
  Most Great 3, 10
  of Tests xiv
  of Wisdom 128
tact 128, 141
Taherzadeh, Adib 22, 37, 55, 75, 87, 95-6, 130, 140, 142, 144, 186-7
Ṭáhirih 52, 104, 121-2
temperance 122, 164
temporal lobe 179
Ten Year Plan (Crusade) 6, 9
Teheran 23, 71, 75, 77, 82, 84, 86, 88, 101
terminology 147, 157
test(s) x, xiv-xvii, 1, 10, 20-23, 31-3, 42, 49, 53, 66, 82-4, 90, 92, 93-4, 113, 133-5, 161-2, 174-5, 177, 195
  of faith 57-8
theocratic government 7, 34, 74
Thompson, Juliet 35, 102, 104, 187
Thonon-les-Bains, France 27, 188
Tillich, Paul 67
'traditionalists' 167
transformation xiii, xiv, 3, 23, 40, 48, 51, 67, 101, 104, 115, 123, 131, 141, 144, 158, 164, 169, 174
  of attributes 70
  of hate into love 69-70, 77
transmutation of elements 114
trauma 69, 80
tribulation 31-2, 33, 45, 50, 51, 66, 70, 73-4, 85, 101
tolerance 124, 147, 166, 169
  of suffering 66-8, 77, 81, 89, 92
torture 20, 29, 33-4, 41, 44, 67, 70-74, 78, 88, 91, 96-7
Trocadero gardens 27
trust 22, 38, 65, 81, 93-4, 139, 180, 183, 194

trustworthiness 79, 90, 93, 162, 165
truthfulness 12, 79, 126, 162, 165
Turk, the 38
turquoise 175

unification of nations 33
United Kingdom 7
United Nations 78
United States 7, 75, 102, 103, 129-30, 133-4, 189 *see also* America
unity xiv, xvi, 4, 12, 16, 29, 34, 45, 53, 56, 60-61, 63-4, 98, 103, 111, 120, 133-5, 137, 159, 181
safeguarding 4, 14, 19, 117, 150, 159
Universal House of Justice 3-4, 10, 13-15, 151, 155-7
see quotations throughout

Vaḥíd 121-2
Varqá, 'Alí-Muḥammad 87-8
Varqá, Azízu'lláh, 87
Varqá, Rúḥu'lláh 84, 87-8
veil(s) 5, 35, 43, 63, 118-19, 121, 129, 135, 143, 154
violence 40, 42, 46-7, 50, 62, 69, 70, 73, 77, 80-81, 100, 163, 164
vitality 19, 143
vulnerability xvi, 51, 66, 79

warrior 41, 178
Washington 28
Water of Life 19, 125
West xiv, 7, 12, 26-7, 31, 46, 48, 50, 62, 64, 66, 75, 81, 97, 99, 123, 134, 135, 149, 164-5, 170, 177, 188
Will and Testament 3, 10-15, 19, 106
wisdom xiv-xv, 3, 11, 31, 33, 35-8, 47, 50, 60, 70, 87, 92, 100, 110-12, 114-15, 118, 123, 127, 131, 141-2, 153-4, 175
Word of God 12, 14, 34, 36, 47-8, 60, 91, 106, 110-11, 121, 126, 149, 186, 193-4
world civilization 4, 7, 11, 111
World Baháʾí Commonwealth 6-7
World Order of Baháʾu'lláh xiii, 11, 14, 16, 33 40, 43, 91, 158, 169, 173
World War I 105, 189
worship 118, 175

Yaḥyá Azal, Mírzá 24
Yaḥyáy-i-Darábí, Siyyid (Vaḥíd) 121-2
Yaran 90
Yazd 63, 104, 141
youth xiv, 29, 34, 82, 85, 87, 101-2, 126, 160, 164-5, 177, 179-83
Yúnis K͟hán 185

www.ingramcontent.com/pod-product-compliance
Lightning Source LLC
Chambersburg PA
CBHW060116170426
43198CB00010B/913